Cat Tails

Heart-Warming Stories about the
Cats and Kittens of **RESQCATS**™

Jeffyne Telson

Library of Congress Control Number: 2017912491

ISBN number: 978-0-692-93368-8

Printed in the United States of America

Front cover photo and author's photo by Catalina Esteves Dachena
Inside cover photo of RESQCATS by Daryl Metzger
Book and jacket design by Demi Anter

All profits from the sale of this book directly benefit RESQCATS, Inc. RESQCATS™, founded by Jeffyne Telson in 1997 in Santa Barbara, California, is a non-profit organization dedicated to the rescue, care and adoption of stray and abandoned cats and kittens.

For more information or to make a donation, please visit:

www.resqcats.org

Dedicated to my soul mate, "Miejek."

In memory of my best friend, "MisJef."

Contents

Prologue

My compassion for animals goes back as far as I can remember. My parents loved animals, so I grew up with cats and dogs, although it seemed that animals always just "showed up" at our house. At one time, we actually had ten dogs in our back yard. That included the box of six puppies that my dad found on the side of the highway when I was five years old. Later, when I was in elementary school, my mother took pity on a stray pregnant cat named Snooky and she became part of our family. A few years after that, a neighbor asked us to take their cat, Soldier, when they relocated out of state. Then, Autumn liked our house better than hers and moved in while I was in high school. When my best friend visited and found Cricket in our front courtyard, my mother invited him inside and he never left. That was when I was getting ready to leave for college, so the timing of Cricket's appearance probably helped my mother through her empty nest concerns. There is no question, I learned compassion for animals from the fine example my parents set in our home.

There is one incident, however, that clearly marked the beginning of what was to become my life's passion. When I was in my twenties, I took up jogging. On Saturday mornings, I would often run at White Rock Lake, a beautiful lake with a great running path located just a short distance from where I lived in Dallas, Texas. I had just finished a leisurely six-mile loop with Mitch, the man who would eventually become my husband, when I noticed a box in the parking area. As I approached, I heard scratching and mews. To this day, I remember opening the flaps and gasping when I saw five kittens inside...some heartless person had apparently just dumped them. At that time, I had no experience to know that anyone was capable of such a horrible thing; abandoning six-week-old kittens in a parking lot! Without a second thought, I loaded the box into my car and drove directly to the local humane society. The staff was courteous and thanked me for saving the kittens. They explained that they would provide medical care for the little kittens and then they requested a donation to help with their expenses.

That was my first contact with a non-profit organization. Of course, I had no foresight that I would spend much of my time raising funds for kittens just like those when I started RESQCATS many years later.

I carried my driver's license and a credit card in my wallet, but I did not have even a dollar in cash. Before I left the humane society, I promised the lady behind the counter that I would return the following Monday during my lunch break with money to put towards the kittens. I doubt that the employee believed me; she had probably heard that line before and was accustomed to people never returning. But I have always been a person of my word and I had every intention of keeping my pledge. The same lady was at the front desk when I appeared on Monday with a twenty dollar bill in hand. She looked pleasantly surprised and was still thanking me as I walked out the door.

ૉ

I worked as a graphic designer for several years and then in 1986, at the age of thirty, I married the man of my dreams. Mitch and I share the same compassion for animals. Over the years, we have shared our home with more than seventy-five cats, thirty-one collies and fifteen giant African sulcata tortoises.

Soon after Mitch and I married, I began rescuing cats that lived on the ocean jetty by our home in San Diego. It was then that I realized that I wanted to make a difference in the lives of stray and abandoned cats and kittens. I began to think about creating my own rescue for cats. I dreamed of what it would be like to spend my life caring for animals. I was determined to, somehow, make my dream become reality.

Several years later, when Mitch and I moved to Santa Barbara, California, my dream did come true. In 1997, I started my own non-profit organization called RESQCATS. My mission was to rescue, care for and adopt stray and abandoned cats and kittens.

I began publishing newsletters three to four times a year to raise funds for the cats and kittens in my care. At first, I personally wrote every article. I sent the newsletters to previous adopters and people that I thought would be interested in donating to the organization. The first publications included information about RESQCATS, donor recognition, statistics, and an occasional short story about some of the rescued cats. In those earlier years, newsletters were rarely more than eight pages.

But as time passed and RESQCATS became a recognized name in the community, the length of the newsletters increased. It seemed I had a lot to say...and many more stories to tell! I also took every opportunity to educate readers about spaying and neutering, the cornerstone of all rescue groups. I began to express my thoughts and opinions about some of the challenges I faced. And as my confidence grew, I felt more comfortable sharing my opinions on subjects that I felt passionate about in the rescue world. Today, newsletters are no less than twelve pages and some are sixteen pages long!

I had always felt vulnerable expressing emotions about animals because I feared being told that I was too sensitive. I discovered that writing about the cats and kittens was a way to share my feelings of affection, joy and grief in a manner that was non-threatening. Writing offered a way to articulate my thoughts without feeling judged. Putting pen to paper gave me the opportunity to share my experiences of love and loss safely; that ultimately helped me heal from the grief that so often accompanies rescuing animals. I also began to realize the life lessons that the animals were teaching me. Sharing my insights with readers became a creative and therapeutic outlet.

For years, my good friend, Carolyn Sacks, encouraged me to write a book about RESQCATS. For a long time, I resisted the idea. I lacked the confidence that I could undertake such an endeavor. But Carolyn had read and praised the stories in the newsletters. She was touched by the articles about the special cats and how they influenced my outlook on life. She continued to try to persuade me until finally, I took her up on the challenge. I set it as a personal goal and committed to writing a book but without a clue as to the enormous undertaking. As you read this book, you will come to understand that when I make a pledge to do something, I follow through! It has taken four years for me to complete the book. I thank Carolyn for her encouragement, support and love throughout the many years of our friendship.

Time constraints were a major factor in bringing the book to completion. The busy kitten season at RESQCATS consumes nine months of the year. My days are very long... "dawn to dusk" is how I best describe them! It is difficult to find the time to write even the newsletters during the kitten season, much less write a book!

In recent years, I have taken the winter months off and spend them at my second home in Oregon. It is there that I can rejuvenate myself and vacation with Mitch, although most of my time off in the last four years has been spent writing, rewriting, editing and perfecting this book. It has been a challenging learning process and one of the four most difficult things I have ever done in my life. If you are curious about the other three, well, here they are: getting Mitch to marry me, hiking the Grand Canyon from rim to rim in a single day, and completing a college chemistry class in a five-week summer session! I have imposed on Mitch and his down time by asking for his feedback and guidance in finding the right words to communicate exactly what it is I want to express. He has been there by my side the entire time and this book would not have been possible without his dedication, time and patience. During the third winter of working together, Mitch realized my willpower was as strong as it had been when I dreamed of starting RESQCATS. I remember saying to him, "If something happens to me tomorrow, it's my hope that my book will be published." Mitch understood my determination and has made tremendous effort and sacrifice to help fulfill my dream. I am grateful for his devotion, patience and love.

Every book in progress needs someone to read it with a fresh set of eyes. There is grammar to check and spelling to correct. It is essential that the message I want to convey is clear. I owe much to Janet Dewey and Christine Orchard for their commitment to make sure that I accomplished that goal.

There have been many volunteers, too many to list, that have contributed to my experiences. They have been the heart and soul of RESQCATS. One, in particular, has been with me since the beginning in 1997. Erika Sacks started as a ten-year-old girl and has continued to volunteer every year. Janet Dewey, Susan Leroy and Denny Epperson began as volunteers but have also become dear friends, offering constant support and unconditional love. Many volunteers have come and gone, but each has given the precious gift of their time. I cherish every one of them.

Few people have had as profound an impact on me as

Wayne Pacelle, the President and CEO of the Humane Society of the United States. I met him during the signing of his first book, *The Bond*, in 2011. Like Wayne, my life is dedicated to animals and their well-being. At that time, I had operated RESQCATS for fourteen years and did not realize that I was teetering on the edge of burn-out. I had allowed the expanded duties of managing a well-established, growing organization and people to exhaust me. I had less time to do what I started RESQCATS for in the first place; to nurture cats and kittens. I missed that hands-on time. My desire to make a difference is passionate and my commitment is unwavering. I thought something was wrong with me because my feelings about animals were exceptionally strong and extremely sensitive. Mostly, I felt alone.

That day, Wayne talked about his book and the treatment of animals. He offered ways to make changes in order to create a more compassionate society. He talked about being a vegan...I was vegetarian at the time but have since become a vegan. He educated his audience about transitions that everyone can make to benefit the well-being of animals. His talk was heart-felt and most importantly, he was not afraid to express his views. After listening to Wayne's presentation, I realized that he and many others share my mind-set. I was not alone! I felt a sense of hope and rejuvenation come over me. I credit his presentation as the beginning of my recovery from compassion fatigue.

ꙭ

I had many stories about special cats and kittens from years of writing the RESQCATS newsletter. As I reviewed them, it was extremely difficult to choose which ones to expand on for the book. While I have chosen only a few from the hundreds of cats and kittens to share with you, I am indebted to all of them. They have taught me some important life lessons about courage, unconditional love, patience, acceptance and joy.

It is my hope that this book will encourage you to expand your compassion for animals and discover a greater appreciation for the important life lessons they teach us. If I touch the heart of even a single reader, then I feel I will have accomplished this goal.

— Jeffyne Telson

Years before I began to dream of starting RESQCATS, I shared my home with a cat named Tattoo. I cannot imagine writing a book without including her. When I lived on my own after graduation from college, she was my first cat. Tattoo was by my side for all of the experiences during my new found independence. And for that reason, she will always have first place in my heart!

ONE

Tattoo, My First Cat

As a little girl, I grew up with outdoor cats that were never allowed in the house. Perhaps that was what most people did with their animals back then or maybe my mother just did not want pets in the house. It was not until I moved out that Mother allowed our family cats to be indoors. I have no idea what changed her mind about having the cats come inside. Maybe she suffered empty nest syndrome and needed the presence of another living being besides my father in the house. Or perhaps by the time I left for college, people were becoming more educated about the dangers to pets left outdoors. Since then, our cats have been indoor cats.

My parents worked hard at making sure that I got an education. Their goal was to make me fully prepared for life and that meant I would attend college and obtain a degree.

My father paid his way through college, working three jobs while raising a family. My mother never went to college. When given the choice of having a shiny new car or going to a university, Mother chose the car. It was a decision that she regretted throughout her life. She attended business school and was employed as a part-time secretary. Her main priority was motherhood. Working reduced hours meant that she had to go to work after I left for school, complete the job and arrive home before I returned in the afternoon. Mother and Daddy worked diligently to ensure that my brother and I had everything we needed and almost all we desired. However, as with many middle-class families, money was always tight. They felt that a college education would insure that my financial future would not be as difficult as theirs had been.

I graduated from Texas Tech University in Lubbock, Texas in 1979 with a Bachelor of Arts degree in Graphic Design.

When I chose my college major, my parents were baffled. While both had always been supportive of my artistic talents, they did not quite understand what a graphic designer was or what one did with such a degree. So they encouraged me to get a teaching certificate in art. My mother felt that a teaching certificate always gives a woman something to fall back on after she has raised her family and needed to return to work.

In my best interest, my folks had my future mapped out in full detail. The plan was to get a college degree, find a good job, stay with the same company for years and climb the corporate ladder.

It was a great plan until I got married, bought a house with a white picket fence and had children. Staying true to the course meant mandatory time off to raise my kids. Once the children were old enough, I had the option of returning to work if needed. At this point, the teaching certificate came into play.

Maybe this was how it was for women back in the 1950s. Perhaps that is what my mother could have done if she had gone to college instead of opting for that shiny new car. Regardless, their predetermined plan was not my plan!

ໄ

My first job out of college was at Neiman Marcus in Dallas, Texas. The job description included fashion layout for newspapers nationwide and direct mail design. I also did freelance package design for Neiman's epicure shop to make extra money. Designing cookie tins, labels for thirty-five different flavors of expensive gourmet popcorn and packaging for a variety of other epicurean delights was most enjoyable. The freelance projects and the creativity they inspired were more pleasurable than my salaried job. Specifying type and fitting fashion drawings into newspaper layouts for advertising was not what I envisioned myself doing forever. I desired a career that would be more graphic design oriented. So I set out to find another job.

After two interviews, Susan Crane, a company that designed gift wrap for national department stores, hired me. The job seemed more suited to my talents and the salary was even better.

I left Neiman Marcus on good terms. The art director assured me that there would be opportunities to continue to do freelance package design for them. I was happy to continue having that creative avenue available.

My folks did not understand why I would leave a job after only a year. It was obvious to all of us that I had already found flaws in their plan. Our conversations were dominated by the fact that I did not have a teaching certificate on which to fall back.

Within a year of leaving college, I began my second job. My father felt this quick jump did not represent a good reputation in the working world. As my parents, they had always realized my free-spirited nature. Now I was proof in the making.

My second interview at Susan Crane was generally an introduction to the other employees. It was then that the new boss introduced me to the designer I was to replace. The proposed schedule was for me to start in two weeks, allowing me to give the proper notice to Neiman Marcus.

The exiting designer was pleasant and incredibly excited about his upcoming job opportunity with a large advertising agency in New York City. However, he had a major dilemma. Her name was Tattoo. She was his cat. I do not recall why Tattoo could not go to New York with him. All I remember is that he begged me to take her.

So not only did I have a new job, I got a cat, too!

Tattoo was two years old when we began our life together.

She was an average-sized cat with short, white fur decorated with a multitude of various-sized gray spots. The name, Tattoo, seemed perfectly suited for my new spotted girl, so I kept it. Glistening yellow-green peridot gems best describe her gorgeous eyes. Tattoo was friendly and affectionate, as well as curious and confident; it took less than a day for her to adjust to my apartment. At this point, I had been on my own for a year. I was single with my career ahead of me and entirely capable of taking care of myself financially. I owned my own car and rented a cozy, one-bedroom apartment. But it was lonely sometimes and Tattoo was great company when I was home.

Our weekday morning routine was always the same. Tattoo perched herself on the bathroom counter as I got ready for work. Watching me put on make-up was her favorite early morning activity. She gazed with curiosity as I applied blush and eye shadow followed by liner and mascara. After all, this was Dallas! And Dallas women wore make-up and dressed in the latest high fashion.

On an occasional morning, just for fun, I put blush on Tattoo's cheeks and eye shadow above her lids. When my mother visited, she teased me, "Looks like Tattoo has been in the blush and blue eye shadow again." Yes, admittedly, that was back in the days when blue eye shadow was in style!

Tattoo's favorite toys were the small make-up brushes. The last thing I did before leaving for work was to safely tuck them into the drawer, ensuring there was no chance that she could swallow them while I was away.

Tattoo must have missed me during my long days at work. Traveling time in the morning and evening was an hour each way...if traffic flowed well. Theoretically, I left at seven a.m. for an eight o'clock start time. The job was from eight to five, so I could be home by six p.m.

That rarely happened, however. After all, I was single!

So after five o'clock, my responsibilities were purely social. There were aerobic classes to attend and guys to scope out at the fitness center, although I can tell you my experiences with any jocks at the gym were nothing to get excited about. The athletes were more about themselves, how much weight they could hoist above their heads and how many females they could conquer.

I remember a good-looking guy I met while running on the track. He was quite flirtatious, but seemed nice, so I accepted his offer of a date.

Our rendezvous turned out to be disastrous, at least in my view. Unexpectedly, from the moment I got into his car, he came onto me much too quickly. His uninvited advances continued throughout the entire evening and intensified upon our return to my apartment. At that point, throwing him out was my best move and that is exactly what I did!

He called the next day to apologize for moving so "fast" while vaguely admitting that he sensed my displeasure. I explained, without mincing any words, that I do not move that rapidly, especially on a first date. And you know what he said? "Well, I move fast because I'm a sprinter!" I replied, "Well, I'm a slow, long distance runner." Then I hung up the phone. Needless to say, that was our one and only date!

Other nights were all about "happy hour." Many times, "happy" lasted more than just an hour. I often went with coworkers or met friends after work and cruised the most popular bars for singles. Half-price drinks and free snacks were more than enough for dinner. When the disco music started, we danced the night away...the whole night! I still wonder how I managed to leave the bars at two in the morning and be at work by eight a.m. (Of course, there were times I did not make it exactly at eight!)

Sweet Tattoo met me at the apartment door every evening, regardless of what time I got home. Upon hearing the turn of the key in the lock, she would make it to the door by the time I crossed the threshold. I developed the habit of inserting my foot just beyond the cracked door to gently force her back inside and entered carefully.

The evening, or whatever was left of it, was spent with Tattoo under my feet or by my side.

૽

I should have realized that the days were lonely for her. Many times, boredom motivated Tattoo to unroll the toilet paper and decorate the entire apartment. Sometimes the delicate lace pillows on the bed appeared to have been tackled and kicked like a football into the living room and kitchen. More than once, she had discovered the loose lid on the Q-tips container and the swabs inside had mysteriously disappeared. I often wondered what she did with all of them. Years later, when I moved, I found at least a hundred under my couch!

Tattoo was always there to greet me and I could count on her to welcome me home with open paws...that is, all but once!

I left work, stopped by the deli to pick up dinner and got to my apartment around six p.m. The plan was for a quiet evening on the couch with my cat and a good movie.

However, that night was different. When I opened the door to enter my apartment, I inserted my foot as customary, but there was no Tattoo to block. The apartment was eerily quiet. There was not a mew or a sign of life. I began a hysterical search. I looked under the bed, which always seems to be the first place people look for missing cats! Why is that?

The wardrobe closet was closed, but I inspected inside anyway. The bathroom shower was empty and so were the adjacent cabinets.

I hurried into the kitchen, running towards the pantry.

Upon opening the cupboard, Tattoo's gigantic, yellow-green eyes stared back at me through the dark.

"Tattoo," I shrieked! "Have you been in there all day?!" I think she nodded. I felt horrible, "Oh no, I'm so sorry!"

My poor kitty had been locked in the pantry for eleven hours! What could she have done in there all that time?

I will tell you what she did. Tattoo managed to open the Crisco shortening and break a bottle of garlic salt. Thank goodness she was not hurt. Broken glass from the container covered the floor, but there was no sign of any blood. All four paws, however, were coated in Crisco and garlic salt. Her feet were a mess.

She jumped out and quickly trotted across the floor to her litter box. She left a trail of goocy shortening and stinky garlic along the way. My idea of a quiet night, dinner and movie were replaced with cleaning the pads of her feet, between her toes…and my carpet!

I felt so guilty about the incident. After all, it was my fault! The only comfort was in the fact that it had been a day when I returned home directly from work. I cannot imagine what the pantry would have looked like if I had gone dancing all night!

❧

I spent many weekends creating freelance designs for Neiman's. Today, graphic designers have computer programs that can generate and alter graphics with the push of a key. But back in my day, design work was created at the drawing board or, in my situation, on the kitchen table. Transparent vellum paper enabled me to perfect designs by using overlays. Color changes were not made by a right or left click on the keypad mouse. We used color pens! Thin-tipped markers were for fine outlines and wide tips shaded large areas. I will boast here that I owned a marker in every imaginable color!

My little buddy was always there to help. Tattoo managed to find a spot on the kitchen table where I worked. She removed markers from their container and tossed them around like a soccer ball. Loose pen caps catapulted into the air with a quick flip of her paw. She watched them fall to the floor. Then she pounced! She chased and batted the caps throughout the apartment.

Needless to say, several made their way under the couch with the lost Q-tips, a treasure that I found much later! The expensive markers that had lost their lids during her escapade could only be salvaged by wrapping them in plastic wrap. When Tattoo tired from hunting marker caps, she returned to the table to sprawl out on top of my carefully designed layout.

I have no explanation for what came over me one day when working on a design for a butter cookie tin. Something possessed me to color Tattoo with the markers. Her pure white fur disappeared into a myriad of hues…red, hot pink, yellow, orange, turquoise, blue and purple. When the decoration was completed, she looked like a rainbow-colored cat. And she did not seem to mind. In fact, she liked the attention and we agreed that she looked absolutely beautiful. Grooming over the following days gradually turned the bright colors into a blend of soft pastels that resembled dyed Easter eggs.

Tattoo often joined me for dinner by placing herself in a semi-circle around my plate, as close as possible without actually touching it. Then, when she thought I was not looking, she swiftly swooped her paw across the plate and removed whatever she thought would suit her taste buds.

Moving around the apartment took cautious maneuvering. Tattoo was like a third leg, constantly walking between my legs and under my feet. I am not complaining. My careful footfalls and high-steppin' were a small compensation for all of the time that she spent alone. She craved our time together.

People who love cats are familiar with the phrase "lap cat."

Tattoo defined the term eloquently, without being particular about whose lap she chose. Any lap would do...mine, a friend, a date or a boyfriend. Of course, like most cats, she possessed a talent for picking the one person in a room that was not especially fond of cats. Given a choice, theirs was always the lap she chose!

Bedtime was a ritual for both of us. She carefully found a favored spot and snuggled tightly into a small nook of my body. Other times, she wrapped herself around my head and we shared the pillow. There was never a night that we were not together. And any overnight guests, if you know what I mean, had to share the bed with her too!

ॱ

Asking the landlord for permission to have a cat was not something that ever crossed my mind. It took five years for the management to discover Tattoo.

One day, a notice was posted on my door demanding that I contact the apartment manager immediately. The timing of the notice could not have come at a worse time. My fiancé had just ended our seven-year relationship, only eight weeks before our wedding date. This left me completely devastated.

I suppose the manager took pity on my plight as I sat in her office, sobbing, telling the story of my broken engagement and sharing the fact that Tattoo was my only true comfort.

The manager never asked me to leave or to find another home for Tattoo. I would have had an emotional breakdown if Tattoo had not been there for me. After that experience, it is easy to understand why I am so adamant in requiring RESQCATS adopters present landlord approval.

Tattoo watched boyfriends come and go. She stayed by my side when I was happy, sad, uncertain or with a clear vision. For the first time in my life, I truly understood what unconditional love was all about.

Tattoo welcomed Violet, a kitten I rescued off a busy highway, as easily as she accepted her new home with me. She and Violet made the cross-country trip from Texas to California in late 1985 so that I could marry the man of my dreams.

ɷ

At the age of twelve, Tattoo was diagnosed with hyperthyroid disease and was treated with a radioactive iodine treatment. Fortunately, the treatment was a success. I remember how difficult it was after her return home. The vet recommended limited cuddle time for two weeks due to the radioactivity that could be transferred from her body to mine. Somehow we got through it and she was back to herself. Once recovered, she acted like a kitten again.

Two years later, however, Tattoo was diagnosed with bone cancer in her nose. Sadly, nothing could be done to save her.

ɷ

Tattoo was my very first cat. She was the first cat I ever loved. The first cat I ever had to euthanize. The first cat I ever lost. The first cat I ever grieved for.

She was my first for a lot of things. So it is no wonder that Tattoo has first place in my heart!

It is important to understand that rescuing cats was my "calling" well before I realized it. I did not plan for rescue to become my mission in life, nor did I just wake up one day and say out of the blue, "I'm going to start a rescue organization today." It was the culmination of many things that evolved over the years.

The story of Miss Violet from Texas took place long before RESQCATS was conceived. Rescuing her aroused something in my soul. This tiny kitten on the expressway was to be my first rescue. There was no preparation or scheduling. It just happened, without thought or hesitation. Saving a kitten in peril opened a door of discovery for me. This newfound awareness would ultimately lead me to my mission in life and to the person I am today.

TWO

Miss Violet from Texas

In May 1985, I was single and working as a graphic designer in Dallas. My usual way home was to take the Central Expressway, which was the city's sorry excuse for a freeway. It was, and still is, the only way in and out of downtown from the suburbs. On this particular day, the five o'clock traffic was traveling slowly, an improvement from the usual standstill. The expressway always resembles a crowded parking lot. Since traffic appeared to be moving a little faster along the parallel three-lane service road, I took that route. I wanted to get home quickly, change from my fancy work clothes into the latest trendy workout attire and attend my favorite aerobics class.

Little did I know that my whole life was about to change... forever.

I was making pretty good time on the side road when I noticed something up ahead. It was straddling the painted lane divider. And it was moving!

No one was stopping or even slowing down to go around it. Driving closer, I could see that it was a kitten...and the kitten was alive!

Without thinking, I recklessly drove across three lanes of traffic and parked half on the curb and half in the slow lane to avoid disrupting traffic. Disrupt traffic! That was exactly what I needed to do to save the kitten! I jumped out of my car to stop the oncoming vehicles.

Now for those of you that know me today, you might think this is a common sight to see when I am out on a rescue. But in those days, dressing up for work in order to fit in with the Dallas fashion scene was very important. I made my way onto the service road with full make-up, perfect hair, manicured nails, a designer dress and my four-and-a-half-inch high-heeled red shoes that matched my belt and purse. My attire was quite different from the sweatshirts, tennis shoes, torn bleached jeans, cargo pants and overalls that have become my uniform today! But hey, it was my first rescue!

Somehow I managed to avoid the approaching cars that were rapidly heading towards me in all three lanes. I stooped down on the pavement, oblivious to the danger I had put myself in, to seize the tiny kitten.

I scooped up the small, limp body and made my way back across the road through the oncoming vehicles to my car.

The kitten was dirty and oily from the street grime. It cried faint and pitiful mews. Thank goodness, there was no sign of blood. Back then, I lacked medical experience, but I knew enough to realize that she needed to see a veterinarian right away.

I placed her on the seat next to me, put the car in drive, raced back into traffic and took the first exit off the service road. Then I headed into the nearby shopping area in search of a veterinary clinic. Those were the days before cell phones and cars with GPS. The neighborhood was highly populated with apartments, so I figured that there had to be an animal clinic somewhere in the area.

Luckily, a vet hospital appeared in full view as I turned onto the first major street. I carried the tiny kitten inside to the front desk. Fortunately, the veterinarian agreed to see us without an appointment and with only minutes to spare before his business day ended.

I followed the doctor into an examination room with the kitten tucked in my arms. The vet gently removed most of the street grime with a warm damp cloth revealing her tabby stripes and white markings. He then gave her a full inspection. He said, "This kitten is about nine weeks old."

Once the exam was complete, he reported, "She has a

bruised shoulder and mild concussion but nothing more serious than that." I exhaled with a loud sigh of relief.

The vet looked at me and smiled. Then he began writing his observations on her chart and said, "I can give her an injection to help her feel better and you can take her home. She's going to be fine. The shot will cost $31.00."

At that moment, the reality of my good deed began to set in. There was much to consider. I must have stopped breathing again.

The vet was jotting down notes for the record. When I did not reply, he looked up. So many thoughts rushed through my head as I weighed all of the options. Please understand me; it was not about the money but about taking the kitten home.

"Or," he continued, "I can just go ahead and put her down."

Put her down?! I could not believe my ears! It was true that $31.00 was a lot of money for a single person making her own independent financial way in the world. The charge card in my purse was to be used only in case of an emergency. But clearly, this was an emergency!

I explained to the vet that my real concern was my cat, Tattoo. She had been an only cat during the five years that I had been her guardian.

Besides, my apartment complex did not allow cats. The recent trip to the manager's office, when Tattoo was discovered, had resulted in her being a rare exception to the policy. Now, a new furry, two-pound dilemma had arisen. Was it possible somehow to hide this kitten?

The vet replied, "Well, I can keep her here a day or so and try to find her a home. But if I can't find one, we'll have to euthanize her."

Out came my American Express card.

Violet went home to meet Tattoo.

Surprisingly, the two instantly became the best of friends. Tattoo was what I refer to as a high-maintenance cat because she was constantly in-your-face, under-your-legs and wrapped-around-your-dinner-plate. She craved attention whenever I was home.

My after-work life was filled with social activities. This did not leave much time to spend with Tattoo. I guess I did all those things that single people do…much of which I have chosen not to recall and you do not need to know anyway!

Violet gave Tattoo something to do during the hours that I was working or out "doing my thing." The two played together, slept together and decorated my apartment with rolls of toilet paper on more than one occasion! Tattoo was like a mother to Violet. She groomed her, offered security and lavished attention. She was the best therapy a traumatized kitten could have asked for. It was fun to have two cats and I adored them.

Obviously, this was at a time before I was educated about the benefits of having two cats when you are away from home for long periods of time. Tattoo and Violet were living proof!

❧

Yes, I did the same stupid thing that I now preach to everyone. The rule at RESQCATS is that potential adopters must have landlord approval in writing before taking a cat home.

I was the prime example of not following the rules. I needed to somehow hide Violet from the management. To my credit, however, I did understand the responsibility of making a lifetime commitment to my cats and I was prepared to move to a cat-friendly apartment if caught with the second feline.

❧

There was something very special about Violet. She was quiet and shy, which was not surprising after her harrowing experience on the road. The velocity of rush hour traffic was enough to toss her miniature body between lanes. When I brought her home, she immediately found a hiding place on the bed behind the decorative lace pillows. Only her tiny tabby head could be seen. She looked like a little stuffed toy strategically placed among the fancy pillows.

Something else about Violet touched my heart like no animal had before. It felt good knowing that I had rescued her from an almost certain death. I was ultimately responsible for her being safe, wanted and loved. And the love she returned was unconditional. Violet made my heart sing in a way like nothing had before.

There was no way of knowing it at the time, but she was just the beginning of what would become the mission of my life...to rescue stray and abandoned cats and kittens.

❧

Violet and Tattoo moved to San Diego when I got married in 1986. After the move, rescuing other abandoned cats off the jetty in San Diego began almost immediately.

Violet and several of the rescued cats relocated with us to Phoenix, Arizona when my husband, Mitch, received a "cannot refuse" position with a big corporation. Insufferable heat and menacing allergies became my worst enemies. I found no redeeming value in the harsh desert environment.

Three years later, we happily returned to California and settled in Santa Barbara.

By that time, I had a dream of starting a non-profit organization to help cats like Violet. That vision eventually became a reality when RESQCATS was founded in 1997.

Once RESQCATS was in full swing, Violet overheard all too familiar tales of stopping traffic to save a kitten. She was a witness to many rescue stories...digging litters out of woodpiles, jumping fences to retrieve abandoned kittens, removing cats from unhealthy hoarding situations and kidnapping felines that were mistreated.

From the day I swooped her off the asphalt highway, Violet lived a life of ease. She seemed to appreciate that she had been saved. She welcomed the many rescued dogs and cats that joined the family during the following years.

❦

I still think of her often. Violet's memory is a reminder of my very first rescue. Even today, when I rescue a cat, I experience the same adrenaline rush that I felt when I saved her. And I feel overjoyed when the mission is accomplished!

I wish I had kept those four-and-a-half inch, red high-heeled shoes to memorialize that day on the Texas Central Expressway, the moment when nothing else mattered except saving a tiny kitten from being killed.

Maybe what I really wish is that Violet could have lived forever. She died on October 9, 2003 after eighteen-and-a-half wonderful years.

The loss left my heart broken but with a gift that no other cat could ever begin to equal. Violet led me to my path in life. I am indebted to her, as are the 2700-plus (and counting!) other cats and kittens.

❦

Sometimes you do not realize just how much someone means to you until after they are gone.

It is said that there is a Rainbow Bridge that connects heaven and earth and that our animal friends wait there for us so that we can enter heaven together. When that time comes and I cross that Rainbow Bridge, I will find Miss Violet from Texas and spend all eternity thanking her.

Until then, just her memory can make my heart sing!

The idea for this book actually began two decades ago when RESQCATS was founded; I just did not recognize it at the time. I also did not realize that a tiny kitten named Miracle would set the philosophy for the future of the organization.

Thousands of cats and kittens have passed through RESQCATS since Miracle's arrival. Only a few have been as sick and without hope. Miracle and his struggle to survive have taught me about life, its lessons, many blessings and, most importantly, to truly "Believe in Miracles."

THREE

Believe in Miracles

🐾

In September 1997, a little kitten, just six weeks old, was brought to me with the hope of saving his life. He was not your run of the mill kitten…all cute, cuddly and anxious to play. His frail body barely weighed six ounces and fit into the palm of my hand. A more appropriate weight for his age would have been closer to one-and-a-half pounds. The kitten had virtually no fur and his tail coiled like a piglet. He was so weak that he could barely lift his tiny head.

The kitten was rescued by a well-meaning lady, who had bottle-fed him for four weeks. However, the woman had no experience in caring for a newborn kitten and fed him only three times a day. Orphaned kittens require bottle-feeding, every two to three hours, around the clock, when they are first born and for the several weeks that follow. The kitten had been slowly starving to death and he was now fading fast.

To make matters worse, she had bathed him each time that he defecated. With so little nutrition and the inability to generate body heat, it is amazing that he was not suffering from hypothermia.

I fed the blue-eyed, Siamese-like kitten a bottle of warm kitten milk replacement when he arrived. Then we immediately went to the veterinarian.

The vet made a quick examination and gave me "that look;" you know, the one that says without speaking a word that there is no hope. Even back then, I recognized bad news. The doctor concluded that the kitten was too far gone and that he would not live through the night.

As readers, many of you are just beginning to know me. So please let me explain something. I do not easily accept this kind of information. I saw this as a challenge and an opportunity to save a kitten's life, regardless of what the experienced vet thought.

So I ignored his opinion and went to work. I fed the kitten every few hours and kept his body warm with a heating pad set at a low temperature. In those days, pet heating pads were not activated by the weight of the animal as they are now. I placed him in a medium-sized crate with enough space that allowed him to move away from the heat if he chose to do so. The flannel blankets inside were cozy and offered a sense of security.

In order to keep the digestive system working properly, I used a warm cloth and gentle stimulation to help him pee and poop.

The kitten was my primary focus over the next several days.

My husband, Mitch, was amazed at the turnaround after just a few days of devoted care. And so was the vet!

I decided to name the kitten, Miracle. Some of you may remember the hit song, "I Believe in Miracles (You Sexy Thing)," by the British soul band Hot Chocolate. In fact, over the next sixteen years, it was not uncommon to hear me sing that very tune as I walked through the house looking for Miracle.

❧

As they say, "The best-laid plans of mice and men often go awry." Mitch and I had made arrangements to take a long overdue and well-deserved road trip along the California coast into John Steinbeck country. It had been several weeks and Miracle was progressing well. He appeared to be in stable condition, so our planned trip was a go.

Then the kitten gave us another scare. Overnight, Miracle became dreadfully sick and it looked like we might lose him.

The vet prescribed two antibiotics and we hoped for

the best. Fortunately, after just a few days, he showed great improvement.

We were scheduled to leave in just two days. The thought of leaving Miracle behind with the pet-sitter while in his delicate condition was inconceivable. He was still extremely fragile and continued to need around the clock care.

The vacation involved driving along the spectacular California coast for about a week. After much deliberation, we decided that it might be best to take Miracle with us. Packing all the things a kitten might need was like taking a human baby on vacation! He required a large carrier in which to sleep, a small carrier for transport, a hot water bottle for the car, a heating pad for motel rooms, food, bowls, blankets, toys, baby wipes, a litter box and litter. Miracle's luggage left little room for our own!

There was one particular incident at the beginning of the vacation that I just have to share. About ten minutes into the trip, Miracle passed gas. When the pungent aroma made its way to the front seat of the car, Mitch and I covered our mouths and noses...but to no avail. Then our eyes began to water. There was no escaping the rancid odor.

As we rolled down the windows, Mitch laughed, asking, "How can something that smells so bad come out of such a small kitten?!" My best guess was that it had to do with the medications he was taking. Our next stop was a convenience store where we purchased the last can of room deodorizer on the shelf. Luckily, that was Miracle's only smelly incident, but at least now, we were ready for any similar mishaps with our citrus scented spray.

By this point in his recovery, Miracle weighed just over one pound, making it easy to tuck him into our jackets. He certainly could not be left in the car alone, so we took him with us when we strolled through the towns and visited the sights. As we walked through Carmel and Monterey, Miracle poked his head out of Mitch's jacket, commanding tremendous attention. Many people stopped us when they spotted him. He was irresistible to kitten lovers, but no one realized how lucky he was to be alive.

Sneaking a kitten into a motel room with all his luggage was not an easy task. Not a single motel where we stayed would allow pets. Kitten formula, canned food and a gallon-sized baggie filled with cat litter were hidden in grocery bags underneath the bagels, chips and other human snacks. So as not to be noticed, I covered the small carrier with Miracle inside with a towel and carried it in with our personal luggage.

I set up the motel bathroom as his little home away from home with food, water and a litter box. Then we left the door to his carrier open, so he could come and go within the confines of the room. Although greatly improved, he still did not feel a hundred percent; it was not as if he would be up playing all night. At least, we did not think so.

The antibiotics began to take effect and Miracle felt better with each passing day. Usually quiet and asleep, he was now awake and very active! In the evenings, he romped, bounced, jumped, climbed and ran around the motel room. He kept us awake longer and longer each night. Finally, on the last night of our vacation, Mitch said, "That's it! Miracle gets to sleep in the car!"

❧

Miracle turned out to be a true fighter. The dire circumstances of his first six weeks of life had a definite and lasting effect. His lack of nutrition during that time resulted in partial blindness. While walking through the house, he would uncontrollably swing his head back and forth. His limited vision combined with a quirky personality prompted me to nickname him Mr. Magoo.

He remained a small cat, at least in comparison to many of

our other cats. This was probably due to his less than fortunate beginning. But, despite his size, the word that best described Miracle was determined.

A few weeks passed and all was well. He was our little "miracle survivor" and this became an additional nickname.

❧

The joy of saving a tiny kitten from such hopeless circumstances was only the beginning of my passion in life. RESQCATS had just been approved as a non-profit organization. That happened in November 1997. One can only imagine my enthusiasm and delight. The world seemed full of happiness and promise. However, less than a month later, our bright, happy days suddenly grew dark and grim. Mitch received a call from the oncologist after his yearly exam at City of Hope Medical Center.

For over thirty-five years, Mitch had been a survivor of malignant melanoma. His cancer was discovered at the early age of twenty-one. Each year, he returned to City of Hope for routine blood work, CAT scan and a doctor's visit. The results of the tests had always been perfect...but not today! The scan clearly showed a mass wrapped around his esophagus.

I vividly recall watching Mitch's face as the doctor shared the test results. He nodded calmly, asked some questions and appeared to take the news in stride.

Mitch developed a philosophy early in life when he survived malignant melanoma, which was usually fatal in those days due to a lack of any viable treatment. His philosophy is very simple, "Plan as if you'll live forever, but live as if you'll die tomorrow."

When he hung up the phone and told me the news, my world came to an instant halt. It was like hitting a brick wall, head-on at sixty miles per hour. No brakes. No airbag. Something dark and frightening trembled through me.

I am not as emotionally strong as Mitch. I would, somehow, need to develop an inner strength in order to face whatever was ahead.

Following an aggressive regimen of a proven chemotherapy protocol, I am happy to say that Mitch made a full recovery! He is a fighter…and a survivor!

We believe there was help along the way. His name was Miracle. Just three months before Mitch's cancer diagnosis, Miracle had entered our lives. Little did we know that such a tiny kitten would offer us so many lessons. I now realize that his purpose was to teach us about fighting, endurance, hope and believing in miracles.

I had matching sweatshirts embroidered for us to wear on chemotherapy days. A Siamese kitten was stitched into the fabric with an amazing likeness to our Miracle. The letters underneath read "Believe in Miracles." We still have those shirts today.

❧

Miracle inspired me to write the Believe in Miracles stories for the RESQCATS newsletters. When a sick kitten arrives, I always ask for a miracle from the higher power that guides our destiny. When those wishes are granted, I write about them.

At one time, RESQCATS had a candle called "Believe in Miracles." It was designed just for our organization and was lit when a miracle was needed.

❧

Miracle died on October 15, 2012. All of his days on earth were good. He lived more than sixteen years when his heart abruptly failed. Suddenly, he was gone. It was my fifty-seventh birthday.

His unexpected death left me in despair. I asked, "Why did it have to happen on this day, my birthday?"

My dear husband, in his infinite wisdom, replied, "Sweetheart, now you'll always have a celebration of Miracle's life, and all he symbolized to you, on your birthday." Mitch is right.

Miracle's greatest lesson was teaching me to believe that miracles really do happen. Big or small, you just have to keep your eyes open to see them. Many beautiful lessons have come from that one tiny kitten named Miracle.

Time has passed since his journey to the Rainbow Bridge and with that has come healing. I can once again, sing out loud in celebration of his life, to the tune of Hot Chocolate, "I Believe in Miracles!"

There will always be a special place in my heart for the very first RESQCATS kitty.

Sometimes we dream about things we want, and we hope they come true. I believe that you must have a dream, visualize it, see it clearly in your mind, and be open to the challenges of making it come true. Only then can dreams become a reality.

FOUR

Elijah Blue, the First RESQCATS Kitty

In December 1997, RESQCATS officially became a non-profit sanctuary dedicated to the rescue, care and adoption of stray and abandoned cats and kittens.

Becoming a non-profit organization required months of planning.

To start with, a name for the organization needed to be selected and a mission statement had to be written.

Once the name was settled, I went to the drawing board. Using my rusty graphic design skills, I designed a distinctive logo. A succinct and informative mission statement was developed and put in ink.

It was imperative that I follow a medical protocol for the cats. I turned to my personal veterinarian who believed in my vision of creating a cat rescue. Over the years, he has continued to offer guidance and I give him credit for helping me make RESQCATS the well-respected organization that it is today.

The registration of the trademark was filed with the government and then the long, tedious process of becoming an IRS approved, non-profit organization began.

I found an experienced lawyer who could follow through on all the legal aspects of incorporation and non-profit tax status. His fee was agreed upon and the required paperwork was put into motion.

Then came the long wait for approvals. I am not sure what I expected... instant turn-around perhaps? There are times when I can be an achievement-oriented, control freak and this was one such occasion. For months, I checked the mailbox every day, hoping that the approval papers would arrive.

The wait seemed excruciatingly endless. My lack of

patience led me to wonder why everybody was taking so long. After all, I was an incredibly enthusiastic rescuer who was going to change the world for stray and abandoned cats and kittens. I was ready for action, right now!

In the beginning, every penny needed to run the organization came from my own pocket. Thoughts about finances and the ways a non-profit organization went about raising funds became growing considerations.

The old greenhouse on our property needed a tremendous amount of work in order to be transformed into a cat sanctuary. After all, it was built for plants, not animals! In fact, Mitch and I often wonder what old Mr. Goodspeed, the former property owner, would have to say about the hundreds of cats and kittens that have lived in the greenhouse that he had built for his gorgeous orchids!

My vision was to turn the dilapidated structure into a beautiful rescue sanctuary for cats. Adding a roof, siding, flooring, shelves, ramps, condos, enclosures, furnishings and various cat comforts would be expensive. Food, litter, vet care and medical supplies would be needed. And, of course, we had to be prepared for the inevitable something forgotten, missed or unexpected to come up.

I did not worry much about expenses in those days, perhaps because of my lack of financial experience. To be honest, when I was single and on my own, I went for years without balancing my checkbook and, believe it or not, only one rent check ever bounced!

From the very beginning of RESQCATS to this day, Mitch reconciles the RESQCATS checkbook. My only accounting duties are to enter the proper amounts of the checks I write and record the deposits I make. This may sound simple enough, but I am a total failure at even these small financial tasks.

Every month, I quickly learned to disappear as soon as Mitch asked for the checkbook. I know for an absolute fact that four letter words will soon follow as he discovers my mathematical mistakes. When asked about a missing entry, my reply usually goes like this, "Oh! I must have forgotten that one." While I still write routine checks, I am now no longer allowed to handle the deposits either!

Thinking back, I was naïve about a lot of things. I had no knowledge about all that would be required to operate a cat rescue organization. Fear of tackling any problems that might take place was not a concern. Maybe my creativity and ability to think outside of the box compensated for my lack of experience. Or maybe I was like the bumble bee, which, based on its weight and wing size is scientifically incapable of flying. I guess nobody told the bumble bee that he could not fly, and nobody told me I could not run a cat rescue organization.

There was only one thing I knew for certain and that was my wish to make a difference in the world. This devotion was the fuel that allowed me to face the challenges along the way. My passion for animals was heartfelt. My life's mission was clear and there was no containing my unbridled enthusiasm. The world had better get ready!

One can only imagine my "happy dance" when the corporate documents finally appeared in the mailbox. The non-profit status was approved. Finally, RESQCATS, Inc. was a reality!

Now that RESQCATS was an official 501 (c) (3) tax-deductible organization, donations could be accepted. Now all we needed were cats! It was not long before someone heard about this new Santa Barbara cat rescue group and christened us with our first formal, government-approved, legally-sanctioned rescue.

ॄ

There will always be a special place in my heart for the first RESQCATS kitty. In the winter of 1998, a stray cat was found wandering in an alley in a rundown part of town. The stunning, Snowshoe Siamese-looking cat's fur had tones of white, beige and taupe. His ears and tail were chocolate brown. A dark mask encircled his magnificent blue eyes that looked like a clear summer sky. I named him Elijah Blue.

Sadly, I learned over the years that many cats are left outside to fend for themselves. Most do not have the good fortune of being rescued and suffer needlessly.

Elijah Blue was less than a year old and had already experienced a tough life on the streets. He endured a cold winter, surprising for Santa Barbara, and had suffered from the elements. His fur was dull and matted. He was starving; his body was an emaciated skeleton. For some unknown reason, he also had a sore and bruised back. I wondered what had happened to him. Early in my rescue career, I realized that it is best not to always know the heartbreaking circumstances behind some of the rescues; my time is better spent healing feline bodies and souls.

The ability to mend kitten hearts came naturally to me. From his first day at RESQCATS, Elijah Blue knew he was safe and loved. I reassured him with affection as I tended to his every need. Fluffy pillows and blankets replaced cold asphalt and hard concrete. A padded bed was a welcome substitute for uncomfortable nooks and crannies behind buildings and under cars. Fresh water took the place of dirty puddles and street gutters.

The food bowl was always full. Elijah Blue thought canned

cuisine was a real prize and ate it like there was no tomorrow. In just two weeks, his boney skeleton was replaced with a sinewy body covered with a lustrous coat of silky fur.

Despite the trauma of his life on the streets, Elijah Blue's disposition was sweet and exceptionally outgoing. He loved to play fetch and chase feather toys. He interacted with anyone who entered his enclosure and discovered that the human lap was his favorite place to park when playtime ended. Due to his loving nature, I guessed that at some point he must have belonged to someone.

Elijah Blue was the first RESQCATS kitty to undergo the medical protocol set up by my veterinarian. Every cat or kitten that has come through our doors has followed this regimen. They are examined by a vet and tested for Feline Leukemia and Feline Immunodeficiency Virus (FIV). They are vaccinated and treated with deworming medication. The females are spayed and the males get neutered. Cats are available for adoption only after all of their medical needs have been met.

Healing Elijah's Blue's body proved to be simple compared to many of the other cats and kittens that came to RESQCATS over the years. For Elijah Blue, a mild adjustment with a special tool relieved some of his back discomfort and an anti-inflammatory injection eased his pain.

When it was time to find a home for Elijah Blue, I grew uneasy at the thought of parting with him. I anticipated feeling sad when adoption time came. What would it be like after he was gone? Would I worry about him? Would the adopters want to stay in touch? I reminded myself that the purpose of RESQCATS was to find homes for the cats…not to keep them! This was my first test as a foster mom and it was important that I get it right!

Yes, I passed the fostering test! Elijah Blue found a great home.

A young woman, her husband and their cat, Joey, adopted Elijah Blue. The family understood his significance as the very first RESQCATS graduate. The couple was sympathetic to my attachment and offered to keep me updated.

I felt like I was on Cloud Nine, knowing that he would never suffer on the harsh streets again. Elijah Blue paid his good fortune forward with unconditional love to his new family for many years.

ʡ

As I write this book, more than 2700 cats and kittens have come through the doors of RESQCATS. While I remember many of them, my thoughts always return to sweet Elijah Blue.

Elijah Blue was the first RESQCATS kitty. He remains iconic because he symbolizes my dream that became a reality.

Some may say that Elijah Blue was only a cat, but to me, he was the beginning of my life's work.

I did not create RESQCATS with the intention of keeping any cats. Looking back, I must have been inexperienced and extremely naïve to assume that all cats were adoptable. In 1999, a decision had to be made. What should I do with cats or kitties that are not adoptable?

Many county shelters euthanize cats that they claim are unadoptable. Sometimes, if an animal has not found a home within a certain amount of time, usually only a few days, the shelter kills them.

The philosophy at RESQCATS is that every life is precious. So I chose to keep any unadoptable cats or kittens and make a lifetime commitment to caring for them.

The first cat that became a RESQCATS resident, however, was adoptable. She just happened to have her own agenda!

FIVE

Smudge, the First RESQCATS Resident

The sweet voice on the other end of the phone belonged to a young woman. She called RESQCATS because the construction company where she worked was finishing a year-long project and she was concerned about a stray cat that had made itself at home inside the office trailer on the site. The job was ending in a few days and the trailer would be removed. None of the workers stepped forward to offer the stray a permanent home. She could not imagine leaving the cat behind.

RESQCATS agreed to accept the cat, follow our customary medical protocol and find a suitable home.

The cat had a charming personality and she easily settled into her new surroundings. She had luminous green eyes and thick short fur. The placement of her black and white tuxedo markings gave the impression that she was wearing a white pinafore. There was a cute, little black spot on her white upper lip; you know, the kind that would be called a beauty mark on someone like Cindy Crawford or Marilyn Monroe. I named her Smudge.

The vet estimated that Smudge was about two years old. She appeared to be in perfect health and had been well fed by everyone at the construction site. I cannot remember if she was spayed, but I can assure you that if she was not, she would be by adoption time!

A young couple adopted Smudge almost immediately. It seemed to be a perfect match. When I did not hear from them, I assumed that all was well with Smudge and her transition into their home. No news was good news…or so I thought.

Imagine my surprise when the couple phoned a month later and wanted to return Smudge. Their reason still resonates in my head, "She's not happy here."

During the early days of RESQCATS, no one had ever asked to return a cat. I was not accustomed to hearing all the reasons that people give for not keeping their promise of a lifetime commitment to an adopted animal.

I was more perplexed and confused by the couple's statement. "She's not happy here." At the time, I took a passive role because I could not comprehend their explanation. I merely replied, "Okay. When can you bring her back?"

That was then...my attitude is different now.

Over the years, I have become much more outspoken when it comes to vocalizing my disappointment. The explanations people give when relinquishing their animals are usually inexcusable. While some truly have legitimate reasons for placing their pets in a shelter, most people do not! The comments go like this:

"I'm moving."

"I'm pregnant."

"My new boyfriend doesn't like cats."

"My roommate is allergic."

"The cat I adopted seven years ago is timid and shy."

"It has litter box problems."

"I'm going on vacation."

"The cat doesn't like my new baby."

"The mom and kitten I adopted are knocking over things in my new condo."

"The kitty eats my daughter's hair ties."

"I can't afford to keep it."

"My cat is eighteen and I need to find it a new home."

"My eight-year-old cat doesn't like the new kitten we adopted."

The excuses are endless. You get the idea?

Over the years, my response to a person's perceived lack

of responsibility has escalated. I have heard the same lame excuses over and over again. While I am not proud of all that I have said during a few fits of anger, I can honestly say that my comments have always been based on the cats' welfare!

ê

Once Smudge was returned, I tried to comprehend why the couple thought that this cat was unhappy. She was friendly, purred like a locomotive and immediately plopped into a basket where she proceeded to roll belly-up from side to side, ensuring that I rub every inch of her tummy. Then Smudge stood up and began to knead the soft bedding with her feet, a behavior I call "making biscuits!"

Smudge appeared to be just fine. So I placed her on the "Available for Adoption" list once again.

Callers are pre-screened during a phone interview to determine their suitability as an adopter. A better description would be that I rake potential adopters over the coals! Once the caller has passed the test, I go on to describe the cats that are available for adoption. Then an appointment time is scheduled to meet them.

My description of Smudge went like this, "Smudge is friendly, fond of belly rubs and she's the kind of kitty that will meet you at the door when you come home from work. She loves to play and I even promise to send some of her favorite toys home with you."

Several people made appointments to visit. Based on my description, many presumed they would be walking out the door with Smudge as their new furry family member.

However, during these auditions, Smudge took on a totally different demeanor. The ingénue lay in her basket like "a dead brick," a term I coined to describe her performance. She ignored everyone who entered the enclosure. She showed no sign whatsoever of having the least bit of personality. In fact, with the exception of her half open eyes, she exhibited no sign of life! That cat made me look like a poor judge of cat character. I was shocked the first time she responded to someone in such a manner. Then it became routine at every adoption appointment.

Once the now uninterested parties had gone and the performance was over, Smudge reincarnated back into her familiar, sweet self. The belly-up position was resumed. Her purring echoed throughout the cattery. Finally, after she was done making biscuits and kneading her pillow for maximum comfort, she theatrically plopped into bed. The actress was proud of her accomplishment...she had gained another night at RESQCATS!

After this curious scenario had played out several times, I decided to contact an animal communicator. I asked myself, "What's going through that little cat's head?" I needed answers from someone who dealt with these kinds of issues. I know, many will think I had lost my mind. An animal communicator! Really?

Throughout the history of RESQCATS, I have entertained such a notion on several occasions.

❧

While many claim they can communicate with animals, I believe there are only a few with the true gift.

I had an unfortunate experience with a veterinarian who only thought he had the ability. He was a travelling veterinarian in a mobile vet van and he boasted of his vast training in traditional veterinary medicine, as well as holistic treatments. The shaman claimed that he could converse with animals that were not feeling well, despite the lack of a medical diagnosis.

The self-proclaimed clairvoyant vet arrived at RESQCATS with wooden sticks that resembled dowsing rods, the ones used to find groundwater and hidden objects. The power within the rods would guide him to cats with medical issues. I was not allowed to tell him which cat had the problem.

However, his vibrating sticks led him to the wrong cat… not once, but twice!

The vet was so upset that he began yelling a variety of excuses and explanations. He got so loud and worked up that he frightened me…and the cats! I politely asked him to leave and to never return. He packed his sticks and hightailed it off the property.

On a different occasion, I gave another so-called animal medium an opportunity to diagnose an ill kitten that had me very worried. Customary to the psychic's profession, she was told only pertinent information so that I could analyze her insight skill. It did not take long to realize that she was like a parrot repeating my words. Whatever I said, she would echo back to me. Needless to say, her visit to RESQCATS was very brief!

Years later, I attended a seminar on animal communication that held great promise. The class brochure guaranteed that anyone could learn how to communicate with animals.

The instructor stood before a roomful of eager students that wanted to learn his techniques. He said, "Your first step in the program is to clear your mind completely in order to receive the messages your pets and animal friends send." I failed miserably. I never got past the first step. It was not possible for me to clear my mind. My brain is a busy beehive. I am constantly juggling thoughts, formulating creative ideas, remembering appointments and maintaining a hectic schedule. Frankly, I have never been interested in relaxing my mind. It just seems, well, so futile. Besides, now that RESQCATS was becoming known, we were getting busy. The last thing I needed to do was clear my mind of all thoughts!

Finding a reputable animal communicator is a challenge, but it was not as hard as finding Smudge a home. I wanted to know what Smudge was thinking. Why was this feline thespian putting on a show for hopeful adopters? Fortunately, I finally found an animal psychic who was recognized on a national level. Anna, not her real name, was professional, compassionate and sensitive. I believe that she had that special gift.

Once we connected, Anna requested a photo of Smudge and we set a time for a phone consultation.

According to Anna, Smudge told her that she wanted to live at RESQCATS. She never wanted to leave and that is the reason why she was unhappy in the adopted home. The couple did not mistreat her. In truth, they provided everything she needed, gave her ample time to adjust and showed constant affection. Simply stated, Smudge preferred to live at RESQCATS!

"What?" I exclaimed, "I didn't start RESQCATS to keep cats! This is an adoption organization!"

The thought of such a dilemma had never crossed my mind. I certainly was not prepared to offer homes to cats that just did not want to leave!

The animal communicator suggested a resolution for Smudge with several steps. First, a special blend of herbal essences was formulated. Second, I was to communicate with Smudge in a particular way. The purpose of the talks was to remind Smudge that RESQCATS was not her final destination and that she needed to be open to finding her own home.

I did as directed. The psychic shipped the herbal mixture that she had developed. Appropriately, it was called "Transition." Each day, six drops of the special potion were put into her water dish. Then, several times during the day, I followed the communication instructions. I was to find a quiet time to speak to Smudge through my mind and my heart. I stated telepathically and very emphatically, "Smudge, this is not your final destination. RESQCATS is only a stepping stone in your lifelong journey. You will find a home and you are leaving." To be on the safe side, I repeated this out loud.

Smudge just looked at me with her steady and intense gaze. She spoke through her heart and her mind and stated very distinctly, "I am not leaving."

ₑ

Over the next four months, numerous attempts were made to introduce Smudge to potential adopters. While this may not seem like a long time, kittens were being adopted at a record pace. I grew concerned when a cat or kitten stayed at RESQCATS longer than a few weeks.

It became increasingly clear that I had lost the battle. While I would like to say I was the one who decided that Smudge could stay, most people would disagree. So let me just say that Smudge and I came to a mutual understanding.

On the day I admitted my defeat, I cautiously opened the door to Smudge's enclosure. She now had full access to the entire cattery. She was able to meet and greet the other cats that lived at the facility. Smudge became the very first official RESQCATS resident in 1999 at the age of two.

Other resident cats were added over the years. However, unlike Smudge, all were truly deemed unadoptable due to health, age or personality issues. Smudge remains the only cat to have clearly followed her own agenda!

For a time, Smudge lived happily among the other cats.

ₑ

There is a certain phenomenon that occurs when several cats live together. As the population changes, when one passes away or another is added, the dynamics of the established hierarchy shift. Some felines become more assertive and rise in the chain of command when a cat dies. Others find themselves demoted in the pecking order with a new arrival.

Often, one can determine the hierarchy in a feline population by observing where a particular cat perches. The established leaders will strategically place themselves on the highest level of a condo. Cats that have been put in their place, or just do not care, will find a position that is physically lower. Some seek a hiding place out of fear. The entire chain of command often changes with the addition of a new resident.

Unfortunately, Smudge found herself on the lowest rung of the ladder. I am uncertain as to why. She became frightened, reclusive and retreated to the outdoor enclosures. She hid and would not come inside to eat or play.

One day, things changed for the better when out of fear, Smudge refused to come in from the rain. Who knows? Maybe she was acting again! Regardless, her performance was rewarded with a private suite. Her furnishings included a large dog crate filled with fleece bedding, a running water drinking fountain and a high-rise kitty condo that offered a view of the entire cattery. A driftwood ramp led from the floor to an upper shelf where a cozy basket awaited her. A covered tunnel led to an outdoor enclosure that measured eight feet by eight feet with ramps and shelves for basking in the sun. She had several fashionable sets of black and white blankets, custom made to coordinate with her black and white markings.

Smudge was one spoiled, happy cat!

Her lasting stay presented a policy dilemma. What are our conditions for permanent residence? What do we do about cats and kittens that are not adoptable?

I believe that every life is precious. I do not condone the commonly held policy that euthanasia is the answer if a cat or kitten is unadoptable. Having my own organization allows room for those individuals. It gives me the latitude to make those decisions.

While I understand that not all shelters have the space to keep animals indefinitely, they often mislead the public on their euthanasia policies. The nationwide trend is moving towards shelters that proclaim to have a no-kill policy for adoptable animals. However, there is no fine print to educate the general public on the definition of adoptable.

The prevalent meaning of adoptable is that an animal must be at least eight weeks old, sociable and healthy. Therefore, a litter of abandoned, newborn kittens may be euthanized as they do not meet the age requirement. They could also be killed if there are no resources, such as a foster home or available finances to bring them up to eight weeks of age.

What is a healthy animal? What happens when a seventeen-year-old cat develops kidney disease? Or a two-year-old suffers from pancreatitis? Is an animal with ringworm considered unhealthy and doomed to die? In many shelters, cats with medical issues, even though they are treatable, are euthanized.

Sociable is another term that needs clarity. Many animals are terrified in shelter conditions. Most often, they need time to adjust in order for their true disposition and potential to emerge. Sadly, too often, frightened animals are quickly assessed as unsocial and euthanized.

The ambiguous definition of no-kill misleads people into thinking that an animal can be dropped at a shelter in any condition and it will not be euthanized! That is simply not true!

I take every available opportunity to educate the public about this lack of transparency. I am proud to share with everyone who visits RESQCATS, "We are truly a no-kill sanctuary! If a cat is too old, too feral, too shy, has too many health issues or is too anything, the cat lives out its life at RESQCATS!"

The only exception to the rule was Smudge!

❧

Smudge lived to be eighteen years old. She never suffered from any long-term illnesses. She became sick unexpectedly and left for the Rainbow Bridge in the summer of 2015.

Her only difficulty was that she became forgetful at times. She failed to remember that I had just given her treats or "cookies," as we call them at RESQCATS. I referred to her memory lapses as "sometimers." Sometimes she remembered and sometimes she forgot! Whenever anyone entered the cattery, Smudge would resort to a pitiful meowing, as if to complain, "I haven't had any cookies today!" She was the volunteers' favorite resident and they played right into her paws. Smudge indulged in an unlimited supply of cookies up to her very last day. On second thought, maybe she was not a "sometimer." Maybe she was just acting!

Her passing was a loss to all of us at RESQCATS.

For weeks, my sadness was overwhelming. I cried until I thought there could not possibly be any more tears.

Mitch asked me one day if I had allowed any kittens to occupy her enclosure. I told him I had not. He said, "Jeffyne, you need to put some life back into her space." He was right. Seeing new lives where she once held center stage has certainly helped heal my heart. Still, there is not a day that I don't miss her...and her dramatic performances!

Rescue work is a twenty-four hour a day, seven days a week job, particularly when orphaned kittens need to be bottle-fed! Without any warning, my life instantly changes when newborn kittens are discovered without a mother. Every day, a precise schedule of mixing warm kitten milk replacement and feeding the kitten, or litter of kittens, at three-hour intervals must be followed.

Caring for such young ones is a rewarding experience, but it is also an exhausting one.

By the third night, I find myself wishing there was an available surrogate feline mom to do what comes so naturally. A nursing mother cat is always better for the kitten. She provides continuous warmth and unscheduled feedings that allow the kittens to suckle as long as they desire. This is preferable and natural, unlike a set schedule offered by a human foster.

Seldom are kittens so fortunate. This is the story of a feline that did get lucky and how he "paid it forward."

SIX

Ted

In the fall of 1999, I received an urgent phone call from the local after-hours emergency veterinary clinic. The panicked voice on the other end of the line said, "We have a baby kitten that someone found under the bushes and brought to our hospital. We can't locate his mother! Can you take it?"

Within thirty minutes, I held the tiny gray kitten in the palm of my hands. His coarse, curly gray fur could best be described as a Brillo pad. He weighed a mere six ounces. Both eyes were closed. His ears were folded tightly against his head, indicating he was about a week old, certainly not more than ten days. Kittens' eyes begin to open at ten to fourteen days of age and their ears are fully upright at three weeks.

I named him Ted.

When newborn kittens arrive without moms, I become the surrogate mother and caregiver. The days and nights are scheduled around bottle-feeding a formula that is designed to mimic the mother's milk. Kitten milk replacement is mixed, warmed and put in a soft-nippled bottle with the hope that the kitten can suckle. Feeding is required around the clock for several weeks until the kitten can be gradually weaned onto regular canned food and kibble.

I always set an alarm clock in order to wake up to feed every three hours. But by the time I get up, warm the milk, feed and go back to bed, I cannot sleep for worrying about snoozing through the next alarm. By the end of the first week, it feels like I have been to seven consecutive nights of slumber parties!

Mother cats stimulate their babies to urinate and defecate.

During those first critical weeks of life, the only source of nutrition for the babies is the mother's milk. Kittens' digestive systems are not ready for solid food until they are four to five weeks old. When there is no mother cat, stimulating the kitten to take care of Mother Nature's disposal systems becomes my job. I keep a large supply of baby wipes on hand to help with the bathroom duties. Hopefully, the kittens at RESQCATS appreciate the fact that I have invested in a baby-wipe warmer!

Once the kittens are eating on their own, and enough time has passed for me to catch up on some much-needed sleep, I look back at the hard work and long hours as a wonderfully rewarding experience.

Of course, the best formula in nature for a kitten is to have a real mother and her milk. A lone kitten also greatly benefits from the company of siblings. Unfortunately, this is not always possible.

❧

When Ted arrived, RESQCATS was caring for a semi-feral mother with three kittens. The babies' eyes were open and they looked like miniature, navy blue marbles. Their ears had already unfolded and were almost in their full upright position. I estimated them to be about three weeks old. Although mom was watchful, she trusted me to pet her babies.

Occasionally, when the mother cat was feeling less suspicious, she even permitted me to touch her. I was cautious when I approached. I whispered softly and gently reached inside the crate where she felt safe to caress her silky coat. I hoped to eventually be able to pick her up.

The volunteers had named the kittens Piwacket, Neesia and Snoopy. Piwacket was a solid black bundle of fearless energy. Neesia was a long-haired black and white girl whose curiosity took precedence over everything. She could not resist the need to know all that was going on around her. Snoopy was a painfully shy black and white tuxedo boy. He had six toes on each front paw. The unique genetic deformity of having extra toes is called hyperdactyl.

The kittens had started to walk, although, wobble was probably a better description. They amused themselves and became curious about their surroundings. I always find it entertaining to see a kitten discover toys or a sibling's tail… or sometimes their own tail! Minutes can easily turn into hours watching them as they quietly roll, tumble, and wrestle in what appears to be a silent action movie in slow motion.

In 1999, RESQCATS was still a new organization, so there was more time to observe the activities of each litter than there is today.

However, with the arrival of Ted, I quickly realized that I could no longer sit and watch Picwacket, Neesia and Snoopy for hours. My time and attention needed to be focused on bottle-feeding and caring for him.

At that time, I had no experience bottle-feeding kittens, but I had all the confidence in the world that I would be successful. I wanted to make sure that everything was in order, so I called my veterinarian for advice. He confirmed the appropriate formula, the proper amount and number of feedings that Ted needed to not just survive, but also to thrive.

Then the vet had an idea. He suggested putting Ted with the semi-feral mother cat and her litter. He thought it would be better for the kitten to have a feline mother where he would receive antibodies through her milk. Ted would also have playmates. I followed his advice hoping that the mother cat would accept him.

The mom quickly fell in love with her new baby. She immediately developed a strong bond with Ted. Caring for him became her job. In fact, she became so protective that she never allowed me to approach Ted or her kittens when they were close to her. She let me know of her disapproval by hissing and lashing out with her extended claws.

The kittens grew quickly over the next few weeks. Ted's size and weight even surpassed his adopted brothers and sister that were at least two weeks older.

Ted particularly liked his new brother, Snoopy. His gregarious personality was contagious, so Snoopy seemed to forget his fears when Ted was around to instigate mischief. He helped Snoopy feel at ease. They explored the enclosure and travelled up and down the driftwood ramps together. The two boys spent hours hunting fake mice and chasing balls. They pounced on imaginary toys that only their feline eyes seemed to see! The two entertained each other for hours.

Ted and Snoopy became quite the pair. It was hard to imagine them ever being separated. I told potential adopters that they had bonded, even though they were not biological brothers. Within minutes of observing them, anyone could see how close they were. I hoped that an adopter would come to the same conclusion. Otherwise, I would have to find a way to say, "No, I'm sorry, but I can't separate these two."

In the early days of RESQCATS, I was much more accommodating with people. I founded the organization to take care of abandoned cats and kittens. I was a novice at the whole adoption process and quickly found myself thrown into the unknown territory of interviewing potential adopters on the phone. I had to determine whether or not they would be appropriate care-givers before ever meeting them face-to-face.

My nature is one of non-confrontation with a strong desire to please. Yes, I was fully capable of saying "No!" but I did not have as much practice at it then as I have today. I was naive to the dishonesty of people telling me what they thought I wanted to hear in order to adopt. I did not realize that people would actually lie to me! But I have always believed that finding the best qualified homes for the cats and kittens is much more important than pleasing everyone.

❦

Happily, Ted and Snoopy were adopted together by a wonderful family. They kept me up to date on this exceptionally bonded pair. They reported, "The boys are always into something and Snoopy is far from the shy little boy he once was. They're still inseparable!"

Ted was a lucky little kitten to be discovered that day under the bushes. His good fortune continued from the moment he was adopted by a feral mom and her kittens. He was blessed with the nurturing love that only a mother could give.

In return, Ted gave a feral cat purpose as a surrogate mother. He helped his shy little brother feel secure and evolve into a fun-loving, outgoing kitten. And with Snoopy by his side, he gave his human family unconditional love.

❦

I wish we could all be a little more like Ted. When someone does something nice for us, we in turn should "pay it forward" by doing something nice for somebody else. A single kind gesture that is passed on to someone, who then passes it on again, results in a continuous flow of positive karma. Just think about the rewards if everyone paid a good deed forward!

More people like Ted the cat would certainly make our world a better place.

My favorite quotation can be found on a greeting card that I keep posted on my bulletin board. There is a photo of a tiny, orange, tabby kitten looking at himself in a full-length pedestal mirror. The reflection the kitten sees is that of a large regal lion with a stunningly beautiful mane. The quote is particularly meaningful to me and reads, "What matters the most is how we see ourselves."

SEVEN

Blink, A Lion in the Mirror

It was the spring of 2002. RESQCATS had been in operation for five years. The organization was well-known and highly respected within the community. We had already found homes for hundreds of stray and abandoned cats and kittens.

By this time, I was very familiar with caring for kitties that had come from terrible conditions. Days were spent treating sick kittens and aiding malnourished mother cats that were doing their best to care for their babies. I was bottle-feeding newborns whose mothers had abandoned them or had met horrible fates.

Every day is a challenge in rescue. This particular season had truly been one test after another with many compromised moms and kittens. About the time one cat was out of danger and on the mend, the next ailing litter arrived.

The medical care that RESQCATS provided had already cured many little feline bodies that spring. The love that the cats received had helped heal broken spirits. My tireless work was rewarded each time a happy and healthy kitten went to a new home.

The week had been quieter than usual. I actually thought there might be a bit of a reprieve and some light at the end of the tunnel. It is odd how life seems to give you a little break before the next challenge comes plummeting towards you at full speed.

This time, the challenge was a tiny gray and white kitten. He arrived at RESQCATS along with his brother, three sisters and their sweet mom. The mother cat was extremely weak and so malnourished that her rib cage almost punctured her skin. Fortunately, a compassionate lady discovered the abandoned family after their uncaring owner moved and left them behind.

ໃ

I cannot fathom how people can abandon animals. There will never be a bone in my body that could comprehend such cruel behavior, so I do not even attempt to understand it. I feel it is better to focus on those who are compassionate and try to forget the heartless people of the world.

ໃ

An enclosure was prepared for the family's arrival. A large crate, filled with fresh blankets, allowed plenty of room for mom to nurse her babies in comfort and safety. I kept the mother cat's food and water containers filled at all times. A heaping bowl of kibble was something she obviously had not experienced in a long time, if ever. However, canned food was her preferred cuisine. The tasty chunks in gravy disappeared instantly when it was put in front of her. I made certain that her favorite canned food was always accessible.

Even though the kittens were still too young to play, I put several toys nearby. My theory is that the balls with bells and fake fur mice should be available as soon as the babies are old enough to start exploring their new world.

New Age music from the CD player echoed softly throughout the cattery. The tranquil tunes were soothing to the mother cat compared to the coyote howls and street traffic noise that so often accompany stray life. The trickle of running water fountains offered peaceful background sounds.

The kittens were just beginning to interact with each other. They tumbled and rolled inside the crate without a sound. I find it amusing that so much commotion can occur, and yet, the kittens are so small that there is virtually no noise as they play. Watching them at that age, as they discover the world, is like watching a toddler take his first step.

Based on their activity level and appearance, I estimated

them to be about three weeks old. The kittens' ears were still half folded. Their navy blue eyes were fully open with the exception of the little gray and white male. One of his eyes was crusted shut, so I used a warm washcloth to gently cleanse the area. I intended to apply an antibiotic once it opened. Goopy, runny eyes are common in little kittens, so I was not overly concerned.

By the following morning, the kitten's eye had opened. However, it was a horrendous sight, unlike anything I had ever seen. The eye was cloudy and swollen. Worst of all, no pupil or retina was apparent. The condition certainly must have been causing excruciating pain.

Sadly, the vet confirmed my suspicions. The eye was severely infected and the kitten's vision had been destroyed. There was nothing resembling an eyeball left inside the socket. What did remain would have to be removed and the socket would need to be sewn shut.

Before leaving the veterinarian's office, I named the kitten Blink.

The following days were spent making multiple trips to the vet in hopes of finding relief for Blink. His eye had swollen to four times its normal size and was so irritated that it had started to bleed. To complicate matters, the doctor felt it would be best to postpone surgery until he was at least four months old…six months would be ideal. The lengthy anesthesia time that was required for the surgery would be better tolerated when he was older.

"But he's in pain. What about now?" I asked. The veterinarian suggested injecting antibiotics directly into Blink's eye using a minuscule needle. The medication would dry up the infection, shrink the eyeball and, hopefully, give him relief from his constant pain. I cringed and almost fainted at the thought of a needle in this tiny kitten's eye!

❧

As a child, I had a tendency to faint at the mere sight or thought of a needle. My first recollection of having a needle phobia was when I was eight years old. My mother had taken me to the doctor for a routine injection. I cannot remember what it was for, probably a childhood booster. However I do recall my unexpected visit to the floor!

It happened while Mother was writing a check to pay the bill. I was standing between her and my younger brother, Stan. I do not know whether it was the medicine in the syringe taking affect or if I just had ample time to think about the needle. But all of a sudden, my knees weakened and my head began to spin. My body broke into a cold sweat, and in what seemed like slow motion, I gradually slid down the side of the counter shouting, "M-o-t-h-e-r!" as I collapsed into a heap like a pile of dirty laundry.

My mother assumed that Stan had pushed me and was fully prepared to reprimand him. However, a nurse who was making her way from one exam room to another saw exactly what had happened and came running to my rescue. Today, Stan would say that she saved him, too!

The nurse escorted me to the nearest chair in the closest exam room. She fumbled through a drawer, found what she was looking for, unwrapped it and gave me a big piece of hot-pink bubble gum. The sweet sugar from the gum did the trick. Within a few minutes, I was back on my feet.

My phobia for needles has continued into adulthood. But now, more often than not, I recognize the signs of an oncoming fainting spell because of that childhood experience.

As an adult, I have had my ears pierced six times. Following each piercing session, I needed to sit for a while until the dizziness dissipated.

I also had my belly button pierced a number of years ago as a surprise for my husband. Of course, that was a time when I still sunbathed in a bikini. After my 50th birthday, the bikini and tan disappeared along with the girlish waistline. But that's another story.

My good friend, Erika, escorted me to the belly button piercing appointment. At the time, she was just fifteen and had recently gotten her driving permit which allowed her to drive with a responsible adult present. The piercing procedure went fine…that is, until I sat up! Then once more, that all-too-familiar sensation took over. The room began to spin. I felt a cold sweat come over me. I knew if I stood up, my knees would buckle under me and I would end up on the floor again like that proverbial pile of laundry. Poor Erika was more fearful than me. She actually thought she might have to drive home. Thankfully, the room stopped rotating within a few minutes and I began to feel well enough to take the wheel.

If we can skip the conversation about my apprehension when I have my blood drawn, I might save myself the embarrassment of passing out right now!

I give the credit for overcoming my needle phobia entirely to RESQCATS. The fact that I can now listen to a veterinarian talk about putting a needle in a kitten's eye, administer subcutaneous fluids and vaccinate kittens myself shows that I have "come a long way, baby!"

❦

Blink was a little trooper during his vet visits. He took all the poking and prodding in stride, never wincing when the antibiotics were injected into his eye. Thankfully, the procedure was successful. He was no longer hurting and I felt tremendous relief for him.

However, my worries about his discomfort were replaced with different concerns. Eye surgery would be expensive. How could I possibly raise the funds for such a complicated operation? Would Blink stay at RESQCATS until he was old enough to undergo the procedure? Who would adopt a kitten knowing he might end up with only one eye? And if he did remain at RESQCATS, was there someone who would adopt him when he was six months old with a sewn shut eye?

Sadly, within my first few years of doing rescue, I learned that most people would see him as a kitten with a defect. Other kittens that had no abnormalities would be adopted more quickly.

Blink, however, was totally unaware that he was different. Like all kittens, he loved to play, romp, chase feather toys and tackle his siblings. He was outgoing and super friendly with people. In his mind, he was absolutely normal and had everything going for him.

I lost count of the number of potential adopters who passed on adopting Blink. Regardless of everything he had in his favor, his appearance was less than perfect, at least in their narrow vision! Finding Blink a home was beginning to look like an unattainable task.

Around that time, a friend who stopped by to donate blankets, towels and bedding had an unexpected gift. She was in a hurry, so there was not an opportunity to introduce Blink or to share his story.

I quickly thanked her for all the donations, said good-bye and returned to put away the fresh smelling towels.

To my surprise, I noticed an envelope on top of the linens addressed to RESQCATS. I opened it immediately. Inside was a sweet note and, amazingly, a check for an amount that would cover the cost of Blink's surgery. Coincidence? I do not think for a minute that it was luck. As I said earlier, I believe in miracles!

ૂ

Adoption appointments proceeded as usual. I introduced every person that desired a kitten to Blink. Unfortunately, because of his appearance, no one wanted him.

It was not until weeks later that Reid, a twelve-year-old boy, and his mother came to RESQCATS in search of a new feline member for the family. Like every potential adopter, they were introduced to all the kittens and then I left them alone to visit with each litter. I feel strongly that it is important for adopters to have private time without me there to influence their decision.

I returned several times during the next hour to check on Reid and his mother. Every time I came back, Reid was in the same enclosure. Whenever I checked in, there he was sitting on the floor playing with the same kitten! He had fallen in love with Blink. I overheard him say, "Mom, you can pick any kitten you want to adopt as long as I can have Blink."

Reid found no flaws in the one-eyed kitten. He saw a new fur buddy that loved to play, pounce and chase balls. When playtime ended, Blink climbed up Reid's pant leg as if it was a ladder, settled into his lap and quickly fell asleep.

Blink was adopted that afternoon along with a playmate that Reid's mother had chosen.

The following months for Blink were uneventful from a medical standpoint. But according to the reports I received, kittenhood was like second graders heading to the playground for recess. The two ran, jumped, pounced, tumbled and entertained themselves nonstop!

When Blink reached six months of age, Reid, his mom and I met at the veterinary clinic for a scheduled follow-up visit and pre-surgery exam. My friend's donation had been set aside to cover the estimated cost of surgery and any needed after-care.

Miraculously, the vet felt that Blink's eye was doing exceptionally well. Since it was not causing any problems, he saw no reason to do the operation. Sight in his damaged eye never returned and the socket remained open, but that did not seem to bother Blink or his human family.

During the following years, Reid and his Mom continued to keep me up to date. They shared many wonderful stories about Blink and his adopted sister. I was delighted each time I received an update.

❧

I often reflect on what Blink has symbolized to me over the years.

Time and again, people question my passion for animals. They ask, "Why don't you spend more of your time helping people in need instead of animals?" My feelings about not consuming animals but rather choosing a vegan diet are frequently laughed at and often criticized. A few people even go so far as to ask, "Why aren't you a real mother to a human baby instead of caring for cats?"

At those moments, I return to memories of Blink and his insightful gifts. Blink saw himself as a normal kitten... fun, loving and perfect in every way. It made no difference to him if he had one eye or three! When I think about Blink, I remember that his lessons in life were very clear to me from the first day I saw him.

Perceptions of ourselves should not be based on the judgment of others, because, just like Blink and the little kitten on the greeting card who saw his reflection in the mirror, "What matters the most is how you see yourself."

Reid's lesson took a little longer for me to comprehend, but it is just as important. Perhaps the fact that I do not have human children of my own is partly responsible for taking more time to realize his significant message.

Reid's gift is a humbling reminder from which we can all benefit...there is an innocence in childhood that sees no differences, passes no judgment and loves unconditionally.

With five years of rescue experience under my belt, I thought I had seen just about everything, but Mother Nature always has a way of presenting new challenges. Although I have never proclaimed to know everything, even those with much more experience are surprised by some of the unusual medical issues that manifest themselves in animals.

Patience is not one of my virtues. Sometimes, a quick fix is not always possible and therein lies my personal lesson. Waiting until the opportune time for a procedure can be risky, but postponing surgery can pose a much greater danger. However, with the best of intentions, it was a chance we had to take to save a kitten named Isabel.

EIGHT

Isabel, My Lesson in Patience

In the first few years of operating RESQCATS, I had gained a lot of experience. Although I had faced many kitten health issues, it seemed that there was always a new challenge.

Jezzie was a sweet mother cat who had been living in a colony of feral cats with her five kittens. The four boys and a girl were about four weeks old. Jezzie was tame, so I suspected that she had been dumped. She did not hiss, lunge, bite, scratch or exhibit any of the behaviors that are common among feral cats. She was outwardly friendly as she greeted everyone that entered her enclosure. Although I would never know her particular circumstances, two things were certain: Jezzie was not feral and she had gotten knocked up!

It is a fact that older kittens are harder to tame if they have not had the benefit of human touch. With every passing week, the success of socialization decreases. Kittens that have not been exposed to people should be easier to socialize at four weeks old than at eight weeks. My experience has also led me to believe that a kitten's prenatal environment starts to play a role in socialization. Beginning in the womb, feral kittens often take on the stress that their mothers feel. For example, if we are relaxing in a yoga class, meditating on a mountain top or taking a stroll on the beach, different hormones are released than those produced when we are feeling anxious. It is the same for cats.

A feline living in a comfortable home with plenty of food, safe surroundings and human companionship is less physically and emotionally stressed than a cat living on the street constantly searching for food, water and shelter. The differences in the environment that a pregnant cat experiences can have a profound effect on the kittens she is carrying.

For instance, I have socialized feral kittens as young as two weeks of age that never quite got past being timid and cautious, regardless of the number of hours I spent with them. So whether it is a house cat or a street cat, the stress a kitten experiences from conception can have a direct bearing on its lifetime disposition.

ॄ

Socializing Jezzie's kittens would be easy since she had such a sweet nature. Because she was so friendly, her kittens would most likely become outgoing, social butterflies like her.

Jezzie and her babies were covered with fleas when they arrived. Mom was treated with a topical solution, but her kittens were too small to tolerate chemical treatments. A bath was in order for the little ones.

Denny, a longtime volunteer, helped bathe the kittens.

ॄ

Denny joined RESQCATS as a volunteer more than fifteen years ago. Initially, I was hesitant because I had never had a male inquire about volunteering. I do not know if it just seemed odd that a man would want to work around a bunch of cats and women, or if I had just not given any thought to having men volunteers. I interviewed him on the telephone, as I would any applicant, and suggested that he visit RESQCATS before he made a commitment.

I was quite apprehensive and thought it best to tell Mitch about the interview. I said, " A man called today and he wants to volunteer. He sounds nice, but it seems strange to me to have a male volunteer." Mitch had the same concern and replied, "Just make sure I'm here to meet him."

Denny certainly was accomplished. He had a PhD in

physics and was a practicing patent attorney. He was also a certified pilot. With that level of intellect, I could not imagine what I could offer that would challenge his mind and keep him interested in volunteering.

As it turned out, Denny was not looking for anything intellectually stimulating, but rather just the opposite, a place away from the stresses of career life.

His first job at RESQCATS was socializing kittens. During each visit, I introduced him to the kittens and told him which ones were the most fearful and needed human attention. I came and went into the cattery putting up laundry and dishes as a way to check on him. Most often, I heard him gently talking to frightened kittens and quietly laughing at the playfulness of others.

I soon discovered that Denny was also a great maintenance person. He could fix broken latches and replace faulty light switches. I was even able to recruit him to repair leaky faucets. But Denny found his real niche in bathing kittens! Over the years, he has bathed literally hundreds of kittens while also becoming a dear friend.

{

The job of getting rid of every single flea is an arduous task. Not everyone steps up to volunteer to bathe kittens, so I try to make it fun. To entice Denny's help, I make him an offer he cannot refuse! I serve him the richest chocolate brownies he has ever tasted. That sweet indulgence is served with a hot chai latte made to his liking. The thought behind the treats is to ensure that he has enough of a caffeine buzz and sugar high to do the job!

Denny generally sets out the needed grooming supplies for nail clipping, bathing and drying. I gather the scale and worksheets to record weights and dates for worming and vaccines. While bath time is accompanied by a lot of talking and laughing, we both agree that there is something very therapeutic about bathing a kitten. A soapy bath followed by a gentle massage with soft towels serves to calm the kittens as we get rid of the fleas. Denny usually does the bathing. The blow-drying and hair-styling are left to me!

There is one occasion that I will never forget. Denny arrived to help bathe a litter of seven kittens. But since I had him cornered with enough sugar and caffeine on board, I thought I could slip in a few more. Five hours and sixteen cats later, he left frazzled and exhausted but with a smile on his face. Denny has always been a real trooper...but especially on that day!

Denny removed Jezzie's only female kitten, Isabel, from the carrier. As he began to bathe her, he suddenly became quiet when he noticed a huge protrusion from her belly. It was different than anything we had ever felt or seen. The lump was the size of a large plum. Fortunately, it did not seem to be painful. The fun and laughter of the moment was immediately replaced with deep concern.

I scheduled Isabel for an appointment with the veterinarian that afternoon. She was diagnosed with a hernia, a tear in the abdominal wall. Many kittens are born with umbilical hernias that are not problematic. But the doctor agreed that Isabel's hernia was unlike anything he had seen during his thirty-year practice. He suggested that she see a board certified surgeon.

This was the first time in the history of RESQCATS that a cat or kitten had been referred to a specialist. Even back then, I knew such a referral might not result in good news. The prognosis could be bad and I was frightened.

Veterinary medicine has grown in proportion to the

significance of pets as family members. Every specialist in human medicine has a counterpart in veterinary medicine. Over the years, I have become evermore grateful for cardiologists, orthopedic surgeons, eye specialists, oncologists, dermatologists and other veterinarians who are experts in their particular field. The additional years of education and dedicated study in order to become knowledgeable in a specialized area of veterinary medicine offers the opportunity to save many more animal lives.

❧

The surgeon was astonished at the size of Isabel's hernia. He thought a complicated operation might be required. The extent of the surgery could not be confirmed until he opened her belly to see the damage and how to repair it.

The operation and the prolonged anesthesia time was more than a four-week-old kitten could withstand. The doctor suggested waiting until Isabel was at least twelve weeks old. By that time, her body tissue would be stronger and able to hold internal sutures. There would also be a better chance of surviving the lengthy anesthesia. As long as Isabel showed no signs of distress, a delayed operation would increase her chances for a successful surgery and a normal life.

Eight weeks seemed like an eternity to wait and hope that Isabel would continue to do well. The pressing danger was that her intestines could suddenly twist and cause a blockage. If that happened, emergency surgery would have to be performed and her chance of survival would decrease dramatically.

❧

When I describe myself as "proactive," I really mean "impatient." I am someone who sees things as black or white. Even my moods are best described as simply up or down. There is no in-between with me. I have no gray area. And now, Isabel had created a huge gray zone. She challenged my natural state of being!

I never considered pre-adopting Isabel. Many people inquired and were very interested in giving her a home after surgery. But I felt that it would be unfair to have someone fill out the adoption papers and visit her week after week knowing that something could go terribly wrong. Dealing with an adopter's grief, not to mention my own, would be overwhelming.

The volunteers also had a connection with Isabel. Her favorite spot was on their laps. She captivated their hearts and they all loved her. I could not imagine how I would console them if something happened to her. I knew I was doing everything the vet recommended, but I would have to reassure them that everything possible had been done for her. That was a day that I hoped would never come.

Fortunately, Isabel thrived during the following weeks. She managed to keep up with her brothers, who were much bigger and stronger.

Kitten energy is like flipping a light switch between on and off. Kittens in the "on" position are romping, running, chasing, playing and tumbling. When they are in the "off" position, nothing can awaken them from the sweet calm of a kitten slumber. It is a sight to behold!

Isabel watched as her brothers were adopted. Jezzie also found a new home which left Isabel all alone. There was nothing I could do about the timing of her surgery, but I could cure her solitude. Her loneliness was remedied by moving her next door into an enclosure with healthy kittens. She made friends instantly. When that litter was adopted, I moved her again to another enclosure with new playmates. She got along with everybody.

Finally, the day of surgery arrived. Isabel was now twelve weeks old and doing well. She checked into the hospital with the heartfelt love and good wishes of the volunteers. Everyone was optimistic and looked forward to a triumphant outcome.

Surgery took over two hours! Two hours and twelve minutes to be precise! I know the exact time because I waited in the hospital lobby very impatiently. There was a big clock on the wall which only served to remind me of just how slowly time passed. Each tick was followed by a seemingly endless pause before the inevitable tock. Tick…tock, tick…tock, tick…tock. Were there only sixty seconds in a minute? And remind me; are there just sixty minutes in an hour? Why did the hospital put a clock in the lobby anyway? It seemed like time crept by at a snail's pace!

After what felt like an eternity, the surgeon appeared from the operating room with a big smile on his face and happily announced as he came down the hall towards me, "All went well!"

Those three words had barely passed his lips before I leapt from my chair and sprinted across the room, wrapped my arms around him and gave him a mammoth hug! I just could not help myself. I was so relieved.

The vet thought Isabel had actually suffered a traumatic injury that could have broken her back and pulled the muscles on one side of her body. His best guess was that another animal had caused the injury. Perhaps she had been attacked by one of the feral cats in the colony? I will never know for sure.

Isabel was released from the hospital the next day and returned to RESQCATS. Preparations for her recovery were already in place. The rehabilitation plan was to wait on her "hand and paw." Isabel played and greeted us with happy mews as if nothing had happened. And as usual, she kneaded her own brand of buttermilk biscuits on our laps with her tiny feet.

Four months had passed since Isabel's arrival. She finally had a clean bill of health. Now the time had come to find her a home. But she was five months old and I feared that she would be passed over by potential adopters who wanted younger kittens.

❧

Human nature tends to mislead people when it comes to adopting. The tiniest kittens are usually the first ones to leave. The bigger, older Isabels are frequently left behind.

I have spent years trying to figure out that side of the human psyche. I have come to realize that my perspective on adoption is quite different than most people. How others think when adopting an animal has been an enlightening learning process for me.

I was very naïve in my early years of rescue. Everyone who visited RESQCATS in search of their furry family member was able to see all the cats and kittens in the facility.

Nine-to-ten-week-old kittens were available for adopters to take home that very day because the medical protocol we follow was complete.

Seven-week-olds could not leave for at least another two weeks because they were not old enough to spay or neuter.

Six-week-old kittens were a full three weeks away from being able to go to their new home.

And for newborns, the waiting period was two months!

It was maddening to watch people pre-adopt the six-week-old kittens first. The next to get pre-adopted were the seven-week-old ones.

By the end of an adoption day, many of the youngest kittens had homes, but they would not be ready to leave for days or even weeks. I was left with the older kittens, the nine and ten week olds that could have been providing love and companionship to their new guardians that very night!

To add misery to madness, those who had pre-adopted the younger kittens insisted on visiting them at RESQCATS every week, sometimes even twice a week…or more!

In an effort to solve the problem, I decided to try my hand at some marketing techniques. I hung signs on the enclosure doors that informed visitors which kittens were available to go home that day. The idea was that the signs might satisfy the "instant gratification" trait that seems to have consumed our current population. But unfortunately, people either did not see the signs or they just ignored them. It seemed that everyone still wanted the smallest kittens!

When my first attempt failed, I decided to divide the cattery into sections. I set up a partition that separated the available litters from the ones that were weeks away from adoption. This tactic was only slightly more successful.

Since RESQCATS operated on an appointment only basis, I tried another approach. Before adopters arrived, kittens that could not leave for homes that day were placed in carriers and hidden in my garage. But thanks to my husband, this tactic was also unsuccessful.

I recall one particular afternoon when I was showing cats. Mitch walked into the entrance of the cattery and loudly announced in a voice that everyone could hear, "Hey Jeffyne, do you know there's a carrier with kittens in the garage!"

I have no idea what prompted him to do such a thing. He might have been shocked to discover kittens in carriers stacked in his garage. Maybe he really thought I did not know about them. Regardless, I shoved him out the door as swiftly as he had appeared when making his uninvited announcement. He had jinxed my plan! His punishment was that he was banned from the cattery during adoption appointments!

To make matters even worse, despite having a wonderful, compassionate heart, he does get carried away. Mitch would like to keep every kitten he sees. Since RESQCATS has adoptable kittens from March through November, it is now an unwritten rule that the cattery is off limits to him during kitten season.

If he was left unchecked, I shudder to imagine how many more cats we would have!

Unbeknownst to me, a new volunteer had fallen hopelessly in love with Isabel. Kay had never mentioned anything about her profound affection. Maybe she thought it was against the rules as a volunteer to favor a particular kitten. Or perhaps she wanted to make sure that Isabel survived. Whatever the reasons, she approached me one day and asked, "Jeffyne, Isabel has captured my heart from day one. Can I adopt her?"

Isabel went home with Kay. Only two weeks later, Kay's nineteen-year-old cat died. She was especially grateful to now have Isabel there to help her through her heartache.

Shortly after Kay adopted Isabel, Ferdinand, a handsome buff and white purring machine from RESQCATS also joined her household. And then, two years later, she added a third feline, Blessing, to her family.

Kay continued to volunteer at RESQCATS for many years.

Although Isabel is one of many kittens that have passed through RESQCATS, she is truly one of the most memorable. She taught me a great deal. She gave me a better understanding of what it means to be patient. She reminded me that fixing something quickly is not always possible. And she helped me to understand that everything is not always black and white, but rather, many shades of gray. These are lessons that I continue to work on and accept as part of life.

Animal rescuers are always "on call." When an animal needs help, we stop whatever we are doing because nothing else in the world seems more important.

Saving animals is our calling in life. In our minds, the words "animal rescuer" are invisibly printed after our name.

We go to great lengths to safeguard animals. I can say from experience that rescuing brings on a euphoric emotional high.

However, rescue takes on a new dimension when it comes to someone who never saw herself as a rescuer of animals. This is the story of a woman who heard and answered the cries of a stray cat.

NINE

Polar Bear, the Best Cat Ever

It was winter 1999. The night was especially cold and damp for Santa Barbara. A young woman named Susannah was awakened by the cries of an animal outside her bedroom window.

She recognized the pitiful sound as meows of a cat in distress. Within seconds, she had slipped on her robe and ventured into the chilly night to investigate. She followed the cries and discovered an unsightly cat that had probably once been a majestic creature. It did not take a mastermind to see that he had been down on his luck for a very long time. Somewhere beneath the street dirt was what appeared to be a white cat. But his fur was no longer the color of glistening snow. It was dirty-gray, matted and greasy. He was so emaciated that every rib was visible through his skin. His jowls were thickened with scar tissue from the wounds of past street fights. His tired, dull eyes lacked sparkle. Outside Susannah's bedroom window was the end of his road...or so it seemed.

Susannah carried the listless body into her house. She offered the cat what was probably the first real meal he had eaten in weeks, or perhaps months. She gathered a thermal blanket and set it in front of the furnace where the cat settled into the make-shift bed and slept quietly through the night.

Susannah acted on impulse when she ventured into her back yard to answer the cat's cries. Unlike those of us involved in daily rescues, Susannah, in her haste, had no plan for what to do with him. Her only thought was, "Here's a cat that needs my help. And he needs it now!" Her actions came from her kind heart.

The next day, Susannah took the stray cat to the closest animal hospital, which coincidentally happened to be one of the veterinary clinics that works with RESQCATS.

After the vet examined the cat, he phoned me and said, "Jeffyne, I have a really nice kitty here that one of my clients found and he sure needs your help."

Although the cat was in poor shape, his physical exam was promising. His feline leukemia and FIV tests were negative. There were a few scratches on his face and he was underweight, but there was nothing seriously wrong that could not be cured with time and good nutrition. The vet offered to neuter the cat and take care of some minor dental issues at no charge if I would take him.

I brought the cat to RESQCATS the following day. He immediately made himself at home and seemed grateful for his first-class accommodations. Although several comfortable baskets and a large crate were available to him as sleeping spots, he preferred a chair that I had placed inside his enclosure. I had put it there for me to sit on when I visited him, but from the start, he made it clear that it was his chair! It was where he wanted to rest! I thought, "After everything that cat has been through, he deserves to sleep anywhere he wants!"

At that time, there was no electricity in the building. Since I could not plug in a heating pad, I placed a hot water bottle under a blanket on the seat. The warmth must have been comforting to his weary body. He seemed quite cozy.

I kept bowls of dry kibble, canned food and fresh water available at all times. As he began to settle in, he appeared more and more contented. I believe that somehow he knew that his luck had changed.

Since he occupied the chair, I sat on the floor next to him. I wanted to get acquainted and have a closer look at his face. When our eyes met, I felt an overwhelming sadness engulf me. Although I would never know everything that the stray cat had endured, it was apparent that he had once been a strong, handsome feline. But now he was tired. His body was physically battered. And I had no way of knowing how injured his soul might be.

I gently picked him up and stroked his fur. Tears filled my eyes. I took his sweet face in my hands and put my forehead against his. I placed him in my lap where he snuggled into a comfortable position. As I softly spoke to him, he peered at me through one blue and one green eye! I had never seen a cat with different colored eyes. Then, he began to purr.

I tried to envision such a lovable stray attempting to survive in a coyote-inhabited area with no food or shelter. The thought of what he must have experienced was beyond my comprehension. Was he lost? Had anyone looked for him? How long had he been on his own? How could he remain such a gentle spirit? Although I would never know the answers, I promised I would find him a safe place to call home where he would never want for a full food bowl, fresh water and, most importantly, love.

I named him Polar Bear after Cleveland Amory's cat in his books, *The Cat Who Came for Christmas* and *The Cat and the Curmudgeon*. I have read all of Amory's books about a stray white cat that he rescued, including his last book entitled, *The Best Cat Ever*. Funny, I have never been able to figure out why Cleveland Amory thought he had the best cat ever because, with all due respect to Mr. Amory, I knew I had the best cat ever!

Polar Bear spent the next month at RESQCATS sleeping on his favorite chair. The only time he stirred was to eat or when I shifted him from the chair and offered him his other favored spot...my lap. Gradually, with proper and regular nourishment, he started to gain weight. His white fur began to glisten like freshly fallen snowflakes in moonlight and his eyes became clear and bright. Through it all, Polar Bear's sweet disposition never wavered.

It was now time to search for a special person who would offer him the home and the cushy lap he desired. His adopter would be required to keep him indoors, not only because he had suffered enough outside, but more importantly, because his pink nose and white ears made him highly susceptible to skin cancer.

Several weeks passed before a young woman replied to a newspaper ad I had placed in the "Pet of the Week" section. I described Polar Bear's rescue to her in detail. "I'm guessing that Polar Bear was abandoned or got lost because he has a sweet disposition and he's not afraid of humans," I told her. The lady said that she had been searching for a white cat on behalf of her retired father whose own white cat had recently died.

I replied, "Polar Bear might be perfect for your dad because he's definitely a lap cat." In fact, I emphasized that a lap was a prerequisite. The woman agreed and said that she and her elderly father, Dick, would like to visit Polar Bear.

As soon as Dick laid eyes on Polar Bear, I could see that it was love at first sight. But there was one problem. Dick was a very large man. When he sat in the chair and I started to put Polar Bear in his lap, something unexpected happened. His lap disappeared under his huge stomach! Gone! Non-existent! I knew I would have to overlook that requirement since Dick and Polar Bear had bonded instantly. I presumed they would work it out...somehow!

Dick wanted to take Polar Bear home. I explained to him that Polar Bear needed additional recovery time and more veterinary care. He offered me reassurance when he said, "That's okay with me. I understand it's part of the responsibility of having a pet."

Polar Bear left RESQCATS that very day. It took him

no time to adjust to his new home. He made friends with Dick's other cat and the two even slept together on Dick's bed. Polar Bear was safe and loved.

I never did find the courage to ask how the lap issue worked out!

Dick stayed in contact with periodic updates on how he and Polar Bear were getting along. Polar Bear had earned a special place in my heart and I loved hearing stories about him. During one of our conversations, Dick exclaimed, "My Polar Bear is the best cat ever!" I will never forget the irony in that statement!

Three years later, I answered an unexpected knock at our front door. I immediately recognized Dick and his daughters, but who was that cat they were holding? Could it possibly be Polar Bear? This cat looked quite different. It had a large tummy, just like Dick's. But as I took a closer look, there was no doubt about the beautiful white feline staring at me through one blue and one green eye. The rumbling purr confirmed it. It was Polar Bear!

After we chatted for a while, Dick's daughters pulled me aside. They wanted me to know that Polar Bear had saved their father's life. Dick had suffered from severe depression since the loss of his previous cat. Polar Bear had lifted his spirits and given him new purpose.

Their surprise visit was one of my happiest moments ever. Once I realized it was Polar Bear, I began to weep; just as I had the day Polar Bear arrived at RESQCATS. But this time, they were tears of happiness and gratitude.

Polar Bear spent many years with Dick. When Polar Bear died, I wanted to do something to remember him and to honor the family that gave him such a wonderful home.

Polar Bear had required continuous veterinary care, even after he went home with Dick. He never fully recovered from his injuries. He walked with a slight limp, a condition I had never witnessed with him. Remember, at RESQCATS, Polar Bear rarely left his chair except to eat.

I thought that RESQCATS would benefit from having a fund for cats and kittens that required medical care beyond the normal protocol. I established the Polar Bear Fund in memory of Polar Bear...the best cat ever.

Since its inception, the fund has helped cats and kittens with critical eye surgeries, emergency blood transfusions, vital cardiac procedures, life-saving tumor removal, and other highly-specialized veterinary care.

The Polar Bear Fund is still active today and has saved the lives of many felines who found themselves on a downward spiral. These cats were the lucky ones; someone heard their cries...just like Susannah once heard Polar Bear's.

Rescuing cats does not always go according to even the best laid plans. It can be an emotional roller coaster of ups and downs, often one with uncertain and unpredictable medical problems. However, the health issues that kittens face can usually be overcome with the appropriate treatment, diligent care and boundless love.

Sometimes, the scars left behind are reminders of the miracles that take place along the way!

TEN

Luke, Nike, Otto, Feather and Falcon

It was mid-November in 2001 and RESQCATS had experienced a longer than usual kitten season. Fortunately, an end was in sight, or at least that is what I thought.

I received a phone call from a concerned lady who had learned about a litter of kittens and their stray mom living inside an auto body shop. She said that the owner of the shop was well-intentioned, but he was at a loss as to what to do with an unexpected feline family.

A phone call was certainly in order. The caring shop owner said that the cat had appeared one cold morning. He had discovered her sitting on his shop's doorstep. He had no idea where the cat came from, nor did he realize that she was pregnant. Since the business was located in a light industrial area, there were no houses for miles around. He invited the stray inside and set up a place for her in his back room.

There is no question that the cat's luck changed for the better when he brought her into the shop. She was off the streets and out of danger. She had a warm place to sleep, fresh water and a full bowl of dry food.

To his surprise, several days later, the shop owner discovered that the cat had given birth to five kittens! He was a compassionate, well-meaning man with a huge heart. To his credit, he spent the next two months attempting to care for the mother and her babies. Unfortunately, he had no experience when it came to providing properly for kittens. He was not trained to recognize problems that might threaten their health or well-being.

The mother cat was extremely shy and responded only to the shop owner. She appeared to have selected him as her sole caregiver. Cats sometimes do that. They pick us! Believe me, I have been chosen by more than a few!

We agreed that it would be difficult to separate the mom from the only human that she had ever trusted. By this time, the man had come to love her. He enjoyed having a companion and said, "I'm happy to keep her. She'll make a great shop kitty!"

When I picked up the litter, my plan was to make sure the kittens followed the RESQCATS medical protocol: vet exam, leukemia test, vaccinations, worming medication and spay or neuter surgery. By now, the babies were nine weeks old and I felt certain that all five would be enjoying wonderful lives in new homes by Thanksgiving.

The kittens had been living in a dark backroom that reeked of oil and car grease. They had never ventured out of the room, nor had they ever seen the light of day. But they did have plenty of food, water, and a litter box. Most importantly, they had a safe place to sleep away from predators and other outdoor threats.

I made arrangements for the mother cat to be spayed. Once that was finalized, I put the kittens in a cat carrier and quickly headed for the car. I had scheduled an appointment for their vet exams that afternoon and I did not want to be late.

I was excited to look at the kittens in the light. Once outside, I peeked inside the carrier. It was difficult to see them as they huddled next to each other in the back of the crate, but I did notice that their fur looked strange. I thought to myself, "They probably just need a good bath to wash away the grease and grime. Then they'll look great."

The trip to the vet proved me to be very wrong. The kittens were infested with fleas. They also had so many ear mites that their ears had to be flushed not once but several times. The usual topical treatment for earmites was insufficient to kill the tremendous number of pesky bugs, so an injection of Ivermectin, a parasite medication, was administered.

The vet's instructions were to return every two weeks to repeat the injections until there was no sign of the mites.

As if the mites were not enough, the kittens' bodies were also covered with scabs and huge chunks of fur were missing. I knew about fleas, but I wondered if the infestation had caused the fur loss and scabbing. At the veterinarian's office, one glance under a black light exposed the underlying problem. The kittens had the worst case of ringworm the doctor had ever encountered. While ringworm is a treatable fungus, it is difficult to eradicate and is highly contagious.

The vet turned to me and said, "Oh Jeffyne, you have a long road ahead of you to get this under control."

One of the kittens looked like a huge scab. The ringworm and extensive fur loss made it difficult to determine his actual color. He also had a deformed paw that resembled a clubfoot. In order to walk, he placed his weight on the outside of his foot causing him to limp slightly. I suspected that he might have difficulty jumping onto higher ground. But fortunately, his foot did not appear to cause him discomfort. I named him Falcon.

The three remaining brothers became Luke, Nike, and Otto. The tiniest kitten was a female that I named Feather.

While at the vet, blood was drawn from each kitten to test for feline leukemia. I expected the results later that day.

I left the clinic and headed directly home to prepare an isolated area. Because of the ringworm, the kittens could have no contact with any other cats.

Once the isolation room was set, the arduous job of bathing them began. Bathing kittens takes place in a large sink in the laundry room of our house. Each kitten got a flea bath and a blow-dry with a hairdryer set on a low temperature.

The flea bath was followed by a lime sulfur dip that directly treated the ringworm. The dip was bright yellow and smelled like rotten eggs! The odor was so pungent that it caused me to gag. That wretched smell permeated the entire house. The sulfur dip was not to be rinsed off. It was to remain on the skin and air-dry so that it could kill the fungus. The fur that remained on the kittens became a dull yellow due to the sulfur color. I was to continue the dips until no sign of ringworm was visible under a black light.

Oral medications are also available to treat ringworm, but they are dangerous to use on young kittens. The lime sulfur dip was safe and non-toxic and would, hopefully, eliminate the fungus.

It took more than four-and-a-half hours to bathe five kittens that first day. As the weeks went by, I was able to decrease the bathing session to only three hours. The little family now looked less pitiful than when I picked them up at the body shop, but that was not saying much. At least the fleas were gone and the sulfa treatment had alleviated the burning and itching.

The kittens settled into their isolated room. Once out of the carrier, they headed straight to the food bowls. Canned kitten food was a new indulgence; they devoured it in minutes. I scattered several toys around the room for them to discover, but they were exhausted from the very long day. With full bellies, they crawled into their fleece bed, piled one on top of another and immediately fell asleep. I called it "a pile of kitties!" It took another two weeks before they began to explore and play with the toys...and each other.

Since ringworm is highly contagious, it was critical that every precaution be taken to not spread the fungus. Unfortunately, I had learned from a previous experience that I am highly susceptible to contracting ringworm, so I needed to be especially careful.

I devised a precautionary plan. To ensure that no volunteers would be exposed, I was the only person that handled the kittens. It became my sole responsibility to spend hands-on time with the litter, so they would become accustomed to human touch by adoption time.

All my RESQCATS duties that did not involve the ringworm kittens were done first. Cleaning their enclosure was saved for last. In order to eliminate the chance of spreading ringworm spores, I stepped into a shallow tub of bleach water before entering and exiting their room. When I returned to the house, I stripped completely. I dropped my contaminated clothes into the washer that was filled with scalding water and bleach. Then I dashed through the house; it was winter after all, so dashing was a must! I raced through the laundry room, the connecting hallway, past the kitchen, into the living room, and then up the stairs leading to the master bedroom and bathroom where I showered. The entire process had to be repeated every time I had contact with the kittens, which was five or six times a day!

In those days, I was younger and well-toned. Nothing had succumbed to gravity. Imagine my husband seeing my naked, sexy body streaking by several times a day and not being able to come near me for fear of getting ringworm!

When I shared my established protocol with the vet for his approval, I expected he would agree that I was doing everything possible to prevent infecting myself, Mitch or the other cats. He approved, and then teasingly asked, as if he may need to supervise, "Now when are the times that you run through the house?"

The results of one of the feline leukemia tests came as

a shock. Luke tested positive! It was the first time that a RESQCATS kitty had ever tested positive for the leukemia virus.

The standard protocol in most shelters for leukemia-positive cats is euthanasia, but that was never going to be the policy at RESQCATS. Even in my early days of rescue, I was of the opinion that unless a cat is suffering and nothing can be done to help, it would not be euthanized. And a cat certainly would not be killed because it tested positive for this virus.

Research has proven that a feline leukemia positive test means one of two things: 1) The cat is a carrier of the virus and may or may not become symptomatic, but it can infect other cats through the exchange of bodily fluids when the virus is shedding; or 2) The cat has been exposed to the disease and the body is in the process of building antibodies to fight it off. In that case, it could retest negative for leukemia.

Since Luke's siblings tested negative, the veterinarian advised isolating Luke and retesting him in thirty days. I hoped that he would fit into scenario number two. I felt terrible about separating Luke from his brothers and sister since they were the only comfort he had ever known, but it had to be done.

The next month was one of uncertainty. So many questions came into my mind. What happens if Luke tests positive again? How do I find someone who will adopt a leukemia-positive kitten, knowing that the average lifespan is only about three years? Should the siblings be retested? What if all five are positive? Could a separate area be built at RESQCATS for the kittens to live out their shorter lives?

To add to my worries, Luke became a very unhappy

kitten when he was away from his siblings. There are few things more upsetting than a lonely kitten. He let his displeasure be known by mewing relentlessly. This only served to increase the stress on his already compromised immune system. It was hard to imagine how a little creature, with so much energy and such a big voice, could be sick.

Luke's isolation room had four solid walls so that he would have no contact with his brothers and sister. He had plenty of toys, but he was only content when I was there to keep him company. Frequent interaction is an important element for any cat's well-being. Luke absolutely needed regular stimulation to keep up his spirits.

One of my volunteers had a great idea to help Luke. She offered to loan RESQCATS a large wire enclosure that was stored in her garage. She proposed setting it outside the cattery so that Luke could enjoy the sunshine, look at the birds and watch us as we went about our daily chores. The enclosure was assembled in an area frequented by the volunteers. Now they could interact with him with feathers and dangling toys. Of course, the volunteers still had strict instructions not to touch him.

Luke's enclosure overlooked a courtyard where Mitch's adopted African sulcata tortoises live. These slow-moving prehistoric-like creatures gave Luke something else to watch, along with all those invisible wonders in nature that only kittens seem to see!

At night, when Luke was worn out from all the daytime activities, he was happy to retreat to the quiet solitude of his isolation room. He seemed content with the arrangement.

It took nine-and-one-half weeks, sixteen sulfur dips and many hours each day to care for Luke, Nike, Otto, Feather and Falcon. They were my constant focus and concern. I hoped that all the attention and work would pay off and that my prayers for Luke's health would be answered.

As recommended, Luke was retested for leukemia after thirty days. Waiting even the few short hours for the results seemed like an eternity. I tried to think positive and push out my fear of a less than optimistic outcome. At last, the call from the vet came. Luke's test was negative!

The joy of reuniting Luke with his siblings was incredible. His siblings welcomed him and they played for hours as if to make up for lost time. Then, weary from all the activity and excitement, all five curled up in a kitty pile and fell fast asleep. For the first time since their arrival, I was able to sleep through the night.

❧

"The Auto Body Shop Kittens" became the litter's group name. It had taken many weeks to get them on their way to recovery. Despite my diligence with the sulfur dips, they did eventually have to take oral medication to knock out the last of the ringworm. The appropriate doses were compounded for each kitten based upon its individual body weight. Fortunately, by this time, their immune systems were stronger and they were old enough to tolerate the drug.

❧

The Auto Body Shop Kittens were finally available for adoption at the end of January. They attracted some extraordinary people to RESQCATS and all five were pre-adopted long before they were ready to go to their new homes. RESQCATS could not release them until the completion of their on-going treatments. A follow-up visit to the vet would make sure they were entirely clear of ringworm. Each time a progress report delayed their delivery date, the compassionate families showed only understanding and patience.

Otto went to a home where he would have another kitty playmate in addition to his human family.

A very sweet couple fell in love with Feather and Falcon. They did not see Falcon's foot as a deformity. They affectionately referred to it as his "special" foot.

Luke and Nike put on such a show with potential adopters that they also went home together. That same family returned to RESQCATS twelve years later and adopted two more kittens.

Each adoptive family was sensitive to my attachment to this special litter. When I wept as they left, they offered me comfort, reassurance and even granted me visitation rights. I felt it would be too emotional to take them up on their offers, but it meant a lot to me knowing the invitation was extended. It would be impossible to not love them so deeply after nursing them back to health.

Even though I took extreme measures to avoid catching ringworm, several lesions showed up on my hand and wrist. They burned and itched and were very painful. I suffered with just a few spots, so I can only imagine how the kittens felt with sores covering their entire bodies.

Well after they healed, several of the spots left scars on my wrist. But having those permanent marks does not bother me. Instead, they remind me of three miracles...the miracle of Luke, the miracle of healing the body and spirit, and the miracle of compassion that radiated from each of the families who gave homes to these special kittens.

I will always remember Luke, Nike, Otto, Feather and Falcon.

Always!

The length of each kitten season varies from year to year. Usually by the end of November or the beginning of December, all the cats and kittens have been adopted and I am looking forward to a winter break. By that time, I am physically exhausted and emotionally drained. It is then that I normally take several weeks off to recover from the long days that rescue work requires. I am more than ready for a vacation!

However, there was one time when rescuing a cat proved to be much more healing than taking a vacation. His name was Mr. Jingles.

ELEVEN

Mr. Jingles

The phone rang on the afternoon of December 23, 2003. When I answered, a woman's voice on the other end of the line asked, "Is this RESQCATS?"

I thought to myself, "The last kittens of the year have been adopted so this should be a short conversation." If the woman was inquiring about adopting, I could do a quick interview. And if the caller passed my rigorous test, she would be put on a waiting list for spring kittens. I replied, "Yes, this is RESQCATS."

The voice on the phone said, "Well, I have a story for you!"

Before I knew it, the words, "Well everybody does!" had slipped past my lips, followed by a little chuckle.

The woman explained that for the past several weeks, a stray cat had been visiting where she worked. Because of the unusually cold and rainy weather, the employees at the company began inviting the cat inside to eat and sleep. In an effort to find the cat's owner, they had also posted "Lost and Found" flyers around the neighborhood. Unfortunately, the guardian was never located.

The office staff named the cat Mr. Jingles, a most appropriate name as it was just weeks before Christmas. As the days progressed, everyone there became quite fond of Mr. Jingles, so they were dismayed when, one morning, he showed up limping and seemingly injured. They thought he must have been hit by a car. Since no one in the company knew what to do in that kind of emergency, the woman called RESQCATS for help.

My heart raced as she told me Mr. Jingle's story. I leapt into action and explained to her that he needed to go to the vet immediately. If a car had struck him, I was concerned that he may have broken bones or internal injuries. I informed the woman that I could arrange for a veterinarian to see him right away.

When she realized that I was willing to help, I heard her breathe a deep sigh of relief and the panic in her voice subsided. She told me that a man named Adam, who worked at the company, had taken a particular liking to the cat and would escort Mr. Jingles to the hospital.

Although this was the time that I usually take my winter break, this particular year, my vacation had been cancelled. Mitch had suffered a serious back injury. He was completely bed-ridden with a ruptured disc; any movement caused him excruciating pain. We were anxiously awaiting notification of a surgery date. In the meantime, there was absolutely nothing I could do to make him feel more comfortable. As a caregiver, this situation made me feel totally helpless.

ι

Mitch and I have a well-defined division of duties in our household. It is imperative to have a sense of organization and a regular schedule when you share a home with as many animals as we do. In addition to his numerous household duties, he also manages his own consulting business and sits on a number of for-profit and non-profit boards that require frequent travel.

The majority of my day is spent operating RESQCATS.

I do not remember how we decided which chores were Mitch's and which were mine. It just seemed to fall into place. I am in charge of washing and folding the laundry, but Mitch carries it up and down the stairs and puts it away. I load the dishwasher and he empties it. He does dog poop patrol and I monitor the litter boxes. When a dog throws up or pees in the house, it is his responsibility. And if I hear him exclaim, "Uh-oh," it is his loud announcement that one of the cats has thrown up or missed the box and I am the one to report with spray cleaner and a roll of paper towels!

But I distinctly remember how it came about that Mitch does the cooking. In the summer of 1992, I became a vegetarian. My participation in an animal rights group had led me in that direction, but my final decision was made when we were flying to the Olympics in Barcelona, Spain. After finishing a book about the cruelty inflicted on animals in the food industry, I looked at Mitch, who was in the seat next to me, and said, "I'm never eating meat again."

And I never have!

My declaration was followed by a period of experimentation with vegetarian cooking. Mitch has never outwardly admitted which one of my failed attempts at meatless dishes encouraged him to take over the responsibility for our daily meals. It could have been the vegetable kabobs that only absorbed the vinegar from the marinade. Or it may have been the unbelievably dry lentil loaf that tasted like cardboard and would not go down the kitchen disposal.

But I suspect that the final straw about my cooking came when my stepson, Steve, visited. He planned to stay with us for three nights. As a guest, he had no choice but to eat what I prepared...acidic vegetable kabobs on the first night and a brick-like lentil loaf on the second.

As he drove to our house on the last evening of his visit, Steve called and sheepishly asked, "What's for dinner?" It was easy enough to read between the lines and hear that he was actually asking, "Should I stop and pick up some real food on the way home?" I was already a step ahead of him. I told him that I had bought a steak for him to broil, even though it went against my new principles. In my mind, I justified that buying meat for him would guarantee that this would not be his last supper with us!

My workload dramatically increased when Mitch was

out of town, or now that he was flat on his back. His usual daily chores of caring for our own animals had fallen onto my shoulders. I had always been in charge of the twenty-five cats. But now, the feeding and brushing of eight collies also became my responsibility. In addition, we had fifteen giant African sulcata tortoises that required my attention. Truthfully, I was actually okay with the extra animal duties. After all, they are my animals, too.

The challenge was that the unfamiliar tasks of grocery shopping and cooking were now part of my job description. I could not find anything in the store because I had not done the food shopping in years. However, with the help of nearly every store employee, I was able to locate all the items on Mitch's list. Then I had to cart the groceries home, figure out where they went in the pantry and, finally, the real test, "How do I cook all this stuff?" This was all uncharted territory!

ဦ

During this time, my father was also experiencing a critical health situation. He was awaiting major surgery to fix several grapefruit-sized aneurysms. The doctors were not optimistic and gave him only a ten percent chance of surviving. Obviously, I could not be in two places at the same time. Mitch was in serious condition in Santa Barbara and my father was halfway across the United States in Texas.

To make matters even worse, one of my older cats, Neiman, was in failing health and her time was short. Any day could be her last. I felt completely helpless; there was nothing I could do for her either.

If I had taken the time to think about it, I might have realized that life is always filled with challenges and, somehow, it does seem to work out. But with so many added responsibilities, I could not focus on the positive. Unlike my usual upbeat self, I was afraid and fearful much of the time.

My emotions were especially sensitive because I felt powerless to help anyone I loved…not my husband nor my father nor my cat.

ʃ

Within an hour of Mr. Jingle's arrival at the clinic, I received a message from the vet. Her words are still clear in my mind, "Jeffyne, this cat is in bad shape; he's positive for the FIV virus and he's severely bruised and sore. His teeth and gums have a terrible infection. He also has some congestion and is wheezing." She told me that he was about eight years old and not neutered. But she also shared some good news when she said, "I don't see any broken bones and he really is a sweet cat".

I went to the hospital to discuss the case. I realized that Mr. Jingles' FIV status and other medical issues could have been his doom. At many other shelters, he would have been euthanized. I was emphatic about the fact that I do not believe in euthanizing cats because they are FIV positive. I told the vet, "If his other health problems can be resolved, that's what we'll do. Mr. Jingles is to receive the same medical care as any of my own cats!"

A vet tech led me to the back of the hospital to meet Mr. Jingles. It was obvious that he had been on the street fending for himself for a very long time. He was lucky when he chose that company's doorstep. The employees were compassionate people who clearly saved his life.

I opened his cage door and looked into his weary, yet soulful eyes. "You're going to be just fine," I said, as tears filled my eyes. He let me gently pet his head. I moved my face close to his and scratched under his chin. And then, as I cradled his head in my hand, he started to purr. Just as the vet had said, Mr. Jingles was an exceptionally sweet cat. In that instant, he melted my heart.

At the time, I did not foresee how much Mr. Jingles would come to mean to me. He gave me purpose at a difficult time in my life. While it was currently impossible for me to comfort Mitch, my father, or Neiman, my failing cat, I could help Mr. Jingles. Being able to make a positive difference for him lifted my spirits.

He was released from the hospital on Christmas Eve after x-rays revealed that he had no broken bones. Since the anesthesia time was short, he had also been neutered. While Mr. Jingles would certainly feel better after he had dental surgery, the vet felt it would be better to wait until he was stronger and could withstand the prolonged anesthesia. As a precaution, the doctor recommended an indefinite antibiotic regimen.

I set up an isolated area for Mr. Jingles which was the size of a normal bedroom. He had several soft beds, a cat condo and a heating pad to soothe his bruised body. His first-class amenities included plenty of food, fresh water and Christmas music; after all, it was Christmas Eve!

I believe that my love for Mr. Jingles was mutual. He readily accepted affection and my endless kisses on his forehead. From that day on, every time I kissed him, I whispered, "Merry Christmas, Mr. Jingles."

I kept Adam updated by phone, but I felt certain that once he learned about the cat's condition, he would abandon the idea of adopting Mr. Jingles. My experience had been that most people disappear when they realize that a cat is in less-than-perfect health. And at eight years old, Mr. Jingles was already considered middle-aged. I was certainly willing to give Adam the benefit of the doubt, but my expectations were not very high.

Our initial conversation surprised me and made me a bit suspicious of Adam. He said, "I'll be happy to give Mr. Jingles a home if no one else wants him." I explained that Mr. Jingles was FIV positive and that the virus could be spread to other cats. He needed to be not just an indoor cat, but the only cat. Adam replied, "Fine." I was pleased with his answer, but I still had concerns about his sincerity.

After a moment, I continued, "You know, he's probably about eight years old." At that point, I thought Adam would certainly lose interest recalling how difficult it had been for me to place even young adult cats. Adam simply said, "Fine." I could not believe what I was hearing!

When I caught my breath, I said, "Mr. Jingles is in bad shape. He needs time to recover from his injuries. Then he'll need dental surgery, so you can't even think about taking this cat home for at least three weeks!" Again, Adam replied, "Fine," and then added, "As a matter of fact, that'll work perfectly with my upcoming vacation."

I tested Adam one more time. "Mr. Jingles will be on antibiotics for several weeks and he'll have to have another chest x-ray to make sure his lungs are clear." And once again, Adam replied with a single word, "Fine!"

I still could not believe what he was saying. Who was this Adam? Adoptions had proven to be so problematic when it came to adult cats. People have preconceived ideas of what they want. They often go so far as to order the feline of their dreams: "It must be a calico with lots of orange and white." "I want one with blue eyes and a fluffy tail." "It's got to be a brown tabby with a pink nose." Do people really think I have any say about a cat's appearance?

I discovered just what kind of guy Adam was when he first came to visit Mr. Jingles at RESQCATS. When he stepped out of his car, he handed me a colossal bunch of colorful flowers. He had a gentle demeanor and his wide and friendly smile lit up his whole face. I liked him instantly.

It seemed Adam was curious about me, too. He had made several local inquiries. "Who is this Jeffyne? How can she take care of twenty-five of her own cats and manage a rescue organization? What is RESQCATS like anyway? Is it a good place for Mr. Jingles to recover?"

Adam felt at ease when we met and saw the "little bit of heaven" that had been created for cats at RESQCATS. He spent the afternoon visiting with Mr. Jingles. It remained somewhat surreal for me that he had bonded that quickly with a cat that had so many medical issues. But over the years, I have come to believe that there are guardian angels in human form and Adam was unquestionably Mr. Jingles' guardian angel.

When his visit with Mr. Jingles was over, Adam and I walked back to his car to get supplies that he brought. As we collected them, he accidentally dropped a bag of litter on the driveway. When he stooped to pick it up, I noticed he had difficulty retrieving it. He appeared to have limited use of his hand and arm. I also noticed a vague hint of a long scar on his cheek and neck. It looked like he must have endured some kind of serious injury. When I asked if I could help, he said he was fine. That seemed to be his usual response!

He hoisted the bag of litter with his good arm. Despite whatever trauma he had experienced, Adam was strong and confident.

I was curious about how he got his injury. Could he be a war veteran who had sustained a battle wound? Or had he been in a serious car accident? Or maybe he had had a major illness? I took a chance and asked him what had happened.

Adam revealed that he had suffered a stroke. "But you seem so young to have had a stroke," I exclaimed. He looked at me with his bright smile and said, "I'm actually forty, but it happened to me when I was seventeen. I was driving on the freeway in San Francisco when someone drove by and shot me. No reason, just a random, drive-by shooting." Adam said that he had spent three months in the hospital recovering and that the person who shot him was never apprehended.

I was in disbelief. I welled up and, for one of the few times in my life, I did not know what to say. Words escaped me.

I believe that Adam identified with Mr. Jingles. They had both sustained a traumatic injury. Adam understood recovery time. Mr. Jingle's life was not dissimilar to what Adam's life must have been. He had probably accepted what could have been his own uncertain future. Therefore, despite all the unknowns, Adam was able to commit his heart and his love to Mr. Jingles.

The day that Adam took Mr. Jingles home was unforgettable. This time, Adam showed up with two gigantic bouquets of bright multi-colored flowers. My less-than-colorful present to him was a long list of instructions, two months of antibiotics, a schedule of follow-up vet appointments…and a great big hug!

Unlike when I first met Mr. Jingles, today's tears were happy ones because I knew that Adam and Mr. Jingles were truly meant for each other. They shared an unconditional love.

Several weeks later, Adam invited me to his house. It was the only time I have ever accepted an invitation to visit the home of an adopted cat. I realize that there is a time in rescue when it is best to let go, but Mr. Jingles was the exception!

Adam's home was a palace for Mr. Jingles. After his dreadful life on the streets, he had every luxury he deserved. There were cat beds and condos in every corner of the house. Kitty toys were everywhere. He had access to an enclosed balcony where he could freely watch the birds and butterflies. Mr. Jingles even had his own website!

Adam and Mr. Jingles had several wonderful years together.

Sadly, there always comes a time when we have to say good-bye. But for Mr. Jingles, that day arrived much too soon.

Since Adam and I had remained friends, he asked me to join him at the vet's office when he gave Mr. Jingles his final gift…the gift of a peaceful passing. He did not want Mr. Jingles to linger, especially since he had endured so much hardship prior to finding a home with Adam.

In the final moments, Adam and I shared sweet memories and wept together. As Adam let him go, I gave Mr. Jingles a kiss on the forehead, and for old times sake, I whispered, "Merry Christmas, Mr. Jingles."

To this day, I remain grateful to Mr. Jingles. He helped me through a very difficult time in my life by giving me the chance to be part of his. He enabled me to make a difference when I felt helpless. Even today, he is still a humble reminder that the world is full of hope.

Mr. Jingles and I shared one of my most rewarding vacations ever!

How far should one go to save a cat? This is a story that goes back many years. I did not reveal it earlier because the tale involved some undercover detective work and potential illegal trespass. I have to admit that I am proud of myself for taking the risk of trespassing to save a life. And I must also say that there was a kind of "rush" in doing so. It was my first test as to just how far I was willing to go to rescue a kitten.

As the years have gone by, I can now confess that I have had a lot more practice and my investigative skills have improved significantly!

TWELVE

How Jeffyne Got Her Bing Back

It began with the adoption of a kitten named Bing.

A potential lady adopter was invited to RESQCATS after passing her rigorous phone interview. She sounded like an excellent candidate for any of our kittens. In person, she was a vibrant, enthusiastic young woman who immediately bonded to Bing.

Once she completed the adoption application, we went over his medical paperwork. I gave her a sample bag of the food that he was eating and had her choose a new feather toy and blanket to take home. Then she loaded Bing into her carrier. She appeared excited with her new feline addition as they left to begin their life together.

Bing's sister and brother, Cherry and Tang, remained at RESQCATS while I continued to search for good homes for them.

Bing was the shyest member of his litter, so I thought he might need extra time to adjust to unfamiliar surroundings. The process of acclimating him to his new environment was explained in full detail to the lady. I usually wait a few days to give a kitten and a new adopter some time to settle in. Then I follow up with a "how's-he-doing" phone call.

I think it is a good business practice to check in, answer any questions, hear how things are progressing and offer suggestions if they are needed. When I called to inquire about Bing, my voice went directly to an answering machine. I left a nice message and asked the woman to return my call.

I got no reply.

Two days later, I called again and left another message, which was just as polite as the first. I said, "I'm checking in to see how things are going with Bing. If you have any questions,

I'm happy to answer them. Please call me and let me know how he's adjusting." I left my phone number a second time.

Two more days passed and still, there was no response.

I began to feel uneasiness in the pit of my stomach. The gnawing grew stronger each day that she did not return my call. My gut feeling told me that something was not right.

Three more days passed since my last unanswered message. I just could not shake the uncomfortable feeling, so I decided to try once again. This time, the lady answered her phone. I identified myself and told her I was calling to see how Bing was adjusting. I asked, "Do you have any questions about anything? I was a little concerned because I left you a couple of messages and you haven't gotten back to me. I hope everything is okay."

The voice on the other end of the line was very dissimilar from the one I had heard in our previous conversations. As the call progressed, I felt like I was talking to a completely different person. The enthusiasm that she had shown when she first met Bing had been replaced by a rudeness that utterly startled me.

She yelled, "Bing got out the day I brought him home. You sold me a sick cat. His eye was watery and he was sneezing. Now I have a cold that I got from him!" I was quite shaken by her offensive manner, but I remained polite and replied, "RESQCATS does not sell kittens...we adopt them. And if your kitten got sick after he got to your house, as I told you, RESQCATS takes the full responsibility. We're always prepared to pay for the vet expenses to get a cat back on track."

I explained that sometimes a cat can have an upper respiratory condition that is lying dormant. Change, such as the stress of going to a new home, may trigger the infection. And then I calmly told her, "Kitten colds aren't transferrable to humans."

She yelled, "Well, I've had a cold for three days," and then loudly repeated, "You sold me a sick kitten!"

I tried to stay calm and asked, "How did Bing get out and where have you looked for him?"

She answered, "I thought about closing the upstairs window when I brought him home, but I fell asleep and didn't get around to it. I haven't tried to find him." And then, she snapped, "Why are you bothering me?"

I ignored her last comment and exclaimed, "Why didn't you call to let me know that Bing was out? There are methods for retrieving lost cats. I could've helped!"

I thought to myself, "Now it's been a week since Bing escaped. He's been alone outside, without food or water, and the chances of finding him are less with each passing day."

She shouted into the phone, "Why are you harassing me? You have no business selling sick kittens."

By now, I realized that continuing this conversation would be futile. Not only did she not appreciate my concern, but she was overtly belligerent and showed no desire whatsoever to find Bing.

I wondered how had I misjudged her. Had I missed something during the phone interview? Was there an overlooked clue about her upcoming behavior when she visited RESQCATS? Then I realized that it would be a waste of time to revisit those questions. The bottom line was that Bing was missing; the woman did not care and I needed to find him. But how?

I was inconsolable and needed moral support. I called Marsha, one of my volunteers, for ideas on what to do next. Marsha was reassuring and told me, "We'll find Bing… somehow!"

The following morning, Marsha called to tell me that she had driven by the woman's apartment and spotted Bing in the auto repair shop parking lot next door.

We immediately came up with a plan. Our idea was to set a humane trap baited with StarKist tuna. This was a method that worked well for trapping feral cats. By now, Bing was probably starving, so the irresistible smell of canned tuna would certainly entice him into the trap.

Marsha and I had a plan and we were on a mission!

When we arrived, we parked directly in front of the woman's apartment. As we started looking for Bing, we were shocked to see another kitten sitting in her open window. From our vantage point on the street, we could plainly see that it was wearing the red heart-shaped nametag of the other local rescue organization. The woman had not bothered to look for Bing. Instead, she had gone out and gotten another kitten!

It was Labor Day weekend and the auto repair shop was closed for three days. The entrance to the shop had a gate that was padlocked. A seven-foot chain link fence topped with metal spikes surrounded the entire property, clearly designed to deter intruders. There were more than thirty cars and trucks in various stages of disrepair scattered around the lot. Hoods were up and doors were open, so the task of finding Bing amid the jungle of littered vehicles just became that much more complicated. There were probably hundreds, if not thousands, of hiding places for a frightened kitten.

Marsha and I were duty-bound to find Bing. Since an easy point of entry was impossible, climbing the fence appeared to be our best alternative. So over the barrier we went.

Marsha went over the fence first, carefully avoiding the pointed spikes. I then hoisted the large trap to her and climbed over. We baited the trap with smelly tuna and put it in an out-of-the-way spot that offered security for the scared kitten. Now, all we had to do was wait.

Unfortunately, my escape from the repair lot was not as successful as my entry had been. Marsha scaled the fence first and got out just fine. However, as I climbed over the top, I got caught on one of the sharp spikes. Then I heard my shorts rip. As I tried to remain balanced and untangle the fabric, I slipped and came down hard on one of the points. I felt a piercing pain in my buttocks, as if "the guard dog that wasn't there" had bitten me! Ouch!

By the time I returned to RESQCATS, I was a bloody mess. When Mitch saw the torn shorts and blood running down my leg, I felt like Lucille Ball when she had to tell Ricky about her afternoon escapades and he would say, "LUCY! You got some s'plainin' to do!"

But rather than asking for an explanation, Mitch embarked on a long lecture about my need to get a tetanus shot (which I chose to ignore!). Instead, I decided to focus all my energy on seeing Bing amazingly appear in the trap.

After some serious consideration, I decided to call the repair shop. When no one answered, I left a message. I explained who I was, what I was doing and apologized profusely for trespassing. I also left my phone number...just in case!

At 10 p.m., I returned to the body shop hoping that Bing would be in the trap. But unfortunately, it was empty. I came home disappointed, but I still had high hopes that Bing would go into the trap some time during the night.

At 6:30 on Labor Day morning, a RESQCATS volunteer excitedly knocked on my front door. She had gone by the auto repair shop at the crack of dawn and saw that Bing was in the trap! He had been without food for a week, so the tuna had obviously done the job.

I had certainly learned my lesson from the day before and did not want to scar my other "cheek." So before I left to pick up Bing, I loaded a ten-foot ladder into the back of my SUV and drove to the shop. As I leaned the ladder against the fence, I spotted Bing anxiously sitting in the trap as if he was waiting just for me.

He was noticeably frightened. Apparently, his fear had been heightened by the speeding cars and the noisy Amtrak trains that passed nearby.

I leaned the ladder against the fence and carefully scaled the barrier avoiding a repeat of yesterday's mishap. I retrieved the trap and gently handed it over the fence to my willing accomplice. My climb out of the repair lot was, fortunately, uneventful. Bing was extremely quiet on the ride back.

Although traumatized, it took less than a minute for Bing to realize that he was again safe at RESQCATS. He gobbled down a huge breakfast and then re-inspected his once-familiar enclosure. As I picked him up and gently placed him in his bed, I could see in his eyes that he was grateful to be home. I checked on him many times during the day and found him peacefully purring, even as he napped.

The following morning, I put Bing back with his brother, Tang. Cherry had already been adopted to her new home. From the moment the brothers were reunited, they became inseparable. They constantly played with each other, ate together from the same side of the bowl and they even shared their naps wrapped around one another. It was now clear to me that they were intensely bonded and should be adopted together.

ι

Adoptions were going well, but I knew that it could be difficult to find someone willing to take two kittens. Although the reasons for having two cats are almost always positive, it is not something that many people consider when searching for a new feline friend.

Adopting in pairs has many advantages. You are saving two lives instead of one, an only kitten can be lonely if left by itself, and a second kitten keeps the first one out of trouble because they have each other to play with. Of course, while there may be other advantages for adopting two, I think the most important reason is that a pair of kittens is just so much more fun!

ɕ

I shared the story of Bing and Tang's happy reunion with a young couple who had visited with the intention of adopting a single kitten. Bing's story touched John and Emily's hearts and they decided to take both boys home.

The brothers blossomed with their new family. Once traumatized by his earlier misfortune, Bing became more outgoing than I could have ever imagined. He had the company of his brother and the calming kindness that radiated from Emily. Together, they provided a peaceful healing environment.

John and Emily promised to keep in touch and they did so regularly.

ɕ

I knew that Emily and John had recently moved to La Conchita, a small community of one hundred and fifty-six homes. The quaint town is nestled between the mountains and the sea just south of Santa Barbara. It is bounded on the east by hills that are normally covered with dense vegetation, wild flowers and rolling meadows of green grass. On the west, the Pacific Ocean offers glorious views of the tides rolling in and out and magnificent vermillion and purple sunsets.

Precipitation had been below normal that year, so the hills were more like a barren desert than a lush field. Most of the vegetation had died. When the rains finally did come, there was nothing to keep the mountain from sliding. It was a geological disaster that engulfed many of the homes, displaced the entire community and, sadly, took the lives of ten people.

Emily called with panic in her voice.

She told me that she felt the kitties must have sensed the impending danger before the mountain began to give way because they had retreated into the box springs under the bed. Each time John reached for the cats, the brothers clung closer together and moved farther from his grasp. The community had been warned but only had a few minutes to evacuate. John and Emily felt that they had no choice but to leave without Bing and Tang.

However, John was quick-thinking and left the back door ajar so that the boys would have a way to get out. And that is exactly what Bing and Tang did… they escaped!

Fortunately, the house did not succumb to the slide, but no one really knew whether Bing and Tang had survived after their getaway. Emily and I pushed any dismal thoughts out of our minds and began working on a plan to find the boys.

To make matters worse, property owners were not allowed into the area for days out of fear that the mountain might still be unstable. However, County Animal Control did gain admittance and was able to set humane traps. I commend them for doing a great job with their efforts to recover people's pets. For some residents, hope that their animals had survived and would be safely returned became the primary focus of their lives.

After working tirelessly for two weeks, Animal Control needed to move on to other jobs. Emily and John borrowed traps from me, baited them with tuna and set them near their old house. Since many of the homes in La Conchita were now uninhabitable, they had found a new place to live in Santa Barbara. However, they continued to drive forty-five miles round trip every day to check on the traps.

Days began with hope and anticipation. But every evening that the boys were not found ended in disappointment.

I continued to offer words of encouragement. Our frequent conversations confirmed that Emily and John had not given up. I reminded them that, after all, Bing had survived for an entire week by himself at the auto repair shop. Because of their special bond, I instinctively felt that Tang would take care of his brother.

ɞ

If my thoughts had been based on reason, I would have acknowledged that the more time that passed, the less likely the boys would be found alive. But I am rarely rational when it comes to affairs of the heart. I remained hopeful for a miracle.

ɞ

After five long weeks, miraculously, Tang was found in one of the humane traps. John, Emily and I were overjoyed.

The vet reported that Tang had lost four pounds but, considering what he had endured, he looked remarkably well. Tang was one lucky cat.

One cat home and one to go!

Now that Tang was safe with John and Emily, my attention turned to Bing. He was alone, without the security of his brother. Many unanswered questions went through my mind. Could he be trap-shy after his horrifying ordeal at the auto repair shop? Would he ever be found? Would we have to live with the lack of closure if he never returned? I tried to stay true to myself and focus on a hopeful outcome.

Exactly three days after Tang was found, Bing was discovered in the trap!

Despite being a little scrawny, having a few ticks and a minor wound on his forehead, there was nothing seriously wrong. The cut could be easily medicated with an antibiotic. But mostly, everyone agreed that being home with his family, having plenty of food, a warm bed and especially his brother, would be Bing's best medicine.

Throughout what must have seemed like endless days and nights, Emily and John never gave up the hope that their cats would come home.

They are true testaments to believing in miracles.

And remember those shorts that I shredded climbing over the fence at the auto repair shop? Well, they were confiscated, framed and given back to me by the RESQCATS volunteers. Today, they proudly hang in the RESQCATS Hall of Fame in the entryway of the cattery. There is an engraved nameplate on the frame that reads, "How Jeffyne Got Her Bing Back!" It is there as proof of just how far I will go to save a cat!

However, you will just have to take my word about the puncture scar on my behind.

My spirituality is not something that has come easily as I grew up with little exposure to organized religion. It was not until my adult years that I found faith in a spiritual power greater than myself. My growth and beliefs evolved out of necessity during desperate times making it possible for me to emotionally deal with the loss of my pets. The evolution of my spirituality has given me hope for the eternal life of animals.

Today I sincerely believe that, upon my demise, I will join my cats, my dogs and RESQCATS kittens at the Rainbow Bridge.

Do I pray? Yes, I pray to whomever or whatever that higher power is. And sometimes, my prayers are answered...with a miracle.

THIRTEEN

An Answered Prayer for Flower

One day, a dear friend called and I could tell by the sound of her voice that she desperately needed help.

She said, "My boyfriend's sister has just been diagnosed with stage-four lung cancer and her prognosis is not good. She has an adopted six-year-old daughter who can stay with us temporarily, but we don't know what to do with her cat!" She was clearly asking for help. She was my friend and I wanted to be there for her.

Within a few days, Flower arrived at RESQCATS. She was a four-year-old cat whose beauty took my breath away. Her fur was thick, soft and pristine white. She possessed a quiet, gentle demeanor. Her brilliant yellow-green eyes were captivating, but they reflected a confused and sad soul. She seemed lost in her new surroundings.

The beautiful cat arrived with a single wish from her dying owner, "Please find a wonderful home for Flower."

The vet gave Flower a clean bill of health, so the search for a new caring owner began immediately. However, finding an adopter for Flower turned out to be a much longer and more challenging assignment than I had anticipated.

It was June, the height of kitten season at RESQCATS. Usually, there are thirty to forty kittens in our care at any given time. Finding eager adopters for kittens is relatively easy, but placing adult cats is much more difficult. There is something in human nature that instinctively draws people to cute, cuddly kittens. During adoption appointments, the majority of people are oblivious to the adults that need homes. That is a reality I have learned to deal with at RESQCATS.

The heartbreaking truth is that during the four months

that followed Flower's arrival, fifty-nine kittens were adopted!

As the days and weeks passed, Flower grew more melancholy and withdrawn. Then her gloominess escalated into anxiety. She began to tug at and pull out large clumps of her fur. I was worried about her well-being and knew she needed something. But what?

I thought that maybe Flower could use company. Perhaps she would get along with some of the kittens. So I tried something. I introduced her to a litter in the adjacent enclosure. Thank goodness, it worked!

Over the next four months, Flower made friends with many kittens. When she was with them, she appeared to become much more relaxed and content. They offered companionship and gave her purpose.

It was a mutually beneficial relationship. Flower's presence helped shy kittens feel safe and protected. She taught others how to wrestle and play. She nurtured babies that had been separated from their mothers by offering them gentle baths, cuddle time and love.

I hoped that sharing the space with kittens would help Flower to find her own home. Potential adopters would have to meet her when they looked at the available kittens in the same enclosure.

During her stay at RESQCATS, many of Flower's kitten friends came and went. I believe that she sensed that adopters did not want her and, feeling rejected, she acted out. Each time a kitten friend was adopted and Flower was once again alone, she reverted to over-grooming and pulling out her fur. I knew what Flower really needed was her own home with her own special human.

Several volunteers stepped forward to help with Flower's desperate search. One photographed her. Another created a flyer telling her story; it had the simple and touching headline, "Flower's Wish." Other volunteers helped by posting the flyers in every coffee shop, pet supply store, vet office and business that had a bulletin board.

I also said many prayers hoping that just one might be answered.

Exactly four months to the day after Flower's arrival, I received a phone call from a man who had noticed her flyer in his vet's office. He was genuinely touched by her story and wanted to know more about her.

I told him Flower's family history and how she had come to RESQCATS. I explained how she had nurtured many kittens during her stay and her subsequent depression every time one left. I confessed that I was deeply concerned about her well-being.

I was also forthcoming about the fact that she needed to be strictly indoors since cats with white ears and light-colored noses are highly susceptible to skin cancer.

At that time, I only suggested to adopters that cats and kittens be kept indoors. Since then, I have made the indoors-only requirement our absolute policy.

The man listened attentively as I rambled. I fervently hoped that something I said would inspire him to meet Flower. I was so intent on not leaving anything out that I did not give him a chance to slip in a single word!

Finally, I took a quick breath and shifted from informative particulars to interview mode, asking him questions to determine whether he was a suitable adopter. But I still did not give him any time to answer with more than a short "yes" or "no." I was determined not to overlook a single attribute of this special cat.

When I finally paused, there was a brief moment of silence, which gave him a chance to speak. He told me his name was Father Jim and that he was a Catholic priest.

I was stunned. I opened my mouth to speak, but no

words came out. It felt like my throat had closed and I could not utter a single sound.

After what seemed like an eternity, I was finally able to say something, "I've been praying for Flower. Could you really be the answer to my prayers? And if not, I don't think there could be a better person than you to pray for her."

Father Jim came to visit Flower the following day. As soon as he entered the cattery, I could tell that he was a kind and gentle man. He lit up the place with his gracious smile and calm demeanor. As he approached Flower, I could not help but imagine St. Francis of Assisi and his compassion for animals.

Flower responded immediately to Father Jim. His soft voice and tender touch soothed her. I thought to myself, "Could he actually be an incarnation of St. Francis?" I left the two alone to get acquainted.

When I returned, Father Jim said that he knew he could give Flower the home she desperately needed. I also believed that his love would enable her to find happiness once again.

Father Jim told me that he had four rescued dogs and three other cats, so he needed a day or two to prepare for Flower's arrival.

Surprisingly, after he left, I noticed a remarkable difference in Flower. Her spirits had changed. She was no longer melancholy. She was happy, playful and attentive. It was as if she realized that a wonderful, new life lay ahead. Two days later, when Father Jim returned, Flower was eagerly waiting to go to her new home.

We agreed to talk during the week to make sure that Flower was adjusting well to her new home. A few days later, Father Jim called and happily reported that she was fitting in perfectly with the rest of his animal family. They seemed destined to be together.

ৎ

I have always believed in the healing power of animals. Research has proven that petting a dog, a cat or even a rabbit can lower heart rate, reduce blood pressure and decrease stress. It has been well documented that when someone loses a partner, the remaining person tends to live longer when they have an animal to love. Animals can truly heal the human spirit.

The reverse is also true. Like St. Francis, some people possess the power and the kindness to cure the broken spirits of despondent animals.

Father Jim was one of those people.

Unquestionably, he was Flower's miracle...and the answer to my prayers.

To ensure the well-being of all their animals, what must be foremost in rescuers' minds is each animal's health and the potential health risks it may present to other animals in their care.

The survival of rescued animals depends on objectivity and on following an established medical standard.

Some people who save animals have hearts of gold but lack experience. They do not realize that pursuing a healthy protocol is imperative. Others make decisions based on their hearts without fully considering the animal's best interests. As a result, the animals and those of us who ultimately care for them are left to deal with the consequences.

FOURTEEN

Eight Miracles to Be Exact

By the time Betsy, a mother of triplets and an unrelated litter of kittens arrived at RESQCATS, the harm had already been done.

Mary (not her real name) rescued five kittens whose mother had been hit by a car. The kittens were about ten days old and were scheduled for euthanasia due to a lack of space or resources at a county shelter. Lack of resources refers to not having the revenue to provide food and housing or staff to bottle-feed orphaned kittens. In my view, both of these reasons are inexcusable, but that is exactly the scenario that prompts many of us to rescue from county shelters.

Mary said, "Betsy's kittens are six weeks old. They drink milk from a saucer and it should only be a few days until her babies can be weaned and introduced to canned food." In Mary's mind, it was okay for Betsy to nurse the ten-day-old litter of five from the shelter. She could avoid the time and commitment of bottle-feeding, so she put the five orphans with Betsy and her three babies. The following day, Mary brought the mother and eight kittens to RESQCATS.

When they arrived, I was shocked to see Betsy's condition. She was painfully thin...less than six pounds. It was very obvious to me that she did not have the strength or the body mass to nurse eight kittens.

To make matters worse, it was impossible to determine which three kittens were Betsy's biological babies and which five were the orphans. They all appeared to be the same age, which was quite different than the information Mary had given me. In reality, Betsy's kittens were no more than two weeks old. Their eyes had barely opened. Their ears were still partially closed and they each weighed less than ten ounces.

If they had truly been six weeks old as Mary had indicated, each one should have weighed well over a pound.

Betsy's original litter was more than enough for such a small cat to care for in her compromised condition. Now Mary had added five more for her to feed! It was clear that both litters were close to the same size and age, so what on earth made Mary believe that Betsy's litter was six weeks old? She had rescued animals for years. What was she thinking? Did she not recognize the hardship she had placed upon an almost gaunt mother cat?

Mary's behavior could have been chalked up to inexperience, but she had experience! Most animal rescuers are passionate and well-meaning, but too often, they follow their hearts when decisions related to the health of the animals should be their priority.

We brought Betsy and the kittens into the isolation area of RESQCATS and removed them from the carrier. One look and I thought to myself, "Where has Mary been keeping these cats?" They were filthy. Dried feces were wedged in the pads of their feet and gummy gunk was lodged under their nails. They reeked of dirty litter and dried urine.

Clearly, Mary had not properly cared for the cats.

I examined each one and noticed, because of their grossly enlarged scrotums, that seven of the eight kittens were boys. I had never seen such swelling in that area. I could not imagine what the cause could be, but I did realize that I needed to clean them right away.

I was extremely upset by their neglected condition, but I remained calm, at least in my outward appearance. I told Mary, "I'll take care of everything."

I was grateful that the extended family had come to RESQCATS when they did. I could support Betsy by feeding her a high protein diet and supplement the babies by bottle-feeding them with a commercially produced kitten milk replacement.

I decided to let Mary escort herself back to her car. While I felt it was important to start bathing the kittens immediately, I also wanted Mary gone for fear that I might lose my composure. As she was closing the door on the way out, she remembered something and called back, "Oh, I have some nose spray to leave with you. Betsy's sneezing." She handed me a small spray bottle and left.

When I heard those words, the blood rushed from my head. I imagined the worst. Had the newborn litter of five been exposed to an upper respiratory virus? Unlike Betsy's offspring, her foster litter would have no antibodies to fight the virus.

I would like to think that Mary had good intentions by letting the five babies nurse from a surrogate mother. After all, bottle-feeding kittens every three hours around the clock for several weeks is not an easy job. But either Mary lacked judgment, or had not taken the time to objectively evaluate the situation. Her decision was not a healthy solution for the cats and, without being overly judgmental, she took the easy way out.

I had a bad feeling about what may lay ahead and, unfortunately, my intuition was correct. Within two days, three of the five surrogate babies were sick with an upper respiratory virus. It would be difficult for the newborns to fight the infection since they had not received Betsy's antibodies.

When they began to sneeze and have difficulty breathing, I rushed the tiniest and weakest little boy to the vet. Despite the emergency efforts to save him, his tiny lungs filled with fluid, he turned blue and died within moments.

I was right there when it happened. It was one of my worst days. I was overcome with a feeling of absolute helplessness. Under the circumstances, I do not think the kitten had a chance, but that did nothing to comfort my broken heart. I tried to reconcile that his biological mother, who had been killed by a car, needed him to join her on the Rainbow Bridge, the bridge that connects Heaven and Earth where our animals wait for us...and she waited for him. The image of the mother and son reunited was the only way I could deal with the sadness of losing such a young kitten.

Another kitten, that I had named Honey Bear, was able to ward off the virus with supportive care. The broad spectrum of antibiotics that I gave him also helped fight potential secondary bacterial infections.

Suga' Bear, however, was headed down the same dismal path as his deceased brother. He was the sickest five-and-a-half ounce kitten I had ever seen. Everything seemed to be wrong with him.

Suga' Bear's lungs were congested, making it difficult for him to breathe. His stuffy nose blocked his sense of smell, so he had no interest in taking a bottle. His right eye was horribly infected. The inner lid was inflamed and painful. It was so swollen that I could barely open it to medicate without hurting him. The vet was uncertain that his eye could be saved. But the greatest urgency was that his extremely low body temperature indicated that he was beginning to shut down.

Suga' Bear spent the next five days at the vet clinic in intensive care. He was able to come home at night where I had set up my own critical care unit. My alarm clock rang every two hours so that I could bottle-feed him. I heated subcutaneous fluid bags in the microwave, wrapped them in baby blankets and placed them around him to keep him warm. It was crucial to keep Suga' Bear's temperature close to normal to prevent his body from failing. I administered lukewarm subcutaneous fluids through a tiny needle under his skin to keep him hydrated.

Do I even need to say that I cuddled, rocked and loved him? There is a healing power in love and it is always the easy part of the prescribed treatment for sick kittens!

Suga' Bear's condition was critical. I realized that his survival would be an uphill battle. His recovery seemed so remote. I needed to be prepared to potentially lose him, but I also knew that I was doing everything possible to give him a chance.

Now I just needed for him to fight.

Two weeks of intensive care paid off. Suga' Bear grew to nine-and-a-half ounces. He was now strong enough to be reunited with Betsy and the rest of the kittens. He was a great deal smaller and played a bit slower than the others, but his siblings seemed to understand his weakened condition and made concessions. All the kittens were looking good. I felt that we were finally out of the woods. I was elated to see the extended family back together again.

I still had concerns about the unusually large scrotums on the boys. I became more alarmed when I detected that all the kittens, even the single girl, had developed enormously bloated bellies.

I immediately took the kittens to the veterinarian for complete examinations. When the doctor discovered fluid in their abdomens, our fear was that the foreign liquid was caused by feline infectious peritonitis (FIP), which is a 100% fatal virus. The vet followed up with x-rays and an ultra-sound. He drew a sample of the abdominal fluid and sent it to the lab for a pathologist and an oncologist to review.

While the results of the tests were not totally conclusive, the good news was that it was not FIP. However, the report did indicate that the bloating could be the result of an unidentified abdominal virus. Viruses, unlike bacterial infections, are not treatable and must run their course. In the worst-case scenario, this condition could be fatal. To preclude any secondary bacterial infection, the kittens were put on a regimen of supportive antibiotics.

I left the hospital with the vet's words of warning resonating in my head. "I'm sorry Jeffyne, but you could lose every single one of them to this unknown virus…all seven kittens…and Betsy, too."

❧

Over the years I have witnessed some amazing recoveries at RESQCATS, so I do believe in miracles. But I do not take them for granted. I actually feel that miracles are all around us; we just have to be open to recognizing them. My belief encourages me to pray for one whenever it is absolutely necessary. I knew that Suga' Bear's recovery from his upper respiratory virus had been a miracle. Do I dare pray for eight more…one for each kitten and another for Betsy!? Why not?

While I understand that prayer is very personal, I still asked the volunteers, the vet techs and the veterinarian to pray for a miracle to whomever or whatever higher power they believed in. To be exact, I asked them to pray for eight miracles.

❧

I frequently wear a necklace that has two silver rings, each engraved with a single word. One of the words is "believe" and the other is "miracles." As a symbol of hope, I removed the necklace and hung it on the door of the feline family's enclosure.

My grandson, Hayden, was visiting at this time. He was just nine years old and loved being my medical assistant. He took his assigned duties very seriously. He medicated the kittens with antibiotics that I had premeasured into oral syringes. He personally named each kitten and put his heart and soul into helping with their care. Hayden spent hours playing with and loving the animals. He was an amazingly compassionate boy and even added his own good-luck charm to the necklace.

ॽ

I was encouraged that none of the cats were acting sick. Betsy and her kittens were playful and full of energy. With the exception of their unusually bloated bellies, they appeared to be a normal, healthy family. After an additional two weeks of antibiotics, the cats were thriving. They were finally out of danger.

ॽ

Betsy was adopted with one of her biological babies and one of her surrogate kittens. Another of Betsy's kittens found a home with his foster brother.

The only female kitten went to live with people who had adopted from RESQCATS three years earlier, so she had a cat playmate and two children that she entertained!

Suga' Bear continued to have on-going eye issues. Although, his eye healed and I was no longer concerned that he would lose it, it still appeared that he would require surgery. However, he would need to be older and stronger to withstand the lengthy anesthesia time to remove some of the surrounding tissue that obstructed his vision.

I concluded that his possible surgery was a good excuse for Suga' Bear to stay with me. Since eye surgery would be sometime in the future, I convinced myself that most people would not want to adopt him now knowing that. And his damaged eye appeared less than perfect, so many potential adopters would pass on giving him a home anyway. Besides, how could I let him go anywhere after all we had been through together?

I searched for any justification for him to stay. Truthfully, it would have been heartbreaking for me to part with this kitten who I now lovingly called Suga'.

So now you know, even I fail at fostering! Then I told myself that it was unfair for Suga' to not have a play buddy. I felt bad when I thought of him being alone. After all, he was accustomed to a big family with lots of brothers and a sister. I tried to rationalize that I needed another kitten, but the real fact was that Suga' did need a pal!

It was true that I had other house cats, but most were grown and well past the playful stage. Some were too shy to come out from their secure hiding places. I felt that none of them would be a suitable playmate for Suga' Bear.

The choice of a playfellow was easy. Honey Bear, Suga's birth brother, suffered from megacolon, a condition that was completely unrelated to any of the litter's earlier health issues and rare in kittens. The medical description of megacolon is when the muscles and/or nerve endings in the colon do not work properly. The bowels cannot move without the aid of medication. Honey would require a prescribed drug twice a day for his entire life.

I was fully prepared to make the pledge to Honey Bear. I could not fathom anyone else making that commitment.

In all honesty, I never even searched for anyone!

My "bears," Suga' and Honey, live with me to this day. Suga's eye surgery was not as successful as we had hoped, but it has never seemed to bother him. And Honey, well, he takes his medicine twice a day, every day, like a real trooper. And not a day goes by that I am not grateful for them.

To me, these boys are miracles...two of eight miracles to be exact!

Many of the calls I receive at RESQCATS are from people who have lost their beloved furry friends. Their hearts are filled with sorrow because they miss having a cat by their side and the unconditional love they offer.

Grieving the loss of a pet is part of the healing process. Grief allows us the opportunity to search for meaning in our own lives. It also offers us the chance to examine how a particular loss may influence our spiritual growth. This insight can generate important life lessons.

This is the story of Marcus and my path of discovery after he went to the Rainbow Bridge.

FIFTEEN

Our Cats as Teachers... Marcus

Marcus was always everyone's favorite cat. I have had many cats over the years, but he always took first place in the hearts of everyone who met him.

Marcus came into my life well before I founded RESQCATS in 1997.

In the early years of my marriage, Friday nights were spent going out to dinner and a movie. I am not sure why Mitch and I felt that our "date night" always needed to end with a trip to the grocery store for our weekly shopping, but I suppose that the definition of a date does change a bit after marriage. With their extended hours, the stores made it easy to shop late, and 10 p.m. supermarket trips were often part of our Friday evening ritual.

Today, however, by ten o'clock at night I have already gotten in at least two hours of sleep; that is, if I count my dozing on the couch!

One date night, as we approached the entrance to the food market, we noticed two young girls sitting in front of the doorway with a cardboard box between them. Mitch and I share a kind of radar when it comes to animals in need, so with no words spoken, we automatically headed for the box to see what was inside.

The younger girl reached into the box and lifted out one of two, tiny kittens. The older girl, as if on cue, said, "If we don't find a home for these kittens tonight, our Mom's going to take them to the pound!"

I looked at Mitch and said, "Oh sweetheart, we have to get one."

He looked back at me and emphatically exclaimed, "Oh, no, we're not going to get one! We have to get both of them!"

That is how Neiman and Marcus came to be part of our family. Their names had special meaning for me since my first job out of college was as a graphic designer with the Neiman Marcus department store in Dallas.

❧

Over the years, despite being littermates, the brother and sister pair grew to despise each other. Anyone who visited never actually witnessed even the slightest hint of their hostility because they did not physically fight. Instead, Neiman let Marcus know of her disdain by hissing, spitting and growling, as if she were saying, "Don't even think of coming near me, Marcus!" He submissively obeyed her forewarnings.

I have no idea what prompted the behavior or how their contempt for each other began, because, when they were little, they were inseparable. But I suspect that Marcus was the instigator. He just seemed to bring out the worst in Neiman.

❧

The problem with Marcus was that anyone he met saw only his best side. He was a big, gray, fluffy furball with a little "got milk" mustache perfectly positioned on his upper lip. He craved attention and did not hesitate to ask for affection from everyone who entered his domain. As a matter of fact, he insisted on getting noticed and resorted to calculated methods to get it. He began by following visitors wherever they went. If he was not immediately noticed, he would accelerate his short legs in order to get ahead of them. Then he plopped on the floor like a glob of Silly Putty, so no one could get by without doting on him. He loved all humans and had a way of making everyone feel like they were his new best friend.

After humans, Marcus' second favorite companion was his

brush. The moment he sensed it coming out of the drawer, he assumed the belly-up position. Once he enticed someone to brush him, he would roll from side-to-side to make sure that not a single square inch of his tummy was missed. This endearing behavior earned him the nickname, "The Rotisserie Man." There was no doubt that Marcus had the best-looking, brushed belly of any cat in town!

❧

Even in cats, there are degrees of intelligence and Marcus certainly was not the brightest cat I have ever known!

When Mitch and I were first married, we lived on the beach in San Diego and our cats were allowed to go outside. It was a time before I understood the dangers to cats that roam outdoors.

We lived in a two-story house with a recessed upstairs balcony. Our terrace overlooked the wide, sandy beach that hosted countless volleyball tournaments, sunbathers, and what my cats perceived as the world's largest litter box! The upstairs sliding door was kept open during warm, sunny Southern California days for the cats to come and go as they pleased.

It was simple enough for them to descend to the patio roof, cross over to an adjacent fence, jump down to the ground and be off exploring the beach and neighbors' yards in less than thirty seconds. When it was time to come back inside, they only had to follow their trail in reverse. Easy enough!

Well, it was simple for everyone...except Marcus. I wondered if he did not remember how to get back to the upstairs balcony or if, for some reason, he was unable. Maybe it was due to his lack of normal feline intellect! Marcus could always be found sitting at the downstairs door meowing to come back inside. The mews were silent to us of course, as they were through the closed sliding door; but there he was, opening and closing his mouth, letting me know of his displeasure. I can only imagine what he sounded like to the runners and passersby on the beach boardwalk.

Marcus found it amusing to go out through the upstairs balcony, head directly to the downstairs slider and then start meowing loudly to come back inside. I lost count, but I can tell you that he played this game at least two dozen times, every day! No sooner had I let him in than he headed up the stairs, out the upstairs door, onto the patio roof, across the fence and back to the downstairs slider! It was obvious that something needed to be done.

To solve the problem, Mitch designed and constructed a ramp for Marcus so that he could return to the house the same way he had left; that is, through the upstairs balcony. He covered the ramp with indoor-outdoor carpet. If Marcus' issue was that he was clumsy, the wide ramp with its textured surface provided both grip and balance. Once the ramp was installed, I laced it with his favorite treats to entice him to return from his outdoor adventures the same way he had left...through the upstairs door. In hindsight, that ramp probably saved me thirty minutes of needlessly opening and closing the sliding door every day!

❦

Despite his shortcomings and apparent lack of basic feline abilities, Marcus was always loved and appreciated. His demeanor was sweet and gentle and he appeared to be in harmony with his world.

Marcus, however, had a darker side to his usual docile personality. As the years passed, and more unadoptable cats became residents, he became more like Dr. Jekyll and Mr. Hyde. He picked fights and marked his territory by spraying the walls and urinating in the shared cat beds. Perhaps he missed being the main attraction as our feline family grew, or maybe he felt threatened when I shared my affection with the other resident cats. He was particularly jealous of a new member of our menagerie named Wizard.

While none of the cats particularly liked Wizard when he moved in, Marcus was especially vehement when acting out his disdain for him.

The two fought constantly. Day after day, I would find tufts of Marcus' gray fur scattered about. His collar could often be found lying within inches of Wizard. Frequently, Wizard's collar was nowhere in sight, yet clumps of his black and white fur were everywhere. It was like entering a room after a black, white and gray feather pillow fight. The difference is that pillow fights are fun!

The unrelenting altercations continued for almost three years. I seriously doubt that there was ever a true winner; at least I never determined one. Luckily, despite their combative brawls, neither cat was seriously hurt or needed to see a vet for a physical injury.

Imagine my surprise, when one day, I entered the cattery and found Marcus and Wizard curled up in a basket together that was only large enough for a single cat. I could hardly believe my eyes! But there they were, nestled together, cheek to cheek. I could not have pried them apart if I had tried. Despite their tumultuous past, that is how Marcus and Wizard slept from that day forward...in the same bed, virtually inseparable. They never had another fight and, I would even go so far to say, that they came to love each other.

ર

I never understood what happened to change things between the two. Maybe it does not matter for us to understand how they worked it out. Maybe it is more important that we learn something from our feline friends.

I believe that Marcus is a reflection of my own personality. I see myself as a sweet, gentle person who wants to be loved. I aim to please. I strive for peace and harmony in everything I do.

It follows that I want everyone to get along and show respect for each other. I recognize that people have different personalities and needs, but achieving that rapport between individuals is not always easy when you manage an organization like RESQCATS.

I become uneasy when there is conflict and unhappiness among my volunteers or other associates. My discomfort escalates, especially when disagreements are petty. I often say, "Why can't everyone just get along and be here for the cats?" After all, the cats are our priority!

Finding common ground between individuals with differing opinions sometimes seems impossible and causes me additional anguish. My innate nature of wanting to make everyone happy often sets me up for disappointment. I realize that not everyone can be pleased, but I sure try. Frequently, an issue becomes so overwhelming that I just need to shut down and walk away because I am not a person who handles conflict well.

However, I always feel better after I take a walk and have had some reflective time. It gives me the opportunity to clear my mind and see things from a different perspective. Time alone provides me the chance to resolve things within myself. But despite my personal resolution, I do understand that there may not be an absolute answer.

While there are some situations in which we may never find compromise, we need to remember that there are always choices in how we handle them.

Perhaps I learned that lesson from Marcus.

Lashing out is an option. We can engage in a fight, scratch out eyes and pull tufts of fur from the ones we see as our antagonists. That, of course, would be most inappropriate! Or we can remain angry and give someone the silent treatment. That too, is not a viable solution. Both actions create "no-win" situations.

A better approach is to learn to appreciate the differences

in others. We each have our own gifts that make us unique individuals. Recognizing and respecting these qualities in others can help us find peace and harmony within ourselves.

Admittedly, I have not found myself cuddling in the same basket, cheek to cheek, with those that I can never please. I do, however, take inspiration from Marcus and try to follow his example of acceptance.

❧

Marcus lived a long, happy life, well into his teen years. He fought bravely when he was diagnosed with triad disease, which affected his liver, pancreas and digestive system. His treatment was successful for a while, but ultimately the illness was more than he could endure. It was very difficult to let him go. Many sorrowful days followed his passing. I missed his physical being, the feel of his soft fur and, of course, his belly-up rotisserie brushing.

But time has passed and Marcus now touches me in a different way; I imagine his spirit surrounding me and he speaks to my heart. I am reminded of his presence through his lessons of acceptance, respect, forgiveness and love. Whenever there is an issue between people, I think of him and his wise lessons. Perhaps Marcus was smarter than I originally thought!

Wizard and I spent a lot of time together after Marcus passed. I knew that Wizard missed him too. Eventually, he did make friends with another cat named Greyco and they often shared a bed.

I do not have proof, but I suspect that Wizard found Marcus waiting for him on the Rainbow Bridge when he left me several years later. Today, I can imagine Wizard and Marcus together...curled up like spoons in a basket just big enough for one...for all eternity.

The volunteers at RESQCATS love their job of socializing the kittens. This important interaction teaches a cat to be comfortable with human contact.

With the socialization aspect of the job covered, I can dedicate my efforts to the medical needs of our cats and kittens. Since these duties consume most of my time, I do not have to become so emotionally involved with every cat and kitten that comes to RESQCATS. As a result, my heart is not broken each time one is adopted.

Every once in a while, however, there is a cat that has a special need, not in a medical sense, but in a different, more emotional way.

As humans, we suffer from the loss of a loved one, but we need to understand that animals also grieve. Recognizing that fact was just as important in saving Misty as providing her with the proper medical care.

SIXTEEN

Misty's Loss

Misty was a six-year-old cat that lived with a single, older woman whose health was failing. The woman had a daily caregiver to assist her with the regular chores of cooking, laundry and other miscellaneous tasks. When the helper arrived on this particular day, sadly, she found that her patient had passed away. It was estimated that the lady had been gone for about an hour. Misty was perched on the woman's lap, yowling at the top of her lungs as if she were in great pain.

When the lady's family arrived to take care of the funeral arrangements, they removed what they wanted from the house...photographs, family heirlooms and other valuable belongings. As the relatives left for a final time, they gave instructions to the caregiver, "You can get rid of Misty. Just take her to the pound."

As with many other shelters in our country, cats are euthanized if they are not adopted within a limited time period. Since the local pound had a grace period of only a few days, Misty's fate would most likely be determined before she even went to the shelter!

I am always taken aback by family members who show no compassion for the animals that their loved ones leave behind. When my mother passes, hopefully many years from now, she has requested that her cat, Tattoo, comes to live with me. She dearly loves that cat and I cannot envision the arrangement being any different. I imagine that I will find great comfort in knowing that a part of my mother will be with me through Tattoo.

❧

Fortunately, a longtime RESQCATS volunteer heard of Misty's probable fate and rescued her. Once the cat was safe at her home, she called and asked if Misty could come to RESQCATS. When I heard her story, I answered, "She certainly fits under our mission statement of being abandoned. How quickly can you get her here?"

Misty was delivered to RESQCATS later that afternoon. She was a sweet, petite girl with long, silky fur. She had beautiful, but sad-looking, eyes. She seemed to be confused and depressed, as if she were grieving for her guardian.

Despite her mournful expression, Misty was interested in her new surroundings in a quiet, yet curious, way. She did not hide as many adult cats do when taken from their familiar environment and moved to a strange place. From the outset, she loved to be held and cuddled.

On the day following her arrival, I took her to the vet. Because she was six years old, in addition to a routine physical exam, I requested that blood work and a urinalysis be done. I wanted to make sure she was healthy. I expected the test results to be normal and, fortunately, there were no surprises.

It was clear that Misty had been a well-cared for cat. Her blood work and urinalysis were perfect. Everything indicated that I could immediately begin to search for her new home.

However, during her first week at RESQCATS, Misty began to decline. She refused to eat anything, including her customary diet. I offered her baby food, cut-up chicken and StarKist tuna. I tempted her with every flavor of Fancy Feast that the supermarket had to offer, but nothing appealed to her.

Although Misty remained responsive to my touch and

affection, she nevertheless became quite melancholy and unusually quiet. I realized that something was terribly wrong.

It was Sunday, the day that all of the local vet offices were closed. I am careful not to abuse the privilege of having my veterinarian's personal cell number, but this was an emergency. In desperation, I called for his advice. He recommended that I administer subcutaneous fluids to make her feel better and hopefully, stimulate her appetite.

I spent the entire afternoon with Misty. My intuition told me that she missed her owner and that her broken heart needed mending. I settled into a comfortable spot with Misty lying across my lap. From all appearances, she seemed to enjoy my company. With every stroke of my hand across her body, I spoke softly to her. I told her I understood how much she missed her owner and that I was certain her human was grateful not to have died alone.

The hours passed much too quickly and before I realized it, the afternoon duties of feeding, medicating and litter box scooping had arrived. Before leaving, I gently picked Misty up, held her close to my chest and quietly whispered, "Your lady is in a good place, Misty. Now it's time for you to let her go. It's okay to move on and make someone else happy."

When Monday morning arrived, I felt it would be wise to rule out any physical causes of her depression, so I took Misty to the vet again. Blood work indicated that her protein levels were slightly low due to not eating, but from a medical perspective, there was nothing seriously wrong.

We returned to RESQCATS and spent the remainder of the morning and early afternoon together. The hours passed swiftly, just as they had the day before. Sitting with Misty, I realized that the grief she felt from losing her companion was no less painful than the sorrow I experience after the loss of one of my cats or dogs.

I believe that animals suffer from grief just as humans do and now, here was Misty as living proof. I could see that she was marooned in her misery and I realized that I needed to help her get through her mourning.

We had another long talk about freeing her heart from such profound sadness and loss. Again, I reminded Misty that her owner was grateful that she had been with her when she passed away. I told her, "One day, you'll be reunited on the Rainbow Bridge."

Perhaps it was fate, or maybe it was just coincidental, but that afternoon, Misty started eating normally. Follow-up blood work a week later indicated that she was back on track.

ɔ

Misty had a charisma about her that was sweet and kind. She loved spending time with the volunteers as they talked to her and gently brushed her coat. Everyone was happy when she responded to their attention. But what we really wanted for Misty was a home she could call her own.

Misty greeted everyone who entered the cattery as if they were her new best friends. I made certain that potential adopters were given no alternative but to visit with her first. I even made it a point to ignore them when they would say, "I'm only interested in adopting a kitten." It was my imposed requirement for everyone to meet Misty. Hopefully, someone would abandon their preconceived notion that they could mold the personality of a kitten into a sweet, gentle cat. It was obvious that Misty was already what they were seeking...just a little older!

I vividly recall standing in Misty's enclosure, telling a couple her story as their eyes wandered to the six kittens playing in the adjacent space; they were oblivious to everything I was saying. While others appeared to like

Misty, once they saw the captivating kittens, the story was always the same, "I only want a kitten." I tried not to show my disappointment, but I knew that if any cat at RESQCATS needed a home, it was Misty!

ʔ

As I said earlier, patience is not one of my strong points. I endure many sleepless nights worrying about finding homes for adult cats. Waiting for the right person to see how special Misty was and to give her the home she deserved was not easy. If such a person did come along, I planned to promote them to "angel" status! Several weeks later, I opened an email from a lady who had just lost Oliver, her nineteen-year-old cat. Oliver had been her best friend since she was ten years old. He had moved with her many times during her childhood and even welcomed the man she eventually married into his world. The lady and her husband were devastated by their loss, but now some time had passed and they felt they were ready for a new feline companion.

She did not indicate in her email whether they had a preference for a kitten or an adult, so I took the opportunity to tell her about Misty. It was quite a lengthy story because I did not leave out a single detail. But to make sure she visited, I assured her that there were also kittens available for adoption.

The couple replied that they were open to meeting Misty. They were going away for the weekend, so we arranged a time for them to visit on their way out of town.

It was love at first sight! They understood that Misty had suffered from the loss of her long-time companion, just as they were hurting over the death of Oliver. I told the couple about my talks with Misty and how she blossomed when she was lavished with love and attention.

Then I gave the couple some privacy to interact with Misty. I have learned over the years that no one needs to feel pressured when they are making the decision about which cat to adopt. Happily, unlike most adopters who only want a kitten, this couple never ventured out of Misty's enclosure!

After the couple returned from their trip, Misty moved to her new home. I cautioned them that she may cry during the ride home; in my experience, she had yowled non-stop in a high soprano voice during our trips to the vet! Although I felt that the couple could offer Misty a perfect environment, I worried that she might become depressed and stop eating again.

To help with the transition, I sent Misty home with twenty-four cans of her preferred cat food, two bags of her favorite dry kibble and a bottle of Bach Rescue Remedy for stress. I also included three single-spaced pages of instructions detailing everything from introducing her to the house, where to massage her belly, and most importantly, specific culinary recipes to satisfy her finicky palate!

As I gently placed Misty into the carrier for her trip home, I told her that everything was going to be fine. I whispered, "Misty, these are your new people and you have a job. Their hearts were broken too. They lost a very special cat and you can help them heal and be happy once again."

When I opened my email the next day, I read that Misty had lived up to my prediction of singing opera all the way home. Once inside the house, she checked things out and promptly found a safe spot under the bed. But it took only twenty minutes for her to reappear and begin exploring her new surroundings. She was curious and friendly. By the end of the day, she had eaten several times and discovered her litter box.

Following her first day's excitement, she fell sound

asleep on the end of the couple's bed. Apparently though, Misty felt her humans slept too late; she was ready to play at 4:00 a.m.! Hopefully those predawn activities occurred only once, but I never dared to ask! It was clear that Misty had made herself right at home and seemed just as content as her adopters.

❧

I will always have a special memory of Misty. Her journey was an affair of the heart. While Misty grieved, she remained open to the comfort and love that I offered her. She left me with a valuable reminder about living life and dealing with profound loss.

So often, people emotionally shut down and hide from their feelings of loss. In the past, I have been guilty of this. Many times, I have been afraid to share what I truly feel. When I whispered to Misty that it was okay to let go of her previous owner and let someone new in, I was also giving myself permission to risk doing the same. I was sure she would find happiness again... and she did!

While our journeys are not always clearly defined, keeping an open heart can create a new path to emotional healing and renewed happiness. Misty appeared to have discovered this invaluable life lesson...she also taught it to me.

At RESQCATS, the challenges we face vary with the arrival of each new litter. Some are easier to deal with than others.

Kittens with infected, goopy eyes and runny noses can be medicated. A bath can eliminate fleas and street dirt. A healthy diet, probiotics and worming medication can eradicate parasites and diarrhea. Appropriate vet care is an essential for a healthy kitten body.

There is another not-so-obvious aspect to ensuring a cat's well-being. It does not exist anatomically and a doctor cannot cure its symptoms with any medical treatment or prescription drugs. The frightened soul of a feral kitten is hard to diagnose and difficult to heal. Sometimes, the help of an angel is mandatory!

SEVENTEEN

An Angel Among Us

RESQCATS occasionally takes in feral kittens that have had limited or no contact with human beings. We utilize a number of socialization techniques to get these kittens accustomed to human touch. Our ultimate goal is to help them reach a point where they readily accept affection from humans. More often than not, our efforts transform feral kittens from frightened spirits into outgoing and playful kittens that will continue to flourish in adopters' homes.

Timing is an important consideration when taming young kittens. It becomes more difficult with each week that they mature. For example, eight-week-old kittens have a much better chance of socialization than twelve-week old ones. Then again, there is always an exception. I remember one in particular, a four-week-old kitten named Wilbur. Whenever anyone entered his enclosure, Wilbur became visibly frightened. His ears flattened against his head. It was a sure sign that he was afraid and felt defensive. His pasted-down ears protruded from the side of his head and made him look like he was ready to fly to Mars! Volunteers spent countless hours with Wilbur and, while he did improve, he never quite made the leap to become the fun-loving, fearless kitten that we had hoped.

Wilbur led me to develop a personal philosophy about socializing feral kittens. I believe that age is not the only factor. Pregnant feral mothers encounter tremendous stress in their environment and live a difficult existence in their constant pursuit of food, water and shelter. The kittens that she carries experience her stress during their development in the uterus. When they are born, that anxiety can be part of their make up. My theory helps explain the Wilburs of the feline world.

Thankfully, Wilbur was adopted by someone who understood his personality and was committed to continue working with him.

❧

Older kittens and cats that cannot be tamed can lead more contented lives in a feral colony. Across the country, there are organizations that are devoted to the feral cats. They are called TNR groups, which stands for trap, neuter and return. The mission of these groups is to capture the ferals with humane traps, spay or neuter them and then return the cats to their original colony. If for some reason, the feral cats cannot be returned, relocation is a viable option.

However, regardless of whether the cats are relocated or returned, both options are contingent on the understanding that they will be fed and watered on a regular schedule by a committed and responsible individual.

❧

In the fall of 2006, shortly before Halloween, my heart sank when a litter of four kittens, three of them solid black, arrived at RESQCATS. From a rescuer's point of view, I dread Halloween. Each year, around the end of October, we receive suspicious calls from people seeking black cats! All Hallows' Eve is a time when black cats are sacrificed by some extreme cults and pretty sick people who have unspeakable beliefs.

Ironically, during other times of the year, I hear ridiculous excuses from potential adopters telling me why they do not want a black kitten. Many of their reasons are based on superstitions that go back ages when black cats were persecuted because of their association with witchcraft and bad luck. After years of attempting to change some adopters' archaic views, I have come to accept that I am not going to convince them otherwise. It is usually a waste of time and energy for both parties. I just politely listen and nod. Oh, if only I could turn back the hands of time and redo history!

ɞ

This particular litter of four had been fostered for a short time through our local TNR organization, so their socialization process had already begun. Within a few days, the three black kittens were outgoing, purring machines.

The fourth, non-black kitten was a beautiful Siamese-Himalayan with stunning sapphire eyes that complemented the chocolate markings on her face. Because she had been trapped a full week after her siblings, her comfort level with human contact was not near what theirs was. Whenever someone approached her, she hissed and spat and quickly retreated to the farthest corner of her enclosure.

I named her Lila.

Past experience told me that her exquisite looks would captivate adopters; but, like some beautiful people, I knew her beauty would take her only so far. Her sole refuge was in the company of her brother, Huckleberry. She appeared to feel safe and happy with him. My hope was that some of his playful, fearless nature might transfer to her. I knew it would be to Lila's benefit if she and Huckleberry were adopted together.

ɞ

Weeks passed before Lila began to trust the volunteers. Over time, she allowed them to come near without flinching or retreating. In addition to their regular duties, each volunteer was asked to spend extra time with Lila.

Every kitten seems to have at least one favorite thing for us to do that can bring it out of its shell. Sometimes it is as simple as petting a particular spot, such as under the chin or behind the ears. We just had to find Lila's sweet spot!

At first, she was not at all fond of human touch, but

she did love chicken-and-gravy baby food. We offered her this tasty delicacy on our fingers. Lila learned from this that our hands meant no harm. She began to let us pet her. She gradually became more relaxed when we stroked her. Finally, we discovered that a gentle foot massage sent her into purring mode. Lila remained timid, but she showed great improvement in her social skills. She seemed ready for adoption...along with Huckleberry, of course!

Clearly, Lila required a special home with a person who fully understood that the socialization process we had begun at RESQCATS must be continued. She needed incredible understanding, patience and unconditional love from her adopter.

❧

Part of my job is to fully inform potential adopters about a cat's history, personality and what to expect when they take the feline home. Because I strive to make each adoption final, it is crucial that people comprehend the commitment it takes for the kittens to continue to progress socially. I do not pull any punches.

I pictured in my mind what Lila's and Huckleberry's new guardian would be like. Compassionate, accepting and willing to dedicate a lot of time were at the top of my list. I also envisioned the person's appearance. They would be agile enough to be able to crawl under beds, cabinets and other tight places where Lila might take refuge. The ability to reach high and climb a ladder would certainly be a plus. Tough-skinned was unquestionably on the list because I feared that Lila might occasionally scratch, at least in the beginning.

It is a gross understatement when I say that Lila and Huckleberry's person arrived in a very different package!

Lila and Huckleberry, were featured in the "Pet of the Week" section of our local newspaper. The photo of Lila with her gorgeous blue eyes had the RESQCATS phone ringing off the wall.

The callers were captivated by her beauty. Many were interested in adopting Lila, but no one wanted her all-black brother. Not a single caller even considered Huckleberry. Two days of answering many, many phone and email inquires ended in disappointment.

Then Liz called. She said, "When I saw the photo in the paper, I knew that Lila and Huckleberry were meant for me." Liz was enthusiastic and eager to meet them right away. She answered all the interview questions to my satisfaction. In fact, she sounded perfect for the pair. We set an appointment for the next afternoon.

When Liz arrived at RESQCATS, every image I had fabricated in my mind about the perfect guardian for Lila and Huckleberry went right out the window! Her petite stature did not exceed five feet. She wore a deep purple, polyester jacket with matching trousers. Her crocheted hat was a lighter shade of violet. As a final touch, a fine antique watch was pinned on her lapel. She was a lovely lady with class who made quite the fashion statement! She was also eighty-five years old!

I stopped mid-step when I first saw her. I tried to keep my chin from falling to the floor. I was flabbergasted. I politely introduced myself. I could not imagine Liz being the right person for Lila. Was she capable of crawling under the furniture when Lila wedged herself into a hiding place? Even a small secluded spot would be hard for a young, agile person to reach. Did she even own a ladder? What if she got scratched? People Liz's age have thinner skin and cat scratches can be very serious. And I had another bigger concern. Was there even a slight chance that Liz would outlive the kittens? How would I handle this? I do not believe in discriminating based on someone's age.

A volunteer escorted Liz into Lila and Huckleberry's

enclosure. As expected, Huckleberry put on his best show; he was quite the entertainer. Unexpectedly, Lila responded favorably to Liz. Much to our amazement, Lila played with a feather toy and she gladly accepted a foot massage from Liz.

I did, however, frantically try to persuade Liz to consider more socialized cats. I suggested Emma, a mother that loved to curl up on volunteers' laps. I thought Liz's well-seasoned lap would be the perfect place for Emma. Besides, she desperately needed a home since all her kittens had been adopted. Liz had no desire to visit Emma. She was adamant, "No, I like these two." She could not take her eyes off Lila and Huckleberry.

There was no question in my mind that Liz exuded a positive energy that Lila picked up and responded to with enthusiasm. But, despite the interaction between them, I still had my reservations. On the other hand, was it possible that Liz's spunk and sense of humor were exactly what Lila needed?

"Where do I sign up?" Liz boldly asked.

I had her fill out the appropriate paperwork.

To make things easier, I offered to give Liz supplies directly from RESQCATS. I suggested that she get her apartment set up for her new kittens before bringing them home. I asked the volunteer to put together a care package. It included a litter box and litter, toys, a bed and food.

As we headed towards Liz's car with the provisions, the volunteer and I stopped in our tracks when we saw this sweet, little old lady's vehicle. We turned to each other with big smiles on our faces. I am almost certain that our words came out in unison, "She definitely has what it takes for Lila and Huckleberry!" Parked in the driveway was the brightest yellow, hottest sports car I have ever seen. It looked brand new and definitely confirmed Liz's spunk, energy and love for life. I knew then that this adoption was undeniably a match for these kittens.

When I told Liz that I loved her car, she replied, "Yeah,

I'm just a little old lady from Pasadena who still wears tennis shoes!"

Looking down, I saw that Liz was wearing tennis shoes and they matched her stylish, purple pantsuit. Liz continued to stay in touch with weekly progress reports.

After spending time with Liz, I can honestly say that I am not surprised that Lila adjusted so well. The passion that Liz felt for her new family was unmistakable. She even claimed that she could hear Lila and Huckleberry growing!

She always ended our conversations by saying, "I'm a happy camper and I just love them both!"

I have always believed that angels live among us. Liz was proof...she was just the angel that Lila needed.

CAT IN MOONLIGHT

Through moonlight's milk
She slowly passes
As soft as silk
Between tall grasses.
I watch her go
So sleek and white,
As white as snow,
The moon so bright
I hardly know
White moon, white fur,
Which is the light
And which is her.

— Douglas Gibson

EIGHTEEN

A Sign From Snowie

Snowie arrived in the summer of 2001 with four adorable kittens. Just like their mother, they were pure white. At first glance, they all looked the same. But on closer inspection, I saw that they were each very unique...just like real snowflakes. I named them Snowball, Snowshoe, Snowman and Snowflake.

Snowie was an attentive mother and loving mom. She nursed, bathed and tended to the needs of each kitten. She watched them explore the enclosure as tiny four-week-old babies. As they grew, she showed them how to eat on their own and use the litter box. They ventured onto the condos and ramps that led to an upper shelf. They played and entertained themselves for hours. As weeks passed, they became less dependent on Snowie.

I knew that the kittens would be adopted very easily. Even in the early years of RESQCATS, I had heard more than enough times, "I only want a kitten." Sometimes it seems like mother cats exist solely to supply kittens for adopters. Moms often go unnoticed during adoption appointments. As I expected, the kittens found homes as soon as they were old enough to leave their mother.

That left only Snowie. So here I was once again, fretting about what to do with an adult mom. The vet estimated Snowie to be between two and five years old. She was exceptionally beautiful with a thick coat of flawless white fur. Her yellow-green eyes looked like autumn leaves just beginning to change from late summer green to autumn gold. She undoubtedly had good looks going for her. The problem was that Snowie was terribly shy. Even if she had been the kind of cat that just wanted to crawl into someone's lap, finding a home for an adult in the heart of kitten season is never an easy task. Add timid and introverted to her resume and it became even more difficult to find an adopter.

ੈ

Most public shelters have an open-door policy. Potential adopters can come and go during normal business hours. On the other hand, RESQCATS operates by appointment only because the facility is located on my personal property. Potential adopters are pre-screened via a telephone interview. I "rake people over the coals," so to speak, during the interrogation. They must agree to our indoor-only policy and promise to never declaw the cat. I also emphasize that they are making a commitment for the kitten's lifetime, thirteen or more years. If all is in order, we set a visiting time.

The advantage of an open-door approach is that cats are continually exposed to the general public. The more often they are seen, the more likely adult cats will find their forever home. Many people have a preconceived idea of what they are looking for when they visit shelters, but they may actually go home with something very different. I am not saying that does not happen at RESQCATS. However, in reality, most who visit are seeking a kitten. It is rare for adopters to leave with a mother cat when their objective was to adopt a baby.

My sole intention for Snowie was to do my best to find a home for her in a timely manner. I felt there was a better chance for her to be adopted at a public shelter because she would have more contact with potential adopters. My hope was that someone would visit the shelter and become enamored with this stunningly plush, white cat. They would find her irresistible and, ultimately, take her home.

A volunteer, Evie, offered to take Snowie to the shelter for me. I sent her with the important paperwork noting dates of her vet exam, vaccinations, spay surgery and other relevant information. I also prepared a care package with Snowie's favorite food and a few toys.

Much to my surprise, Evie was back within half an hour. She was distraught to the point of tears and said she had been treated rudely by the woman in charge at the shelter. The shelter manager had merely glanced at Snowie inside the carrier and abruptly blurted, "That cat has skin cancer and it will take six months to clear it up." But Snowie's vet exam had revealed no such condition! And Evie had done nothing to provoke such disrespect. I would like to think that the shelter manager was just having a bad day. Still, that was no reason to treat anyone in such an offensive manner. I became angry as Evie told me what had happened. The insinuation that I had sent Snowie to the shelter because of her medical condition was completely untrue.

I got into my car and drove directly to the shelter. This was a matter that I would certainly clear up with the manager. At the same time, I planned to address the disrespect she had shown to my volunteer. Her rudeness was totally unacceptable. On the way I decided that with that kind of attitude, Snowie was definitely in the wrong environment.

When I arrived, I had a stern, yet professional, conversation with the woman. I also brought Snowie back to RESQCATS!

Fortunately, Snowie was adopted a few weeks later by a sweet, quiet, older lady who understood that Snowie was shy. She also realized that it may take a long time for Snowie to adjust to new surroundings.

We had a lengthy discussion about how to introduce Snowie to a new home. She was to begin in a single room. The door to the room was to remain closed. Once Snowie was comfortable in that setting, it would be okay to open the door to the adjacent area. Determining how quickly to increase access to the entire house depended on how well she responded with each added space. As always with cats, it is on their own timetable!

It had been less than a week when Snowie pushed out the window screen in her room and was gone. I was thankful that the lady called immediately to inform me about what had happened. However, I was afraid that the odds of Snowie returning through the same window were highly unlikely. The sweet lady realized that Snowie was not the right cat for her. If Snowie returned, she asked if RESQCATS could take her back.

Fortunately, I was able to trap Snowie and return her safely to RESQCATS.

ℓ

Caring for a resident cat at RESQCATS requires an enormous financial obligation and emotional commitment. That being said, there was not a question in my mind that Snowie could stay at RESQCATS for her lifetime.

One particular volunteer had grown exceptionally fond of her and was elated that Snowie would be a permanent tenant. She drew up a contract and handed it to me just one day soon after Snowie's return. She pledged to provide Snowie with a lifetime supply of albacore tuna in water and her favorite toy... bouncy balls!

ℓ

The first years of Snowie's life had been spent on the streets in sunny Southern California. At RESQCATS, she spent much of her time in the overhead outdoor tunnels that connect the main cattery building to outside enclosures. She enjoyed the warm sun beaming down on her outstretched body and fair-skinned face. As a precaution, we covered her favorite tunnels with shade cloth to protect her from skin damage. But

Snowie sought out even the tiniest spot of bright sun to park her little pink nose and white ears. The cumulative exposure from years on the streets as a stray finally caught up with her. She was at RESQCATS less than two years when small scabs and sores appeared on the outer edges of her ears. Unlike the earlier claim by the shelter, this was the first sign of any skin issues.

A vet exam confirmed skin cancer on Snowie's ears. While we were in the exam room, I reminded the doctor that she had been treated for occasional eye infections. The prescribed antibiotics had not helped. He got out a special optic tool and looked closely at her eyes. "Yes, I see the problem now," he said. "Her lower eyelashes grow inward." The medical term for the condition is entropion. Every time she blinked, the tiny lashes scraped past her corneas causing irritation. Imagine it is like having a piece of sand in your eye that you cannot get out. If left untreated, her eyes could ulcerate. That could cause extreme discomfort and eventual blindness. He suggested that surgery to turn the eyelashes outward would fix the problem.

The veterinarian presented two options to take care of the skin cancer. Neither was palatable. However, if nothing was done, the cancer would certainly continue to spread. The burning and itching would persist and make her miserable. The other option was to amputate the flaps of her ears and prevent future damage and suffering. Believing it was in Snowie's best interest, I opted to have the surgery done. However, I did not truly comprehend the remorse I would feel.

I will never forget visiting Snowie at the veterinary clinic immediately after her surgery. Sutures spanned the entire top of her head, well past where her ears had been. She had stitches under each eye that neatly tucked back the entropic eyelashes. I felt awful for what I had done to her.

Snowie was prescribed heavy medication for her pain. The vet instructed me to continue the meds for several days. I was grateful that there was something I could give her to alleviate her discomfort. But there was no drug to help with the agony I felt for her suffering or my remorse for having put her through such trauma.

I left the vet's office in tears. Guilt weighed heavily on my shoulders. I knew that having her ears surgically removed was the right choice. But it would be years before I recognized that my decision for the surgery was all right with Snowie, too.

I contacted the volunteers when I returned to RESQCATS and forewarned them about how pitiful Snowie looked. I also needed them to be prepared for her depressed state. I told them that the next couple of weeks would be difficult. Lastly, I reassured them that her pain would be controlled with pain medications.

Snowie was able to return to RESQCATS the day after surgery. There was a long list of instructions, which I was happy to follow. In fact, I would have done anything for her to atone for her suffering.

The volunteer who pledged a forever supply of tuna showed up every morning at 6:30 sharp to offer the aromatic treat Snowie loved so much. On days that she did not want to indulge in fish, she enjoyed Gerber's chicken and gravy baby food.

All the volunteers gave Snowie special attention with strict instructions from me. "Tell her that she's beautiful without her ears." I convinced myself that if they said that enough, I might also feel better about my own burden of guilt for what I had asked her to endure.

As Snowie recovered, she appeared to look forward to the volunteers' visits. During the next month, she healed both physically and emotionally. She craved attention and favored belly rubs. She was quick to roll from side to side in her basket as if to say, "Hey, you missed a spot!" She loved to be brushed. Her fur was as thick as a polar bear, so brushing sessions could go on indefinitely.

Her stoic recovery was humbling. Little by little, I became accustomed to her new appearance. She looked like a baby white seal peeking over the edge of her basket. When she popped her head into full view, she reminded me of a white owl with jewel-like eyes.

Once Snowie had fully recuperated, I opened her enclosure door so that she could mingle with the other resident cats. She had gotten along fine with them during her previous years at RESQCATS, but now she was cautious and avoided contact.

Unfortunately, her reintroduction did not go well and I have never quite been able to pinpoint the reason. Some of the other residents saw her release back into the cattery as an invitation to intimidate her. They made it their sole mission to make her feel unwelcome. She became fearful of the other cats and retreated into hiding. She remained in the outside tunnels and hesitated entering the building where she could eat and sleep in a comfortable bed. When Snowie did come in, she could not avoid altercations. In the current set-up, she was doomed to a life of torment.

I knew things needed to change when I found Snowie sitting in one of the exterior tunnels terrified to come inside the building. It was not fair for this sweet cat to be frightened all the time. So we constructed an indoor enclosure for Snowie. An overhead tunnel covered with shade cloth led to a private outdoor area built just for her. The enclosed space outside was constructed in the midst of several avocado trees that provided shade.

Snowie thrived in her solitary space away from the other cats. She spent the warm summer days in an open basket watching birds and taking in the fresh breeze. She could watch the volunteers' comings and goings from a place where she felt safe. On cold and rainy days, she slumbered in her basket with a heating pad in her inside enclosure. She was incredibly content!

❧

In the years that followed, Snowie required several more surgeries to remove additional pre-cancerous spots from her nose and forehead. As she got older, anesthesia presented a higher risk, so the veterinarian suggested some special creams as an alternative to surgery. Treating skin cancer became a routine part of her life. She required continuous monitoring and check-ups every six months. She accepted it with grace and understanding although trips to the veterinarian were always extremely stressful for her.

❧

Snowie captured the hearts of all volunteers over the years and each made a point to spend special time with her.

My visits, however, were not something I talked much about. I felt fragile sharing my feelings of soft-heartedness and vulnerability with the volunteers. After all, I'm supposed to be the boss! I should be able to put on a straight face and handle all situations objectively with decisive strength.

❧

My outlook about exposing my extreme sensitivity was a result of my childhood. I often felt scolded for my feelings, "Jeffyne, you're too emotional." "You wear your heart on your sleeve." "You're too sensitive. People will walk all over you." I perceived that being emotional was a character flaw. In my defense, I felt it was better to be cautious about sharing my innermost feelings with the volunteers. Fortunately, I have a much healthier perspective today. I realize my compassion and sensitivity are part of who I am...and I'm okay with it.

ℰ

The time I spent with Snowie was after everyone was gone for the day, when I could be myself. If I felt like crying, it was safe with no one around. I could speak to Snowie from my heart and hold nothing back. I told her that she was beautiful without her ears. I asked for her forgiveness. I had placed that burden on myself; it was not one that Snowie put on me. The quiet times we shared at the end of the long days gave me the chance just to be in the moment and breathe. That part of my day was something I looked forward to and treasured. I truly loved Snowie from the most vulnerable part of my being.

ℰ

Things changed suddenly on July 5, 2007 when I found Snowie on the ground in her outdoor enclosure. She had collapsed and could hardly breathe. I recognized the signs of heart failure. I rushed her to the vet where she was admitted immediately. Fortunately, the doctor was able to stabilize her. But we needed to know exactly what had happened in order to prescribe treatment.

She had an ultrasound the next day and the results were not good. Snowie's heart was failing. The condition caused her chest to fill with fluid, which made breathing difficult for her. She could have been prescribed three different medications twice a day to lengthen her lifespan. In addition, weekly follow-up trips to the vet to monitor her heart, kidneys and hydration levels would be required.

None of this seemed fair. It was not fair for this to happen. More importantly, it was unfair to put Snowie through all this. Doctor visits had always been incredibly stressful because of her shyness. The increased trips to the vet could certainly send her back into her shell.

According to the vet, Snowie's remaining time on Earth

could be extended. But I just could not imagine putting her through that emotional trauma in order to give her just a few more days...or weeks. We shared a special bond that had taken a very long time to develop. Treating her with medication with an inevitable outcome coupled with stressful vet visits would certainly destroy our relationship of understanding and trust. The regimen was not something I could bring myself to endorse for Snowie. Ultimately, her heart would still fail. If she went into cardiac arrest, she could suffer a dreadfully painful death. I could not envision that for her.

On July 6 at exactly 7:00 p.m., Snowie journeyed to the Rainbow Bridge with the compassionate help of her veterinarian. I remember stroking her beautiful white coat as the first injection to relax her took effect. I could not hold back my tears. Before she was euthanized, I asked the doctor, "Do you think that Snowie will get her ears back when she gets to Heaven?" He looked at me sympathetically and said, "If she wants them back, she'll get them."

Many weeks later, my question was answered and my guilt vanished. It happened during a massage that my good friend, Laura, insisted I needed. She is a wonderful masseuse and I accepted her offer knowing she was right. I have always been able to share some of my most private feelings with Laura. I felt comfortable telling her that sometimes the release of my emotions happens during a massage. I forewarned her, "If I cry during this, don't worry, I'm okay."

I got up on the massage table and lay on lightly scented flannel sheets. Laura went to work, her hands gently kneading my body. She found all the pressure points and concentrated on releasing my built-up emotions and anxiety. I relaxed and fell deep into a tranquil calm. It felt as if I were floating.

My thoughts turned to Snowie. Quiet tears filled my eyes.

A few minutes later, a beautiful vision came to me. There is no doubt in my mind that it was real. I saw myself in a magnificent place in nature. It was calm and warm. There was green grass under my feet and birds singing overhead. A tepid breeze swept across my face. The sapphire-colored sky was interrupted with white, billowy clouds. A brilliant rainbow reached across the heavens. It was a bustling place with all species of animals in the distance. Bustling, yet peaceful.

Some of the animals stopped when they saw me sitting on the grass. A few of them approached and gathered around me. I let them crawl onto my lap. I reached out my hand and invited them to nestle close. I gently caressed their fur. I could hear their serene murmurs of contentment.

When I looked up, I saw Snowie in the distance. I was startled at first and questioned my sight. But there she was! And she saw me too!

As she approached, I could see that Snowie did not have her ears. She could have gotten them back in Heaven if she had wanted them! But apparently, she felt fine without them... and had all along!

At that moment, I forgave myself for what I felt I had done to her...and I began to heal.

As a rescuer, I began with a notion of saving the world and envisioned myself as the savior of all cats. However, I learned early on that not all people care about the fate of animals the way I do. Animals are abandoned every day and many have no way of surviving. They suffer because of what people do to them. While I realize that not all the animals can be saved, I give it my all.

The true heart of a rescue person is tested when an animal needs assistance. It is not always at our convenience when duty calls. Any time, any place, anywhere…you have to be ready and willing.

The story of Nemress and Miracle is about those who came to their rescue. It is a narrative that pays tribute to all rescuers and their appreciation of life through loss, dedication and love.

NINETEEN

Nemress and Miracle

Kitten season normally begins in March and lasts through late October or early November. Female cats go into heat when the weather is warm. The cooler weather in late fall and early winter means that I can look forward to a few months of downtime. By the time we start our preparations for Thanksgiving, the last of the season's kittens have usually been adopted.

When Susan, one of my volunteers, called on a frosty November morning, my enthusiastic anticipation of a break came to an abrupt halt. She sounded panicked and out of breath and her words were practically inaudible. When she did manage to speak intelligibly, the tale she had to tell was a horror story.

Susan grew up in Bakersfield, California. Most of her family still resides there, so she often goes back to visit. She has delivered cats from there to RESQCATS on more than one occasion.

Over the years, Susan and I have collaborated on many rescues. In fact, we have gone to some extreme measures to save cats...some of which I dare not write about. Let me just put it this way; we often refer to ourselves as Lucy and Ethyl!

Susan's story that morning went like this.

On a recent night, her son's neighbor noticed a big box in the middle of the road in front of his house. He thought it would be best to move it off the street, so it would not be hit by oncoming cars. He left it on the sidewalk thinking that if the box had fallen from a truck, the owner might backtrack to retrieve it.

The following morning, the box was still on the sidewalk. No one had removed it and it appeared untouched. The man decided to investigate. The package was tightly sealed with duct tape, but he noticed scratch marks on the cardboard sides. They seemed to originate from the box's interior. There was no sound coming from inside, so he ripped off the tape and opened it. What he found was quite a surprise!

The box contained four kittens. Two were about eight weeks old and two were around seven months. One of the older kittens was so startled that it leapt out and dashed down the street. Unfortunately, despite the neighborhood's efforts, it was never seen again. The man swiftly closed the lid and moved the box with the remaining kittens into his garage. Then he closed the garage door to make sure that no one else escaped. Not wanting to be late for work, he placed a blanket in the box and left. He hoped that while he was away, the kittens would recover from their trauma.

When he returned home and checked on the kittens, there was another surprise waiting for him. The seven-month-old cat had given birth to six more kittens! Sadly, one of the kittens had already died. The neighbor realized that something needed to be done, but he lacked experience with baby animals. In desperation, he telephoned his neighbors… that also happened to be Susan's son and grandchildren!

Susan's family was well aware of her dedication to rescuing cats. She has been a volunteer at RESQCATS for many years and has a lot of experience with young kittens. Her granddaughter called and asked, "Grandma, what do we do?"

As usual, Susan had plenty of advice…and I mean that in a good way. She is a candid woman who is not afraid to say what she thinks. "Get them out of that garage and into your bathroom! It's freezing in Bakersfield! Set up a heating pad for those kittens and I'll be there as soon as I can!"

The drive to Bakersfield is about one-hundred-fifty miles and takes the average driver almost three hours. Now I have been a passenger in Susan's car and one had better buckle up! It took her less than two hours to get to her destination!

While driving to Bakersfield, she called me. Susan knew that kitten season was supposed to be over and I sensed some reluctance in her voice. I try to take a break in the winter months and she did not want to impose on my downtime. But Susan knows me all too well and she had a plan in place if I were willing to lend a hand. Of course, I was more than happy to help the cats... and my friend! We agreed that she would foster the mother cat and the newborns once she transported them from Bakersfield to Santa Barbara. I would take care of the eight-week-old kittens.

By evening, the mom and babies had checked into first-class accommodations, also known as Susan's bathroom. The room was set up like a nursery. Pastel blankets lined the inside of a covered pet house where mom could nurse her five babies in private. Designer bath rugs covered the tile floor. Food and water were set up along the side wall. There were enough toys to fill the shelves in the cat section of a pet supply store! A radio inside the room played ambient spa music. After settling the family into their new quarters, Susan spent the next several hours with the mother and her newborns. As the wee hours of the morning approached, the long day caught up with her and Susan grew tired. She flipped on the bathroom's nightlight and began to head for bed. Susan paused then and decided she should first name the mother cat before retiring; she chose Nemress.

I have no idea, nor do I dare to ask, where Susan's

husband goes when he is expelled from his personal bathroom to make space for foster kittens. He seems to accept it uncomplainingly. I have a sneaking suspicion that he either realizes that he has no say in the matter, or that it is best to avoid a no-win confrontation with Susan. I give him credit either way!

❧

Susan went about her job as foster guardian while I took the remaining two eight-week-old kittens to RESQCATS. Within a few days, they had been provided the usual medical protocol required prior to adoption. It was not long before both kittens were adopted to fantastic homes.

All did not go as well for Nemress and her litter. When Susan called to say there was trouble, I heard the same alarm in her voice as I had when she called from the road. But this time, I also detected a sense of hopelessness in her voice.

Nemress had become pregnant when she was only five months old. She barely weighed six pounds herself and now had five babies to feed. She was a kitten herself...a kitten having kittens!

Due to the stress of being crammed into a box and deserted in the middle of the street in freezing weather, her babies had most likely been born prematurely. They were severely underweight. Despite Susan's best efforts, four of the five kittens died within twenty-four hours. Losing young kittens is never easy; it was devastating for Susan. Her grief was intense and there was not anything I could say or do to console her. That remains the saddest day in our history of rescuing together.

The four tiny bodies weighed less than eight ounces in total. We positioned them together in a small box lined with a flannel blanket. I placed a light pink rose on their sweet bodies. Lastly, I put a feather in the make-shift coffin, so their spirits could fly to the Rainbow Bridge. They were buried in a special place in my yard called Twilight Park. The pet cemetery has filled almost to capacity over the years with angels like Nemress' babies.

ε

It is at a time like this, when lives seem taken so prematurely, that I remember something my mother once said. "Jeffyne, angels are not on this Earth for very long." These kittens were certainly angels. I continue to find comfort in my mom's words even today.

ε

I called the vet looking for answers. What could have happened? Was there anything we could have done differently? Did we do something wrong?

The doctor said that the kittens likely suffered from a condition called fading kitten syndrome. He assured us that there was nothing humanly possible that could have been done to save them. Premature birth, low birth weights, a young mother, stress and freezing temperatures just do not add up to survival.

When Susan returned to the mother cat and her only surviving kitten, she believed that Nemress was fully aware of what had happened. Susan thought she could see actual tears in Nemress' eyes.

Despite her grief, Susan found the emotional strength to continue fostering Nemress and her baby. She named the kitten Miracle. Certainly, having beaten the odds qualified her as a miracle!

Over the following weeks, Miracle grew from a tiny preemie into a full-fledged kitten. She was as active as kittens get! That same kittenish behavior that Nemress had placed on hold during motherhood reappeared in all its glory! She and Miracle wrestled, played and slept together like siblings. Witnessing their bond to each other after such tragedy and loss was heart-warming.

The subject of adopting Nemress and Miracle as a pair never came up in my conversations with Susan. I think we assumed that separating them was not an option and there was no need to even discuss it. As most times, we were on the same page.

Once Miracle was old enough, we began to search for a home. The local newspaper offers rescue groups "Pet of the Week" ads at no cost. I wrote a story about the two cats and submitted it along with a photo of Miracle. The newspaper stipulated that only one cat can be featured in the photo. I considered sending the editor a picture of Nemress. However, from past experience, I knew that the likelihood of people responding to what they saw as an adult may not be the best approach to finding a home for the pair. So I gave them an irresistible photograph of Miracle.

I was not quite prepared for what followed. Once readers saw the picture, the phone began ringing. The calls were coming in faster than I could answer them. It seemed that everyone in Santa Barbara wanted to adopt Miracle. Callers were very sympathetic when I explained the details of Nemress and Miracle's survival. They understood why they needed to stay together. Most, however, could not commit to two cats.

It took some time, but a special person that wanted to adopt mother and daughter finally appeared. Susan thoroughly screened a young woman in a phone conversation. I am certain that she was more than diligent during the interview process! After all, she had invested a lot of time caring for the duo. She felt a tremendous love for Nemress and Miracle.

I know what it is like when a piece of your heart goes with

cats and kittens that you have literally saved from death. It is an emotional roller coaster. I feel happy for the cats, and at the same moment, I miss them very much.

Susan met the lady in person and gave her endorsement. To her delight, Nemress and Miracle went to their new home that very day.

The woman was understanding of Susan's attachment and stayed in touch. In fact, she called Susan several years later to let her know that she and her new husband were moving to Australia...and Nemress and Miracle were going with them!

Hearts never quite heal from the loss of a tiny kitten whose life has been much too brief. But my hurt is lessened when I recall my mother's words of comfort, "...angels are never on this Earth very long."

I learned early on that it is not always better to know what had happened to some of the cats and kittens prior to their arrival at RESQCATS. Some are in poor shape from their misfortune on the streets. They have been deprived of food, water and shelter. Others have dealt with a worse fate. They arrive with broken bones, puncture wounds and many other serious health issues. I cannot help but wonder what unbearable conditions they faced at the mercy of Mother Nature or, even worse, at the hands of abusive humans.

I appreciate that it is sometimes better not to know. Otherwise, I think my heart would just break. That time spent wondering is better focused on caring, nurturing, loving and healing feline bodies.

Sometimes, a cat or kitten comes along that needs more than I can give. Miracles are essential.

TWENTY

The Miracles of Blessing

It was an early summer morning in 2004 when three stray seven-week-old kittens arrived at RESQCATS. If they had not been found, life for them on the street would most likely have been short.

The two boys were handsome Siamese-mix kittens. Their eyes were as blue as Paul Newman's. They were instantly inquisitive about their new surroundings at RESQCATS. It was not long before they discovered balls, feather toys and climbing posts. In their feline minds, everything in their enclosure existed entirely for their entertainment. They romped, played tackle and chased balls to their hearts' content. They ate until their bellies were full. When it came time to sleep off all the excitement, unlike their lives as strays, they had many beds from which to choose.

To my surprise, the brothers were in perfect health. Living on the streets had not been too harsh. They were fat and healthy. Although she was never found, there obviously had been a mother who had cared for them. Their stay at RESQCATS would not be long. Another couple of weeks and they would be ready for adoption. There was no doubt in my mind that these brothers would find homes quickly. For an adopter, they would be what I refer to as "instant gratification" kittens. They had everything going in their favor; they were cute, social, healthy, fun-loving kittens!

The smallest kitten of the three was a female. She was a pretty, dark tabby with long, sleek fur and big, green eyes. I named her Ko.

Regrettably, her fate had not been as fortunate. Ko had a ghastly laceration on her back leg. It was badly infected and required immediate medical attention, so off to the veterinarian's office we went. The vet showed me how to properly clean the wound and explained what to look for that would indicate further signs of infection. He sent us home with antibiotics and instructions to return the following week to recheck her injury.

Ko was very timid compared to her brothers. I presumed that the trauma she suffered may have been part of the reason for her shyness, but she tolerated me dressing her wound without hesitation. She seemed to appreciate my gentle touch and sensed that I was trying to help her. She did not flinch, even when I knew she felt discomfort.

Ko watched me through big emerald-colored eyes. As I cared for her injury, her expression was both sad and grateful. Her watchful gaze reminded me of the adage, "Eyes are the windows to the soul."

&

I know what some of you may be thinking. Seeing expression and emotions in Ko's eyes is considered by some as anthropomorphism. That is, ascribing human characteristics, such as appearance or behavior, to non-human entities.

Some people believe that animals are incapable of showing emotion and that attributing human feelings to them in any form is ridiculous. However, there are many stories and clinical studies to prove that animals do have feelings. Regardless, I do not need scientific evidence to tell me that animals are capable of expressing love, sadness, grief, loneliness and pain. I witness it on a daily basis.

In 2005, a devastating tsunami hit Indonesia ending the lives of over 250,000 people in a matter of minutes. The destruction and toll of human life was felt throughout the world. During the disaster, a baby hippo, whose mother perished in the catastrophe, became stranded in the ocean. Fortunately, he was rescued and taken to a nature park. He was named Owen. Strangely, once there, he bonded with an Aldabra tortoise, Mzee. They became inseparable. Photos of the unusual pair and their love for each other were publicized all over the world. Their story is one of love and friendship between different species.

In 1996, Scarlet, a mother cat, made a daring attempt to save her kittens during a fire in Brooklyn, New York. She had been living in an abandoned building that was a suspected crack house. When fire broke out, Scarlet made five separate trips into the thick, choking smoke and sweltering heat to save her kittens. Once she had retrieved the last one, she touched each one on the nose to make sure they were okay. Then she collapsed and passed out. A fireman noticed Scarlet and went to her rescue. She was severely burned; her eyes were blistered shut, the fur on her face was completely gone and her body was badly scorched. Scarlet would have given her life to save her kittens. She showed the strength and willpower of motherly love. She and her babies were transported to intensive care at The North Shore Animal League in Port Washington, New York. After three months of treatment, she and her four surviving kittens were ready for adoption. Thousands of letters poured in offering homes for the family. The kittens were immediately adopted. Scarlet became a heroine. She was adopted by a kind woman who had survived a serious car accident and vowed to take in a special-needs cat. Scarlet died three years to the day after the brave rescue of her kittens. Those who followed her story grieved and have never forgotten her.

In 2006, a dog named Capitan ran away from home after his owner and best friend died. A week later, he was seen sitting beside his owner's gravesite. Capitan had never been to the cemetery before and no one knows how he found the burial ground or his master's grave. For six years, Capitan roamed the graveyard during the day, but at 6 p.m. sharp, he returned to his master's grave. He lay down and stayed there all night. The personnel said they had never witnessed such grief and loyalty from a dog. The cemetery became Capitan's home and the staff made certain he was properly cared for.

Wounda, a chimpanzee, was found near death in the Congo. She was taken to the Tchimpunga Chimpanzee Rehabilitation Center where Jane Goodall and her team worked for years to rehabilitate her. Wounda was released into a protected chimpanzee sanctuary in June, 2013. Before she bounded back into the wild habitat, Wounda paused and turned to look at Miss Goodall. Then the chimp approached her. When Wounda reached her, she wrapped her elongated arms around Miss Goodall, rested her head on her shoulders and hugged her.

In my view, those who do not believe that animals are capable of emotions are missing out on some wonderful experiences. For others that do believe, you understand when I say that Ko looked at me with grateful sadness.

Ko and I had a ritual everyday. I removed the bandages, washed her wound, applied a topical ointment and gave her an oral antibiotic. My medical duties were always followed with cuddle time and soothing whispers. I held her close and reassured her that everything would be okay.

I tried to block any thoughts from my mind about her past and what might have happened to her. My imagination could lead me to picture the worst. Something in my head told me I did not want to know.

The days went by and finally it was time for Ko to see the vet to have the laceration rechecked. The scheduled appointment time was supposed to be a quick exam of the wound by a vet technician to make sure it was healing properly. I anticipated a brief wait in the lobby. Once Ko was checked, I expected the tech would return with a report and further instructions.

To my dismay, it was the veterinarian who appeared in the lobby. He sat down close to me. I saw deep concern in his eyes. I knew at that moment that something was seriously wrong. He said, with uneasiness in his voice, "Jeffyne, this little kitty's bladder is the size of a tennis ball and we need to find out why. I expressed it and her urine is full of blood."

I had noticed her in the litter box more than usual but attributed it to curiosity. She probably had never seen a litter box before coming to RESQCATS.

When kittens first arrive, they are curious and soon discover that their litter box can serve many purposes. Some are so enamored with the set-up that they spend hours stalking the strange container. Feline curiosity usually gets the better of them. They inspect it from all angles and cautiously bat at it. Suspiciously, they approach the foreign sand-like ingredient inside the box and discover that it moves. The litter becomes their playground. They leap and play in the clay sand and dig as if there is some magnificent treasure buried at the bottom. The litter ends up everywhere outside of the container! The alien box and its contents become their main entertainment. Ultimately, they perceive that the sole purpose of the strange-looking sand is for beach parties!

Recently, I witnessed a young kitten watch his mom as she urinated in the litter box. At least he was polite enough to wait for her to exit before he went in to inspect. He retrieved her clumped urine ball and removed it from the box. He was so captivated by it that it became his knock-around-the-entire-enclosure-toy. Of course, the clump fell apart and scattered across the enclosure floor, which made it even more interesting for the kitten! It is no wonder that the morning cleaning crew at RESQCATS is the least desirable volunteer job!

Some kittens find that after a long, hard day of playing,

the litter box is the best place to turn in for a nap. Funny, I thought that was the purpose of the baskets with cushy blankets! I must be wrong! Hopefully, by the time kittens are ready to go to their new homes, they have figured out that the litter box is meant exclusively for their toilet duties.

ɞ

Ko was checked into the hospital without delay. I left the clinic feeling apprehensive. My gut intuition told me that bad news was on the horizon.

The vet's report and x-rays confirmed that Ko had a broken pelvis and a fractured femur. However, her injury had not occurred in the last few days. Her bones had already fused back together.

What on earth had happened to her? The morbid thoughts I had tried so hard to push out of my mind began creeping back. The pain she had endured must have been unbearable. Was it a car? Could it have been an animal? Had she somehow managed to escape? Was it possible that someone had abused her? Was she still in pain? What could I do to help her?

Ko checked into the hospital where she could be continuously monitored. The vet had to express her bladder since she could not urinate on her own, although she did try. Manually relieving bladders on kittens was not something I had ever done and I knew it could be tricky. This undoubtedly was not the time for me to learn such a procedure. I could not take any chances on doing it wrong, possibly hurting her and causing additional problems.

The veterinarian consulted three orthopedic surgeons. All came to the same conclusion; nothing could be done since the injury was not new and the bones had already healed improperly. Not one of them recommended surgery. The conclusion was that it would be worse to re-break her bones in order to put them back in the right place. Ko was able to walk, jump and climb like any normal kitten. The risk of doing anything to correct the old injury would have caused unnecessary suffering. The chief concern was that Ko could not urinate on her own. If the circumstances did not change, she would be destined to a life of continually needing to have her bladder expressed. Infections were sure to follow and these circumstances would likely shorten her life.

In addition, finding an adopter that was willing to make a commitment to her condition would be a challenge.

The veterinarian, clinic staff and I were dedicated to doing all we could for her. Euthanasia was not an option for me. I could see in his expression that it was not a consideration for the vet either. "What we need is a miracle," he said. I looked him straight in the eye and replied, "Well, I believe in miracles!"

Ko remained in the hospital for several days. The vet technicians administered antibiotics, monitored her water intake and expressed her bladder every few hours. The entire clinic staff spent their breaks playing with her. Everyone loved this irresistible little girl. It was not uncommon to see her perched on someone's shoulder in the back treatment room when I stopped by for daily visits. The longer she stayed, the deeper our love became. The word from the hospital staff was that she would become their office cat before she would ever be euthanized.

Then, one day, to everyone's surprise, Ko urinated all by herself. It was only a tiny amount, but she did it! We were all ecstatic, just like young parents feel when their toddler uses the toilet for the first time.

I swear that for the next three days, I heard my favorite disco song, "Celebration," by Kool and the Gang wherever I went. It played on the radio, in the mall, in the pet supply store and in the bank. It played everywhere! Most certainly, it was not in my head! The entire city of Santa Barbara was celebrating the fact that Ko had peed by herself. Hearing that song wherever I went was absolute proof!

Ko improved daily. After two weeks in the hospital, she was able to return to RESQCATS. I was so overcome with joy that I hardly heard the vet's warning. He explained that the way her broken pelvis fused had displaced her colon. The abnormally healed bones pushed on her colon causing it to bend. That could cause bowel problems. He cautioned, "We better hope this kitty never gets constipated. If she becomes impacted, she could be in big trouble." He recommended a diet of mostly canned food. The extra moisture would help her move her bowels.

I was so grateful for her progress. I felt blessed by this miracle, so I gave her a new name, Blessing.

The shy little girl had blossomed with all the love and socialization she enjoyed at the vet clinic. She was as active as any perfectly normal kitten. She ate and used the litter box regularly. She loved to climb and play. Her favorite toy was a fake-fur mouse with a feather tail. Once she had exhausted every toy in her enclosure, she fell into a sweet slumber that kittens succumb to after a long day of just being a kitten. Her beloved mouse toy went to bed with her. Her brothers had been adopted, but she did not seem to notice.

Blessing spent a few weeks at RESQCATS for continued monitoring. During that time, she captured the hearts of all the volunteers.

When it was safe for Blessing to be spayed, I decided it would be better for her to return to the same hospital for surgery instead of the usual low-fee spay clinic. Her attending veterinarian was familiar with her body from x-rays and an ultra-sound. If there were any surprises during surgery, he was fully equipped to handle the complications.

Her spay operation went well and she returned to RESQCATS that evening. I stayed with her while she ate a small amount of her canned food and drank water. She was drowsy due to the anesthesia, so I tucked her in a bed with a heating pad for the night. As I left, I whispered, "Sweet dreams, Blessing."

Everything was fine until the next morning when I discovered that Blessing had pulled the sutures from her incision. Her internal organs were partially exposed and some of her intestines had been dragged through the cat litter. It was not a pretty sight!

I rushed Blessing back to the hospital. She underwent anesthesia to sterilize the exposed organs, return them to their proper place and stitch her abdomen together again. This time, she was sent home with antibiotics and an Elizabethan collar, a cone that looks like an inverted lampshade, so she could not get to her stitches.

What the vet had most feared happened almost immediately. The pressure of the displaced pelvis on her colon narrowed the bowel passageway. The narrow passageway combined with two consecutive days of anesthesia had caused Blessing to become constipated. Her bowels could not pass and Blessing was in big trouble. She went back to the hospital again where she was administered stool softeners and subcutaneous fluids.

We could only hope for another miracle. Did I dare ask for another one? Yes, of course! It never hurts to pray. I invited the vet staff and the volunteers to join me. Fortunately, our prayers were answered. The medication worked and once again, Blessing returned to RESQCATS.

A second miracle!

Blessing was expected to recover completely, but she was to remain on stool softeners throughout her life. Administering them to her twice a day was the prescribed dosage. It was an absolute necessity to monitor her litter box duties. If there was a problem, she would have to go to the hospital immediately.

Where on earth was I going to find someone to adopt

Blessing and make such a commitment? Many potential adopters visited RESQCATS in search of a kitten. They were touched by her story, but once they understood that medication would be part of her daily routine, they lost interest. She was not the "perfect" kitten, so they passed on adopting her. They did so politely, but they passed, nonetheless. Sadly, that has been my experience with less-than-perfect kittens. I wondered if there would be anyone willing to adopt Blessing.

Little did I realize that the right person had been standing right in front of me all along. Kay had volunteered for RESQCATS for several years. She had also adopted two kittens three years earlier. As part of her volunteer duties, she visited RESQCATS twice a week to help socialize cats and kittens. Kay's favorite expression was, "They just need some loving." She was devoted to making sure that all the cats learned that human touch is nothing to fear. She spent many hours with the most terrified ones. Kay's love transformed many frightened souls into outgoing adoptable kittens.

I knew that Kay was aware of all of Blessing's trips to the hospital because I had kept volunteers updated on her condition. Kay had spent a great deal of time with Blessing on her volunteer days. However, I did not realize how bonded they had become.

That is, until she called me and said, "Jeffyne, I love Blessing and I want to give her a home. I'm fully prepared to give Blessing her medicine twice a day. I also got permission from my landlord to have a third cat. I have it in writing from the leasing agent, too. I love her and I want her to be part of my family."

I should have seen the special bond between Kay and Blessing developing. But I didn't. Perhaps it was because I was preoccupied with the serious medical concerns going on with Blessing during the past weeks. My attention had been focused on trips to the veterinarian, hospital stays, warnings from the doctor, caring for Blessing...and praying for miracles.

Kay has always been such a sensitive and loving person. She is one of the kindest women I have ever had the privilege to know. It should have come as no surprise that she would want to adopt Blessing.

Kay now lives in a senior assisted living facility in Colorado where she is closer to her human family. She stays in touch with me on a regular basis. Kay is always happy to report that as a thirteen-year-old cat, Blessing is healthy and content.

I believe that Kay is Blessing's third miracle!

The arrival of kittens at RESQCATS is always an exciting time. The expectation of the impending birth demands a watchful eye. The gestation period for kittens is only sixty-three days. But when a pregnant cat arrives at RESQCATS, I have no way of knowing when her babies were conceived. That can lead to days or weeks of eager anticipation!

TWENTY-ONE

Lilly's Way

I am an early-to-bed and early-to-rise person who gets at least two hours of work done before most people roll over and even begin to consider getting out of bed. By 6:30 a.m., I had already responded to the email written well after I had gone to sleep the night before.

The subject was "HELP!" The email read, "We found a cat under our car on Easter Sunday and we think she's pregnant. She also has a terrible eye infection. We have her in our apartment, but we're not allowed to have cats. What should we do?" I emailed back, "Call me as soon as possible!"

By late morning, the couple and I had connected by phone. Josh wanted to know all about RESQCATS. I started by telling him that we are dedicated to stray and abandoned cats and kittens. I answered all his questions and, I assure you, he had more than a few! I told him that we take care of all medical needs for the cats. I also shared that my philosophy does not include aborting unborn kittens. While he said everything sounded great, I detected a hint of hesitation in Josh's voice. He needed reassurance that RESQCATS was a reputable organization. Josh asked if he and his girlfriend, Kym, could "check everything out" before leaving the cat in our care.

Later that day, I led the young couple, in their early twenties, on the usual thirty minute tour. I was not halfway through my customary spiel when I noticed the two look at each other and smile. RESQCATS will be the "perfect place for her" they said almost in unison!

Josh and Kym had become quite bonded to the cat in only a few days. We agreed to keep in touch.

The volunteers chose the name Lilly, which seemed appropriate since she had been rescued on Easter.

Lilly was several weeks pregnant, but she did not appear ready to deliver. Most of the time, however, it is hard to tell when a cat will give birth.

I recall a seemingly pregnant cat that arrived a few years ago. She had a big round belly and I expected babies anytime. I was so excited. I prepared a comfortable quiet place in an isolation area, so she could have her babies in peace; that is, away from the other cats in the main building. I anxiously checked on her several times a day hoping to see that healthy newborns had arrived. But days passed and nothing happened. Apparently, I had lost all perspective on whether she was bigger or any closer to delivering babies. In my defense, it was hard to tell since I spent time with her every day. It would be like living with someone and not noticing whether he/she had gained or lost a few pounds. After three weeks of watching, I became concerned. I took her to the vet and to my surprise, he announced that this cat was just overweight!

Lilly's vigil continued. I arrived in the cattery every morning hoping that kittens would be born that day. I imagined the to-be-mom's discomfort when I looked at Lilly's enormous extended belly. She looked miserable in that "ready-to-pop" stage. I wondered, "Is there any way that she can get any bigger?"

In general, when RESQCATS has a pregnant cat, I watch for signs of nesting in a secluded area of her enclosure. This is a signal of an approaching delivery. I happily prepare for the momentous occasion.

Clamps and dental floss are readily at my disposal in preparation. I may need to cut umbilical cords and tie them off if a young mother does not perform that important task. Sometimes, inexperienced cats do not know how to cut the cords.

Other times, mother cats are exhausted after delivering kitten after kitten. They forget to finish the birthing process of chewing the cord and consuming the placenta. I must be standing by to assist! I love being part of the whole experience. As strange as it sounds, when I am lucky enough to witness kittens being born, I find myself pushing as if I am the one giving birth!

I did not have children of my own. Despite what friends and family have said, I have never felt that I missed something. Although I have never asked for anyone's opinions, some people have gone so far as to voice their thoughts on the subject anyway. A few friends have even communicated their views by telling me that I was missing out on the miracle of childbirth. I do not apologize for my seeming lack of maternal instincts.

Having children was never an issue for me for two reasons. First of all, my husband is thirteen years older than I am. He has grown children and he did not want to start a second family. Second, unlike many women, my biological clock never kicked in when it came to wanting human babies.

I do, however, have a very strong mothering instinct, but I have always felt that it was meant for me to nurture stray and abandoned cats and kittens.

I usually wait a day or two before taking pregnant cats to the veterinarian. That extra time gives them a chance to settle into their new surroundings. However in Lilly's case, her eye looked alarmingly bad, so I took her in for a vet check the day she arrived.

Lilly was a beautiful Siamese-like cat with brilliant sky-blue eyes, or at least one of them was brilliant. The other was severely ulcerated. The ulcer protruded from the cornea and appeared painful.

The vet thought that Lilly was about ten months old, which meant she probably became pregnant at only eight months. She was still a kitten herself; another kitten having kittens! An ultrasound revealed at least three babies in her belly. It also confirmed that her due date was still a couple of weeks away.

The vet's major concern was Lilly's eye. It was severely lacerated and needed immediate attention. He instructed me to medicate it with antibiotic drops every two hours around the clock for three consecutive days. "Wow! Every two hours," I repeated. Even doctors working on their residency do not have a seventy-two hour shift! Luckily, the doctor agreed that it would be fine for me to start medication at 6:00 a.m. every morning. As I said, I am an early riser so that would be no problem. The drops should continue every two hours until 10:00 p.m., even though ten is already two hours past my normal bedtime! Then I could doze until 2:00 a.m., sleepwalk into the cattery to give her the drops, return to bed and start all over at 6:00 in the morning.

The vet wanted to see Lilly on the fourth day. I documented the exact minute and hour of each treatment. I took my log with me when I went for her recheck.

The objective of the medication was to prevent scarring from the laceration. With the drops and a little luck, we could save her eye. She got an excellent report, but the eye meds needed to be continued for ten additional days. I was grateful that the time between treatments could be spaced out to every four to six hours.

Lilly's eye continued to show excellent progress. And fortunately, since there was no scarring, her vision remained intact. Although the appearance of her eye remained cloudy, the doctor was not concerned.

Now I just had to be patient and wait for her babies to arrive.

Our grandson, Hayden, happened to be visiting while Lilly was at RESQCATS. He loved helping out during his summer vacations. He was seven years old and had been my assistant since he was four. The anticipation of kittens being born was very exciting to both of us.

Hayden and I did not want to miss seeing the kittens as they were being born. So when they did not arrive during the day, we decided to set up camp in the cattery at night. Not wanting to sleep on the cement floor, I found an air mattress in the back of a bedroom closet. We dragged it into the cattery and asked Mitch to blow it up with his tire pump. We brought out blankets and pillows from the guest room to keep us warm and comfortable. We thought we had everything we needed. Then, at bedtime, room service arrived! Mitch served us vanilla ice-cream covered in chocolate syrup and topped with chocolate sprinkles. Hayden and I agreed that this was the only way to camp out!

Hayden was a little nervous during the night in the open air cattery. Raccoons rustled through fallen leaves. We heard tiny footsteps running across the roof of the cattery, occasionally stopping to feast on fallen avocados. There were also a multitude of other inexplicable night noises! I suppose that the imagination of a seven-year-old boy can be pretty scary. To ease his apprehension, I turned every nightlight in the cattery to the "on" position. We found a package of six brand new flashlights in the garage. They also burned all night!

And then there were the resident felines! They were intrigued that Hayden and I were in their campground and assumed it was all for their benefit. Blackie wriggled deep under the blankets while Greyco played chase with her on top of the covers. Seacliff trekked across our faces several times during the night. I woke to Wizard hovering above me purring and "making biscuits" on my chest. In fact, the cats kept us up most of the night. It reminded me of what it was like to be at a slumber party, the kind we had in grade school when you stayed awake all night with friends. It was fun at the time. But do you remember how you felt the next morning?

Waking Hayden and getting him out of the cattery by 8:30 a.m. before the cleaning crew of volunteers arrived was next to impossible. I dragged my sleepy grandson into the house and made him eat a bowl of cereal for breakfast. Before I realized it, he disappeared into his bedroom and slept until 11:00. As for me, groggy is the best way to describe how I felt for the rest of the day.

Hayden and I spent two nights at our cattery camp-out with the hope that Lilly would give birth. But unfortunately, she did not cooperate and Hayden had to return home before the kittens were born.

ξ

Josh and Kym visited twice a week without fail. They loved Lilly and were committed to giving her a home. They began searching for an apartment to rent that allowed cats. Their visits were spent with Lilly curled in Josh's lap while Kym sat next to him. I was surprised to hear that they were entertaining the idea of two cats. Josh said, "My birthday is April 17 and if Lilly has her babies then, I might just have to keep one of her kittens, too!"

On April 17, I called Josh to wish him a happy birthday. I also congratulated him on the arrival of Lilly's babies that morning! She had three perfect babies!

Oddly, Lilly gave birth in a basket on an upper shelf. What! Of all the plush places in her enclosure, why had she chosen there? She had access to a large crate filled with layers of towels to have her kittens. There was a good-sized condo lined with fleece blankets that would have been an optimum smaller place to deliver if she felt the crate was too spacious. Why on earth had she decided that the spot that suited her most was an unsecured basket on the highest shelf? What if the basket falls? What if one of the kittens is displaced from the basket and tumbles to the ground below? I decided that I had to move them to a safer place.

I must confess that this sort of behavior did fit Lilly's personality. Lilly maintained her independence. She could be head-strong. If cats could have a favorite song, hers would be Frank Sinatra's "My Way" as Lilly certainly insisted on doing things her way!

She also had traits that can best be described as high maintenance. She craved continuous attention. Typical of Siamese cats, she was chatty. "Love me, love me more, love me first!" was my interpretation of her constant verbal commands. She demanded attention every time I entered her enclosure. Her favorite place was a human lap.

I transferred Lilly and her newborns from the high shelf to lower and safer ground. Fortunately, she accepted the new spot alongside her kittens and was perfectly content inside the big crate. It was lined with several clean towels. I draped a blanket over the open crate door covering it halfway, so she would have a sense of privacy and security.

The anticipated birth of the kittens brings excitement to the cattery and now that day had finally arrived. The volunteers made special trips, even on their unscheduled days, to see Lilly and her family. Josh and Kym could not wait to visit. He celebrated his birthday and Lilly's extraordinary gift on his special day. The subject of finding a place to rent that would allow mom and one of her babies was the main topic of Josh and Kym's conversation.

Lilly nursed and cleaned her kittens inside the crate for the following week. However, she never missed an opportunity to come out when she heard someone in the cattery. She would chat, solicit attention, have some lap time and eat...and then eat some more! She ate constantly to keep up with the demands of being a mother.

Now that a week had passed since the birth of Lilly's kittens, it was time for me to get inside the crate, pull out the soiled towels and replace them with clean ones. I was confident that Lilly would allow me to make the exchange without objecting. While a volunteer kept Lilly occupied, I gently lifted and placed the kittens in a basket. Then I quickly replaced the soiled linens with fresh ones and put the kittens back inside the crate.

Like many mother cats, Lilly was very protective of her kittens. She did not like the new towels. She immediately moved her babies out of the crate and into a small condo. I returned the kittens to the roomy crate. She transferred them back to the little condo. Again, I relocated them to the crate. Once more, she moved them to the condo! We repeated this power struggle three more times! I was puzzled. Lilly had cared for the newborns for a week inside the crate with no problem. Why was she being so stubborn? It reminded me of the signs you see in hotels: "Place this card on your bed if you want to save water and protect our precious planet's resources." Leaving the card on your bed meant you would sleep on the same linens again that night. Lilly's message became clear! She glared at me as if to say, "I put that card on my bed and said I would sleep on the same blankets. You just ignored it!"

For the next week, Lilly nursed her babies inside the small condo. It was cramped, but she was set on having it her way. As the kittens got bigger, she settled into a sitting position on the outside so that her nipples were available to her kittens that remained inside of the condo.

Eventually, she decided that the condo was getting tight for her growing family. So, true to herself, in her own time, Lilly moved the babies from her efficiency studio, the condo, back to the one-bedroom apartment, the crate! During the ensuing weeks, I watched the kittens grow to be fat and healthy. Lilly was an attentive mom; however, the stress of being a young mother was hard on her. Nursing took a physical toll. Her fur began to fall out. As a kitten herself, she barely weighed six pounds. She ate constantly, but the nourishment from her food went to producing milk for her babies. I became worried about her well-being. The vet suggested supplements to support her immune system. Thankfully, they helped.

Once her babies were finally weaned and eating on their own, Lilly began to improve. Her fur stopped falling out and she even gained a whole pound!

I had the opportunity to get to know Josh and Kym during their twice a week visits. They were obviously very much in love. They were mature, despite their young age, and understood the responsibility of adopting a cat...or two! They were prepared to make a lifetime commitment to Lilly and one of her kittens. They chose one of Lilly's daughters and named her Tiger.

Kym and Josh found a place to live that allowed them to have cats. They signed the lease, paid the pet deposit and moved in.

When the day finally arrived for them to take Tiger and Lilly home, it was a day of celebration for all of us.

I will always have a place in my heart for Josh and Kym. I remain grateful for the extraordinary concern they showed for a pregnant stray cat and the home that they ultimately gave Lilly and one of her kittens.

ಶ

I still think about Lilly. I imagine hearing her chatty mews for attention when I enter the cattery. I treasure the fact that she was a lap cat. It is not often that I meet a cat that craves so much love but also has so much affection to give.

I can still recall her independent antics. I reminisce about her giving birth. It still makes me laugh when I think about our contest of wills when she moved her kittens to that tiny condo. She certainly did it her way!

One might wonder why I would write about our dogs when this is supposed to be a book about my experiences of rescuing cats.

When we lose one of our collies, a resident cat or a kitten that never had a chance, the heartfelt pain that I experience is dreadfully profound. I have discovered that writing about the grief often helps me with the healing process.

Sometimes all it takes is a rainbow in order to find harmony and joy in life once again.

TWENTY-TWO

In Search of a Double Rainbow

Mitch and I have rescued many collies over the years, but the story of Harmony and her sister, Joy, is unique.

An elderly man kept sixty-six collies on his property in northern California. He had no means to properly care for that many dogs. The animals were kept in unsanitary conditions on concrete that reeked of urine and feces. At feeding time, food was scattered across the floor. The dogs fought over it and many had scars to show for their intense altercations. Not one had ever set a paw on grass or slept in the comfort of a soft, warm bed. To make matters worse, none of the dogs were spayed or neutered. They mated indiscriminately and suffered serious inbreeding health issues.

The owner of the dogs was a hoarder. Many hoarders start out with big hearts and have good intentions to help the animals. But somewhere along the way, they become overwhelmed by the number of animals in their care. Providing for them becomes more than the person can handle. Conditions deteriorate and the hoarders lose sight of the harm they are bringing to the animals. They claim to love their pets, but loving them and properly caring for them are entirely different matters.

The hoarder mentality begins with an obsessive-compulsive disorder and reaches a point that results in animal suffering and abuse. If hoarders do not receive continued counseling, they tend to repeat the behavior over and over to the detriment of all of their animals.

Despite the explanation for their mental condition, I find it difficult to have compassion for any person committing such inhumane acts. As a rescue person, I am witness to how the animals suffer. Those who rescue animals are the ones left to clean up the hoarders' messes at great costs, both financially and emotionally. Rescuers' priority is the animals and we are devastated when we cannot save them all.

In this particular situation, the adult collies were removed by animal control and placed into foster care. Criminal charges were filed against the man who was, in fact, a repeat offender.

❧

Mitch and I drove to Yolo County to offer our assistance. We spent the next few days brushing and bathing dogs that were caked in dirt and feces. Some of the collies had such painful mats that they had to be completely shaved. Others suffered severe skin infections due to their filthy living conditions. Scars covered the long snouts of these gentle creatures from fighting over food. As a result of indiscriminate breeding, a number of the dogs were deaf and/or blind.

It was not surprising to us, however, that the dogs' loving dispositions had not succumbed to all their misfortune; that is just how collies are.

When the dogs were confiscated by animal control, a litter of puppies was discovered inside the man's house. The pups were the more fortunate ones since they had not been exposed to the horrid outside conditions. The puppies were divided amongst several foster homes.

As in most animal abuse situations, it takes a long time for the case to make its way through the legal system. With the Yolo collies, it took more than a year for the charges against the man to be finally settled. Only then could the dogs be adopted to qualified permanent homes. Mitch and I adopted one of the puppies that had been removed from inside the man's house. By that time, she was more than a year old. We named her Harmony.

Harmony fit right in with our pack. Introductions to her new family were without incident. She loved the other dogs and they readily accepted her. They played and romped in our yard. It was a happy daily routine to see six or seven collies run the two-hundred yard width along the ocean side of the property. Sometimes, it was a single line of collies playing chase across the horizon with the Pacific Ocean in the background. Other times, they made big circles on the deck until one or another decided to take the lead across the yard. They ran, leapt and played like kids in the schoolyard at recess.

Harmony captured my heart from the day we adopted her. Her disposition was sweeter than any dog I have ever been privileged to share my life. She woke up happy, never had a bad day and always smiled. Dog people know the look! Her most endearing quality was finding her favorite spot to curl up for a nap...on my lap. Yes, all fifty pounds of her!

A year had passed when we were contacted by the original foster, the director of the rescue organization, about Harmony's sister. She had not found a permanent home but, sadly, had been passed from one foster family to another. She was now two years old and it was a shame she did not have a home to call her own. The director explained that she was not very social, unlike most collies, and hoped we would consider adopting her. A few days later, Harmony's sister joined our family. We named her Joy.

Joy and Harmony were reunited at age two after being separated as puppies, but one would never know they had missed a single day together. The "sista's", as I called them, were instantly enamored with each other. Every leap and bound they made as they ran across the backyard together looked like a beautiful dance in perfect harmonization. They reminded me of synchronized swimmers, like the ones I watch during the Summer Olympics. Mitch and I were amazed by the instantaneous bond that appeared between Joy and Harmony. They became inseparable.

The sisters traveled with us to our home in Yachats,

Oregon. Yachats is a small, secluded town on the central Oregon coast. We have a second home there and it is where we spend the winter months while it is not kitten season at RESQCATS. It is in Yachats that I take time to rest from the physical and emotional demands of the previous year's rescues. The little town is known as the "gem of the Oregon coast." It has become a healing place for me. I love watching the wild winter storms. As the ocean waves swell, crash and return to deep waters, I visualize them carrying my grief from the losses of the past year out to sea.

Many times, rainbows follow the storms. The palette of colors that reach across the sky in a magnificent display takes my breath away. Rainbows are occasional miracles that remind me of the poem, "The Rainbow Bridge." The prose speaks of a beautiful place where our animals wait for us until we join them. When I am blessed to see a rainbow, I imagine my animals patiently waiting.

Joy treasured Oregon as much as I do. She loved people and, in fact, she was anything but unsocial as she had been previously described. She and Harmony were always eager to walk and run on the beach. Joy's personality blossomed as she became more confident with exposure to new environments. It was as if Oregon was home to her.

In fall 2007, as we set out for our first walk along the ocean, Joy appeared to have some difficulty with one of her back legs. She was still uncomfortable the following morning, so I took her to the local veterinarian. Upon examination, he found nothing out of the ordinary. He thought she may have hurt her leg jumping into the back of the SUV. The doctor suggested that she rest and forego her walks for a couple of weeks.

Joy never took her favorite walk in Oregon again.

She became progressively worse and rapidly declined over the next four days. It was unlike anything I had ever seen.

The local vet referred me to a specialist at the veterinary school at Oregon State University in Corvallis. The drive was an hour and a half and under other circumstances would have been enchanting. The road winds through the forest and mountains. The sun beams through the tall firs creating visible rays of light that look surreal. At this particular time of year, the leaves were changing. They were bright hues of red, orange and yellow that not even Crayola crayons can replicate. But today, the trip seemed endless as Joy got progressively worse with each curve in the road.

When we finally arrived in Corvallis, the medical staff was waiting for us at the curb with a gurney. They rushed Joy into the emergency room. By now, she was unable to walk, stand or relieve herself without physical support. The staff worked swiftly to take x-rays and draw blood samples to run tests.

I was absolutely shocked when Joy was diagnosed with spinal lymphoma. Everything seemed unreal as I passed from a state of astute consciousness to unmistakable denial. It was as if some part of my being left my body. The exam room began to spin. I felt like the doctors were talking to someone else. Could there be someone standing behind me? I thought, "This can't be my dog! She was fine just a week ago! How can this be happening?"

By now, it was late in the day. Mitch had remained in Yachats with Harmony, MisJef and Triumph, the other collies that had travelled with us. He suggested that I check into a motel room. He searched the internet and found a room near Oregon State. I wanted to be close in case of an emergency during the night.

The room was comfortable enough, but I still could not sleep. I lay awake praying for a miracle. I filled my mind with visions of Joy coming home the next day, the walks we would take, the people she would greet and her jaunts with Harmony and the other dogs. I imagined her running beside Harmony.

They were in perfect formation. In my mind, it was just like it had always been.

But sadly, by morning Joy could hardly breathe. The lymphoma had taken over her entire body. Her decline had come so fast; I knew that the kindest thing to do was to let her go. I realized that euthanasia would be a gift that would release her from the cancer, although that insightful perception did not make it any easier.

The vet techs and doctors moved Joy to a blanket on the floor where I could be next to her. I held her close, cradling her against my body. I buried my head in her fur and inhaled her sweet scent. I told her how much I loved her, hugged her for Mitch and tearfully sent her on her way to the Rainbow Bridge. I stayed with Joy until her last breath. Then, there was peace for her. For me, it was a devastating day that hardly seemed real.

Joy was only three-and-a-half years old.

When I returned home to Yachats, Harmony sensed that Joy was gone forever.

ι

It was an inconsolable time for Mitch and me. In our minds, it was impossible to grasp that such a young dog could be fine one day and gone five days later. We later learned that twenty of the sixty-six dogs the hoarder had when the county animal control confiscated them had died within that first year. Most of the deceased dogs had been diagnosed with lymphoma or complications from IBD: irritable bowel disease.

Twenty of sixty-six! That is one third of the dogs! Gone! Dead! Within a year! What had this man done? Was there some environmental cause? That could not be the case with Joy; her feet never touched the ground on his property. She had been a puppy in his house. Was it inbreeding? I just wanted an answer! I needed to know why, but understanding never followed.

Sadly, the following summer, Harmony was diagnosed with irritable bowel disease. The veterinarian said the disease could possibly be controlled with diet, medication and immune support supplements. We started her on a maintenance regimen and she did quite well for the first few months. She appeared stable, so we decided to take her to Oregon on our next trip.

But while we were in Yachats, Harmony became extremely ill. She began to decline very rapidly. Upon the advice of her veterinarian, we decided to rush her back to California for treatment.

We left in the wee hours of the morning and arrived at the hospital in the afternoon. Harmony was rushed into emergency, but within fifteen minutes she had to be resuscitated. In the hectic moments that followed, tests were taken to determine her blood values and she was given a transfusion. All the tests came back with the same results…her organs were failing. No matter what the doctors did, Harmony continued to slip away.

Mitch and I realized that her fate was out of our hands. Still, we could not help but feel guilty about not getting her into the hospital sooner. Could this somehow be our fault? Should we have gone back to Oregon State? Would time have made a difference? What if this; what if that? The vet could see our anguish as we asked her question after question. She was compassionate and assured us that nothing could have saved Harmony. Not time. Not medicine. Not love. Nothing could have saved her.

There was no choice but to end her suffering. Harmony journeyed to the Rainbow Bridge to reunite with Joy.

Harmony was four-and-one-half years old.

I do not remember much about the next days or weeks.

The inconsolable feelings of losing Joy resurfaced and once again, I grieved her loss. And now, Harmony was gone. I felt overwhelming sorrow. It was like the light in my soul had been extinguished.

Then I got angry. I blamed the hoarder for the pain he had imposed on the dogs. And now I realized that he had also hurt the people that had adopted his collies.

We returned to Oregon two months after losing Harmony. If there was to be any healing from such pain, it would be in Yachats. I could immerse myself in the winter storms, wild winds and torrential rains. As the storms ended and the sun began to peek from behind the clouds, I looked skyward in search of a double rainbow. I thought to myself, "If I could see two rainbows, I'd know that the sisters were reunited; together on the Rainbow Bridge." I watched the skies continually, but no double rainbows appeared. I gazed in wonder at many single ones, but I yearned to see two...two rainbows together!

Then one day, as I was walking along the ocean, I spotted bands of color shimmering across the sea spray. As the sun's rays reflected off the tops of the waves, I stopped, almost breathless. There in front of me, in perfect rhythm, were rainbows skipping across the surf. Time stood still. As I watched, I began to realize what was happening. There they were, Joy and Harmony, running and dancing across the waves...together again, just as they were in our yard that first day.

ɫ

I see them often now. Whenever I walk that ocean road in Yachats, I know just where to look. And when the sun's rays strike the surf to create a spectacular prism of color, I see them again. I see the sista's dancing in perfect unison. I see Joy and Harmony.

Most people want a cat to be loving, outgoing and eager to crawl into their laps for cuddle time. I get it!

I do my best to satisfy their desires when they are looking to adopt from RESQCATS. However, I never promise that the traits they see in kittens will remain as they grow into adult cats. I chuckle when someone wants their kitten to grow up to be a lap cat knowing that cats are unpredictable and there are no guarantees. They are their own beings for sure!

I have come to honor cats' diverse personalities and respect their boundaries. Learning to appreciate all the mysteries that accompany them and to accept each cat for who it is has been one of the greatest gifts of rescue.

No cat has ever been a more perfect example of the need for that acceptance than Bella.

TWENTY-THREE

Memories of a Free Spirit... Bella

Whenever I see a cat that is that obviously on its own, my world comes to an immediate halt. I feel that it is my moral responsibility to save it. After all, that is what I do...rescue cats!

After seeing a cat hunting along the side of the road adjacent to my driveway several times, I promised myself that the next time I spotted her, I was going to rescue her. She often walked across the road and I feared that she would be hit.

Early one evening, Mitch and I left the house to join friends for the first night of Passover. Dinner was a kosher pot-luck. Our contribution to the Seder was on the backseat of the car. Mitch had made a huge pot of soup and I had baked several flourless desserts. They were secured safely for the short journey to our friends' home. We were looking forward to an evening of good conversation and the mouthwatering delectable fare that is always present at Jewish feasts.

I was in the passenger seat when I spotted the slender black silhouette of a cat in the street. In my loudest possible voice, I yelled at Mitch, "STOP!" I am sure I almost scared him to death with my sudden outburst! He slammed on the brakes and brought the car to a screeching halt.

In the following seconds, everything happened simultaneously. I got out of the car to rescue the feline while Mitch turned to see the soup pot come tumbling forward. Luckily, the pot was stopped by the back of my seat and Mitch caught the lid just before it popped off, thus avoiding spilling any of the hot matzah ball soup. Thankfully, no harm came to any of my luscious desserts either!

As Mitch rescued our Seder contribution, I swooshed the cat from the street and cradled her in a tight squeeze in my arms. Then I returned to the car and positioned her in my lap before she had a clue as to what had just happened. She sat calmly on my legs and nuzzled close to my body as we turned around and headed back up the extended driveway to our home and RESQCATS. That was the only time she ever allowed me to hold her in my lap.

I hurried into the cattery and quickly set up an enclosure for my latest rescue. I felt the same familiar adrenaline rush that I always experience when I save an animal. As my nerves calmed and I proceeded through my routine of preparing an enclosure, a kind of euphoria took over. It was like the high I often feel following a strenuous walk on the treadmill.

I worked quickly to get everything set. I lined the inside of a large crate with blankets and put pillows in a basket, so the cat could choose the spot she found more comfortable. I left a bowl of kibble, a large can of tuna-flavored cat food and a fresh bowl of water. Then, once again, we were off to our Passover dinner.

When I returned later that evening to check the cat's status, she seemed quite settled in her new surroundings.

The next morning, I returned to the cattery to visit Bella, the name I had chosen for my latest rescue. Bella means beautiful in Italian and in my eyes, this cat was gorgeous! Her fur was as black as polished onyx. It glistened and made her luminescent green eyes shine like emerald jewels. She reminded me of Elizabeth Taylor in her portrayal of Cleopatra... deep black hair and captivating gem-like eyes. But then I always had a weakness for black cats, especially since they are usually the last ones anyone considers adopting.

When I tried to pet Bella, she flinched and backed away as if my touch caused her discomfort. The vet found nothing significant during his exam of her. He even took x-rays to try to find the cause of her painful reaction, but there was nothing to indicate serious injury.

Several days later, Bella was spayed and because she was semi-feral, I had her ear tipped. Ear-tipping is a common practice in feral cat colonies. It seems rather cruel to me to cut off the end of a cat's ear. But it has become a standard protocol in feral colonies because it is the only way to tell if a feral cat is spayed or neutered. One can imagine trapping a group of wild cats and taking them in for surgery only to discover that they have already been spayed or neutered.

ʔ

My first cat rescues were in the late 1980's, well before I dreamed of starting my own organization. I lived on the beach in San Diego next to the channel that led into Mission Bay. Frequently, unscrupulous people dumped cats on the rock jetty adjacent to my house. The unaltered cats bred indiscriminately and, at one point, there were over twenty cats living in the rocks. Most of the cats were frightened of humans, so it was rare that you saw them. They only appeared from the deep crevices when someone showed up with food. Several neighbors were compassionate and took it upon themselves to feed the stray cats.

I took it a step further and began trapping the cats to take them in for spay or neuter surgery. But after I brought the same female cat in to get spayed three different times, my vet suggested that I allow him to tip their ears as he completed the procedure. In my defense, most of the jetty cats did look alike since they were all related!

He was polite in suggesting what seemed at that time to be a drastic measure. "Cutting off the tip of a cat's ear!" I exclaimed. "Isn't there something else we could do? What about shaving the tip of their tail?" I asked. Then I quickly realized that the fur would grow back. My mind raced as I tried to come up with a more humane solution, but I thought of nothing. So I reluctantly agreed to ear-tipping.

For someone who does not believe it is right to dock tails and crop ears on dogs so they "look" the way a human wants them, at least I could accept ear-tipping of a feral cat because it serves a valid purpose.

❦

I had every intention of finding a home for Bella. She could be quite affectionate when I first entered her enclosure. She marked me by rubbing against my legs with the scent glands along her cheeks, but the second I reached down to pet her, out came the nails and…SWAT! Bella was hyperdactyl, which means she had extra toes on her feet, so those additional nails dug in hard. She certainly did not fit the usual requests of adopters wanting a lap cat!

To make matters worse, Bella did not get along with other cats either. She informed everyone, felines and humans, of her dislike, even from the confines of her enclosure. She spat, hissed and charged at the resident cats. If she thought they did not heed her warning, she reached deep into her diaphragm and emitted a growl that could only be interpreted one way; "Don't even think about coming near me!"

Bella tested positive for FIV which is not a highly contagious virus but can be transmitted through fighting. While most FIV cats can have normal lives and live many years, they do not have an immune system that is able to defend itself as they age. Bella showed all the signs of being a cat that would instigate fights, so I could not let her have contact with the other residents for fear they would encounter more than a cat with just a bad attitude!

I came to the conclusion very quickly that Bella was not adoptable. She had been an outdoor cat before I rescued her and was accustomed to being a free spirit. To keep her inside in an enclosure all the time would have certainly been stressful for her. Relocating her on the property seemed to be the best option. In order to follow the right protocol and be successful in keeping Bella on the property, I consulted a group in town that relocates feral cats.

A temporary enclosure was set up outside the cattery. It was quite large and furnished with all she needed to make herself comfortable. Blankets lined the inside of a crate, so she could comfortably take in her surroundings at floor level. A shelf was installed where she could survey her new environment from a higher vantage point.

She watched hummingbirds in the nearby feeder. She was curious about two of Mitch's African sulcata tortoises that lived in a yard adjacent to her space. And she saw volunteers as they went about their daily duties.

Bella was fed in the morning and allowed thirty minutes to eat before any leftovers were removed. The same feeding was repeated at night. In the evening, her enclosure was covered with a large blanket that draped halfway down the sides. It kept her warm, but the real objective was to show her that she had a safe, dry place to sleep and would never want for food and water again.

The same routine continued for three weeks before I opened the door to the enclosure and let her explore the property. If the relocation proved successful, she would return in the evening for food and the security of her "little apartment." I could not believe that it really worked! But it did! Bella went out every morning and returned every evening for the next five-and-a-half years!

After I was certain that Bella had accepted her new home, a permanent enclosure was built especially for her on the back side of the cattery. The roof on the existing building had a four foot overhang; this served as the ceiling for her newly constructed space below. It also protected her from rain and provided shade in case she decided to spend part of the day in her enclosure. It was well-equipped with her bed, a heating pad and litter box. I called it "Bella's Apartment." I even had a sign made that said just that!

Bella went out every morning when the weather was nice,

which is most of the time in Santa Barbara, and returned each afternoon when I called her. I was the only person who was allowed to pick her up; in fact, she insisted on it when it was dinner time. Bella came when she was called, stopped ten feet short of her enclosure, parked her little behind and then just sat there. No amount of coaxing would pry her from her fixed position. Her message was quite clear; she expected me to pick her up and carry her into her apartment every night.

Bella was usually the first cat that potential adopters saw when they visited RESQCATS. She roamed up and down the driveway and greeted many visitors as they approached the cattery entrance. Then she joined me as I gave tours of the outside of the facility, showing guests the outdoor enclosures and the overhead tunnels that resident cats enjoy. Her random appearances put me in an uncomfortable position since RESQCATS has an indoor-only policy for all adopted cats. Adopters practically sign away their lives on the adoption contract promising to follow that rule. I often had to awkwardly explain that Bella was the exception.

It became customary, whether or not the question was posed, to explain that Bella was semi-feral and, most likely, previously abused. She appeared affectionate and inviting but could turn in the blink of an eye and strike like a mongoose on a cobra. She never allowed anyone to touch her back without repercussion. She flinched as if it brought back a memory of someone mistreating her. As she curled around visitor's legs, I warned them, "Bella may appear very friendly, but she can turn and lash out in an instant; and it hurts, especially with all those extra toes and claws."

Bella's trips to the veterinarian were very difficult, both for her and the vet! She could not be easily handled and required sedation for exams, vaccinations and other routine procedures. In fact, her chart had big red letters written across it that warned, "CAUTION!" Her attending doctor was always the same. I knew that he had a sweet tooth and loved chocolate. So after each visit, on the day following her appointment, Bella had me bake a batch of rich and chewy chocolate brownies for her vet as a token of our appreciation…and as an apology for the trouble she had caused the previous day!

There were many pans of the warm treats delivered over the years. I believe that the vet actually looked forward to Bella's visits knowing that the decadent chocolate treat and a card that read "Bella's brownies" would follow soon.

It may sound like there was not much to love about this cat named Bella. I admit that it was a bittersweet relationship. Everything was scheduled around being at RESQCATS in the late afternoon to make sure she was safely tucked into her enclosure. I heard my share of growling, spitting and hissing. I always had scratches and bites on my hands and arms due to her unpredictable outbursts. But I loved Bella…and I loved all that she symbolized. Bella was a free independent spirit; and yet she chose to allow me to care for her.

Bella never lost her hunting skills. I despised the fact that she killed the little creatures she hunted, not the least because she left them on the doorstep of her enclosure for me to discover! But I never acted ungrateful for all her special gifts.

I began every morning at RESQCATS by opening her enclosure door. As she ventured out, I called after her, "Have a nice day, Bella." She spent her days roaming and patrolling our property, looking for small animals to tease and birds to taunt. By late afternoon, I only had to call, "Bella, Bella, Bella!" and she would reappear. Then she sat and waited for me to pick her up and place her into her apartment for the night. Our evening ritual ended as I affectionately asked, "Did you have a nice day, Bella?"

That was our routine for over five years.

I was out of town when Bella disappeared. She knew the house sitter well, so her no-show was highly unusual. My instinct was that something terrible had happened. I always knew that she could have a shorter life expectancy because she was allowed to roam outside. I also realized it would have broken her spirit if she had lived any other way.

While I believed that Bella was dead, I found solace thinking that her life had ended quickly. She would not have wanted to endure a long, drawn-out illness. It would have been impossible to treat her easily, if at all, due to her combative personality.

Bella was a free spirit who vanished from my life as quickly as she had appeared.

I truly missed our morning and evening routine. One day, as I stood at her empty enclosure, I thanked her for the years she had permitted me to care for her. After several weeks, I finally removed her bedding and litter box. But I could not bear to remove the sign that said, "Bella's Apartment." Then I closed the door to her enclosure. "Let your soul fly, Bella" were the last words I spoke to her...or so I thought.

Four months later, while I was on a ten-day overseas cruise, a young man left a message on the answering machine. Bella was alive! She had been found under his house. She was wearing a name tag and collar when she disappeared, but I could not imagine that anyone had been able to pick her up and read it. Evidently they had!

According to the message, she was in the people's house. Although the call was from many days before, I returned it immediately. They told me that Bella had escaped on the same day they had left the message. No one had seen her since.

But she was alive! I had to find her and bring her home!

When the family gave me directions to their home, I was astounded to hear that they lived twelve miles away on the opposite side of the freeway. That meant that Bella had, somehow, travelled two miles from RESQCATS down a fifty-five mile per hour, high traffic road. She had then crossed from the south side to the north side of a major highway through one of the busiest intersections in Santa Barbara. And then she had made her way an additional ten miles through commercial areas and busy streets to their distant neighborhood.

I have never figured out how Bella ended up so far away, but I was certain of one thing; she had not done it on her own. Somehow, she had to have been transported. The arthritis in her back and both hind legs would have prevented her from making the long trek. Perhaps she had crawled into someone's car and they had let her out when they discovered her. More likely, because of her biting and swatting, she was thrown out! Or maybe she fell asleep in the back of a worker's truck and woke up later to find herself in a strange place with no way to get home.

All I knew was that I needed to rescue her again. I printed five hundred flyers with her description and my contact information. In my frantic state, it made perfect sense that the more printed flyers, the better chance there was of finding Bella. I gathered three of my friends and we set out to deliver the notices to houses in the area.

The first stop was with the family who had called about Bella. The oldest son informed me that Bella had actually visited them that very morning. He had seen her eating dried bread that he had put out for the birds. He was anxious to help and set out walking the street in one direction while my friends and I split up to cover other routes.

Half an hour into the search, the young man came running towards me yelling, "I just saw her dash into some bushes a few houses away!" I rushed to the shrubbery, but by the time I got there, she was gone. I asked, "Are you sure it was Bella?" He replied, "Yes, part of her ear is missing, red collar and black. I'm absolutely positive."

We returned to the spot, but I could not find her in the underbrush. Where did she go? How could she disappear so quickly? Did she just get beamed up? I was reminded of Star Trek when Captain Kirk says, "Beam me up, Scotty." But in that case, we knew where Scotty went! Where had Bella gone?

My friends and I decided that the best avenue for retrieving Bella was to set a humane trap. Fortunately, I had come prepared to do just that. I folded a newspaper into thirds and placed it in the bottom of the trap, which provided a surface for bait. Then I put tuna in key spots along the newspaper to draw her farther into the trap. My hope was that she would go deep inside, trip the latch and spring the door shut behind her. I draped the top of the trap with a towel to give Bella a secure feeling.

As added insurance, we still went about distributing flyers, knocking on doors and asking anyone that answered if they had seen a black cat. Between house visits, I called out, "Bella, Bella, Bella!" hoping that she would remember my voice and amazingly reappear.

I felt desperate and was reluctant to leave, but we all agreed that we had covered a lot of ground in a single afternoon. I needed to focus on the good news; we had proof that Bella was still alive. One of my friends lived nearby and she eagerly agreed to check the trap later that night and first thing the following morning to see if Bella had taken the bait.

As we approached the trap one last time before returning to our cars, I heard something rattling. The wind had kicked up suddenly, so I assumed that it was the newspaper blowing; but I checked it anyway. I lifted the towel expecting to have to reset everything. To my delight, there was Bella...my beautiful Bella!

It was readily apparent that there was significantly less of her, but it was Bella and I would take her anyway I could. My friends and I were overjoyed. We hugged each other and exchanged high fives. I placed the trap with Bella inside into my car and waved farewell to my friends. It was only then, on our quiet drive back to RESQCATS, that I realized Bella's miraculous recapture meant she would be home with me once more.

On her return, no one minded her unfriendliness and surly attitude. Her hisses, growls and swats meant Bella was back. I was grateful and happy. We once again resumed our daily routine.

ꞁ

As she aged, Bella spent more and more time in her enclosure on her heating pad. The warmth soothed her arthritic joints. Whenever she ventured out, she was never more than a "Bella, Bella, Bella!" away.

She lived several more years after her harrowing adventure, but as she got older, her immune system began to fail. Due to her FIV status, there was nothing that could be done for her.

With the help of her compassionate vet, Bella took her last journey. This time, her adventure was not to a strange neighborhood where she was forced to fend for herself. It was to a beautiful place where she could continue to be a free spirit... but in a different form.

Perhaps unfriendly behaviors such as hisses, growls and spits are allowed at the Rainbow Bridge. I often wonder. But regardless of her attitude, I believe that she was welcomed there; and someday, when the time is right, I will join my beautiful Bella.

They say that things happen for a reason. But do we always get to figure out what those reasons are?

I am uncertain why particular events draw my attention. For instance, why would a car accident that killed a woman I had never met have such a profound impact on me? What brought her cat to RESQCATS? Was it coincidence? Or was it fate?

What I am confident about is that the healing powers of animals are immeasurable. They can help us through our loss and give us a chance to soothe our grief.

TWENTY-FOUR

The Healing Power of Skip

I have two pet peeves at RESQCATS. The first is that the volunteers be punctual. They all understand when they sign up as a volunteer that we start at 8:30 a.m. sharp! There is much work to be done in preparing for adoption appointments which begin promptly at 10:00 a.m. Knowing that, it was highly unusual for all the volunteers to be late on this particular September morning.

By 9:00, one volunteer after another had trailed in explaining that there was a detour off the main road. The alternate route to RESQCATS was long and out of the way, so everyone was twenty to thirty minutes tardy.

Later that morning, I learned the sad reason for the detour. A woman had been hit on the main road by a drunk driver at 7:30 a.m. She and several other ladies were training for a marathon to raise funds for a charitable cause. A few hours after she was struck, the lady passed away at the hospital.

I travel the route everyday as it is the main corridor to my home and RESQCATS from town. On the following day, I could not help but notice a memorial with fresh flowers and a cross at the site of the accident. Most people probably would not have noticed it as they sped by at fifty-five miles per hour, but for some reason, the cenotaph caught my eye every time I passed. I felt peculiarly sad. Although I am an exceptionally sensitive person, I still could not pinpoint a reason for me to experience such sorrow. After all, I did not know the woman who died.

Two weeks after this tragedy, I received a call from a lady asking if RESQCATS could foster a cat until she could find him a new home. "A good friend of mine was recently killed in a car accident and her two beloved felines were left behind," she said. "The female cat, Claire, died just a few days after the tragedy." The woman went on to explain that while Claire's health had been failing, she believed that the cat had actually died from a broken heart. "The other cat, Skip, is by himself now," she continued. "He needs a temporary foster while I look for a permanent home for him."

I offered my condolences and then explained that RESQCATS was dedicated to stray and abandoned cats and kittens.

I was reluctant to accept a temporary foster because of an earlier experience when a two-week foster became a six months resident! In that case, I had agreed to foster the cat of a woman who was going into an alcohol rehabilitation program. She told me she would be back on her feet in a fortnight and would come for her cat then. It was not until six months later that the woman finally felt ready to care for her cat again.

My caller this day understood my position. As I was about to end our conversation, something stopped me. "How old is the cat?" I asked out of curiosity. She replied, "Skip is thirteen years old." Thirteen! She wanted me to foster a thirteen-year-old cat until she could find him a home! I explained to her that it would be next to impossible to find a home for a cat that age. The great majority of people who are considering adopting really want a kitten. At best, they want a young cat with no health problems. Even sweet, young mothers, barely a year old themselves and still kitten-like in their behavior, are hard to place.

I was about to offer a few last words of comfort, say good-bye and wish her luck when an out of the blue thought entered my head. "Did Skip happen to belong to the lady who was hit by a car a couple of weeks ago?" I asked. She replied, "Yes, as a matter of fact, he did. I'm the pet-sitter. Skip isn't doing well now that he's alone in the house." She explained that the woman's family could not give Skip a home and while their reasons may have been valid, it was very sad. I promised to search for someone willing to foster and I committed to staying in touch.

Our conversation weighed heavily on me all that day and into the night. I lay in the dark, tossing and turning, staring at the ceiling and thinking about the other cat, Claire. The pet-sitter's words, "She died of a broken heart," repeated themselves over and over in my head. Now poor Skip was alone. The house-sitter visited twice a day, but she could only spend an hour each visit. Could the same thing happen to Skip? Would that lonely cat also die of a broken heart?

As soon as the sun began to rise the following morning, I called the pet-sitter and announced, "Skip can come to RESQCATS. Somehow, I'll find a home for him." She brought him to me that afternoon.

Skip, a handsome black and white cat, had clearly been well cared for. He was sleek and muscular. He was delightfully friendly and very curious about his new surroundings. Although he was thirteen, Skip was spry and playful. In fact, he appeared as if he was just entering the prime of life. Skip was nothing like I had envisioned a senior cat would be.

I made him comfortable in an enclosure with a large crate, condo, baskets and toys. I had chosen a set of fleece blankets from the cabinets that I thought would complement his exquisite black and white markings. They had whimsical black cats on a white background and the reverse sides were black and white paw prints.

I need to pause this story and explain something. I mentioned earlier that I have two pet peeves. One is that I want everyone to be on time. The other has to do with the blankets!

During our first few years of operation, RESQCATS used donated blankets and towels. I added to the collection when I came across small fleece baby blankets on sale. As time went on, I invested in larger ones that were on clearance at the end of the winter season. While the designs varied, I managed to find several in each color of the spectrum. I collected an array of pretty greens and blues, as well as hot pinks, purples and pale yellows.

In my previous life, pre-RESQCATS, I had worked as a professional graphic designer. I should have realized otherwise, but I subconsciously assumed that everyone, especially the RESQCATS volunteers, would only put coordinating colors and patterns into a cat's enclosure. When they would place a pink polka-dot blanket next to a blue plaid one that was adjacent to a yellow and green floral print, it was a visual nightmare for me!

"Could you at least stay with the same color range when you set up an enclosure?" I asked the volunteer who was particularly guilty of choosing multiple colors and patterns in for a single space. I then somewhat kiddingly suggested, "Choose all pink or all blue or all green blankets to create a sense of continuity. One that doesn't hurt my eyes!" Understand that I was not angry. I realized that the cats did not care about the colors of their blankets. The visual appeal of the enclosures was really for the humans caring for the cats. I honestly wondered about that volunteer's house décor, but did not dare ask!

Getting the volunteers to follow that simple request was a lost cause. For my own sanity, I desperately needed to come up with a solution to satisfy my need for visual organization. I spent my entire winter vacation that year sewing sets of fleece blankets for every enclosure. The project gave me the opportunity to be creative with fabrics. Each set consisted of a big blanket to drape across the top of the large crate inside the enclosure plus four smaller ones for the baskets and condos. The predominant sides of the blankets were printed with cute kitty designs. The reverse sides had coordinating patterns…either striped, or paw prints or perhaps a pretty floral. All were color coordinated!

I instructed the volunteers to put the large blanket over the crates with the cat print image facing up. The smaller blankets could go on either side. From a creative standpoint, I thought it looked wonderful and it certainly pleased my visual scrutiny. To my delight, the matching sets were a hit with the volunteers; of course, the cats never commented one way or another!

To this day, every new volunteer is given explicit instructions about being on time and on how to arrange the blankets!

🐾

Skip settled in nicely. Although he required a special diet and daily medication, overall, he was a healthy cat. Due to his particular diet, it would be impossible for him to become a RESQCATS resident. So I was faced with finding a home for a thirteen-year-old cat right in the middle of kitten season.

The local newspaper agreed to print a follow-up article about his deceased owner and the orphaned Skip. It was a well-written piece along with a great photograph. The strategic placement in the paper meant that it would be seen by virtually every reader.

I knew that a photo of a cute kitten in the adoption section of the paper always attracted a lot of attention. Previously, I had answered fifty-three inquiries in three days for one particular kitten. My hope was that someone would respond to Skip's article and photograph. It was gravely disappointing when not one person called to inquire about him.

Instinctively, I had done the right thing by bringing Skip

to RESQCATS, but I had no idea how difficult it would be to find him a home. The pet-sitter and the deceased woman's family asked everyone they knew, but no one wanted him.

ι

In preparation for an upcoming charity event, the marathon team that Skip's owner had been training with continued their practice runs. One of the participants had seen the article in the paper and was talking about it when another teammate overheard the conversation. Prior to hearing the exchange, the young woman had no idea that Skip had not been adopted.

She called RESQCATS the next day. "I heard about Skip," she said in a quiet voice. "I was wondering if you would do me the honor of allowing me to adopt him?" Perhaps it was intuition; I honestly do not know what made me ask, "Did you know the lady who owned Skip?" There was a lengthy pause before she answered, "She was my friend. I was running just ahead of her when she was hit. I held her hand while we waited for the ambulance to arrive and I was with her at the hospital when she died." At the end of her explanation, there was a crack in her voice. She began to weep.

I was silent. Words eluded me. If she had been standing in front of me, my response would have been to take her in my arms and let her cry. No words would have been needed. My hug would have said it all. I could not imagine what she was going through. Dealing with such profound loss had to be devastating. When I was finally able to speak, albeit through my tears, I told her how sorry I was.

The lady visited Skip that afternoon. He was playful and affectionate and it was clear that he had won her heart right away. I overheard her talking to Skip while he put on his best performance. Most importantly, Skip made her laugh.

Although Skip was the kind of cat who loved everyone,

it takes an extraordinary person to consider giving a home to a senior feline, especially one that requires a prescription diet and daily medications. But here was that special person, standing right in front of me.

The woman was open about her sorrow and seemed excruciatingly vulnerable because of her grief. She said that the loss had been so traumatic that she had sought counseling. She was as kind-hearted a person as I have ever met. Above all, she wanted to do the right thing...give Skip a home.

I gave her a long, heartfelt hug and told her, "You are an absolute angel." She responded, "It's the least I can do for my friend." Skip went home with her that very day.

She called the next day to tell me that Skip was doing great and had adjusted to his new home immediately.

In her memory, a tree was planted at the site where the woman was hit. I often think of her as I drive past it. I regret that I never had a chance to meet her. But I sense we know each other on a different, more spiritual level.

I now know that there was a reason that I was drawn to the lady's roadside memorial. It was Skip's destiny to come to RESQCATS. And it was fate that Skip found a home with the woman's running friend so that he could help her heal from her loss.

It is not uncommon for those who dedicate their lives to rescuing animals to experience burn-out and compassion fatigue. After fourteen years of rescue work and the added tasks that a growing organization required, my responsibilities had greatly expanded. Additionally, dealing with people issues and problems with volunteers was frustrating. I had far too little occasion to do what I loved; that is, spend time with the cats and kittens.

I had always thought of myself as someone who aimed to please, but my inability to make everyone happy exhausted me. I found myself facing many of the symptoms associated with burn-out. I became depressed, pessimistic and began to have some health concerns. Worst of all, I felt like my enthusiasm for rescue had been diminished by some of the people around me.

With the guidance and support of my husband, Mitch, I was able to make changes in the way I managed the organization. The objective of the new direction was to enable me to return to the reason I began RESQCATS...to care for and nurture stray and abandoned cats and kittens. I hoped that my passion would return and restore my optimism.

TWENTY-FIVE

A New Direction

When I founded RESQCATS in 1997, my mission statement read: A non-profit sanctuary dedicated to the rescue, care and adoption of stray and abandoned cats and kittens. That was, and still is, my objective. I spent the majority of my days caring for all those fortunate enough to be saved and enter through RESQCATS doors.

Over the years, RESQCATS earned an outstanding reputation and grew beyond my wildest imagination. With that expansion, my job evolved into more of an administrative position than caregiver to the cats. The growth required me to wear many different hats. I became adoption director, volunteer recruiter, foster coordinator, newsletter writer, marketing person, human resources liaison, fundraising manager, plus anything else that had to be done including the morning cleaning when a volunteer failed to show.

My expanded duties took me far away from the reason I began RESQCATS...to care for and nurture cats and kittens. I sorely missed spending time with them. There was little opportunity for me to go into an enclosure to sit, play and cuddle just for pleasure. The many other things that needed doing to ensure a smoothly run organization demanded the majority of my time and attention.

Of course, I was involved with the sick cats on a daily basis, but the time I devoted to my new responsibilities created a distance from most of the kittens. I was unable to intimately know the animals in my care. I realized during adoption appointments that I had not learned each kitten's personality, its favorite toy, or preferred place to be petted. I missed the cats and kittens! Without that hands-on time, my "heart-light" grew dimmer.

My optimism and enthusiasm waned with each passing kitten season. I had always credited myself with being a person that saw "the glass half full." But as the years went by, I struggled to find the positive in any situation. My upbeat attitude was replaced by an uncharacteristic pessimism. I had become cynical.

The accumulated stress also took a physical toll. For no apparent reason, I would experience shortness of breath. Sometimes, I became so dizzy that the room would spin. Most days, my glass was half empty and on other days, it felt like it was completely drained.

My winter sabbaticals in Oregon were spent wondering if I could continue operating RESQCATS. Mitch and I talked for countless hours discussing alternative ways to run the organization. His continuous encouragement was critical to my well-being. I returned from Oregon feeling re-energized and I told myself that I could do a better job of managing.

Please understand, my frustration was never about the animals…I loved taking care of the cats and kittens. It was all the other "stuff." It was about people. My gentle demeanor is not naturally one of confrontation. In fact, it is quite the opposite. I wanted everyone to like me and to show respect for each other. That quality made it difficult for me to be a good leader to the many volunteers and their varying needs. I felt personally responsible for each volunteer's happiness and took it upon myself to make sure they enjoyed both their assigned duties and the people who worked alongside them. I went so far as to change schedules so that the volunteers would get along. I tried to avoid conflict of any kind.

In hindsight, I failed miserably at management.

In my defense, no one would have been successful with my approach to supervising people. I had no formal training in management. For heaven's sake, my college degree is in graphic design, not business administration!

In addition to my unrealistic desire to please everyone, I still needed to answer hundreds of phone calls and emails, respond to more than three hundred potential adopters, and coordinate the schedules of fifty volunteers. All the ingredients were present and I was the classic candidate for what is known as compassion fatigue; that is, emotional and physical exhaustion caused by the stress of caring for traumatized or suffering animals or people.

For several years, I found a way to push my way through. But, little-by-little, the stress chipped away at me. Within the first six weeks of each new season, I found myself crying and depressed. I knew I was coming to a breaking point and realized that the impossible expectations I had imposed on myself were devouring me.

By 2011, I knew I had to make some drastic changes before I suffered irreparably. It was imperative that I save myself from the emotional and physical exhaustion that was consuming me. I longed to get back to the reason I began RESQCATS.

I spent my free time that winter analyzing the current situation and thinking about what needed to change. By the following year, I was ready to make major adjustments to the structure of the organization. The reformation was difficult at times. When I let some volunteers go, there were hurt feelings; however, most understood and offered their continuing moral support.

Although it took both time and some painful decisions, a new direction for RESQCATS was taking place. I found that having fewer volunteers to try and please was a significant way to reduce my stress. A few chosen people remained with the organization. I recruited new ones, but I was more discriminating and upfront about my expectations. And I was careful in my selection.

RESQCATS also partnered with a local pet supply store to handle the majority of adoptions. I instructed the staff on how to properly screen potential adopters. By having that responsibility handled by qualified interviewers that I had trained, I had more hands-on time with the cats and kittens. In return, the shop had the opportunity for a new customer with each adoption.

My hope was that with this new direction and the reorganized RESQCATS operation, I could continue rescuing stray and abandoned cats and kittens well into the future. I realized that I may never be a great manager of people, but I am getting better.

Change has always been difficult for me. While I realized that the adjustments in how RESQCATS operated were essential for me to continue my life's work, I needed to have a new perspective. I recall seeing a poster at a pet seminar prior to the reorganization that said "obstacles create opportunity." At the time, I was uncertain as to why that phrase seemed so insightful. But those three words guided me through the challenges of accepting new ideas and letting go of the old ones. They gave me hope that somehow, my heart-light would shine again.

TWENTY-SIX

A Gift from Picadilly

It was spring 2012, the first season of a new direction for RESQCATS. The organizational changes we had recently implemented had allowed me to return to being the main caregiver and nurturer of the cats, something I had missed for many years.

Around that time, a litter of four kittens was found living at a winery near Solvang, the famous Danish village nestled in the rolling hills north of Santa Barbara. They were lucky to be discovered when they were because they would have certainly perished from either starvation or predators. Their mother was nowhere to be found. The four rescued kittens arrived at RESQCATS late one Thursday afternoon.

Judging by their size, mobility, and activity level, I estimated the kittens to be about five weeks old. They were definitely old enough to eat on their own although, in a perfect world, they would have still been with their mom for several more weeks to be weaned gradually. Unfortunately for them, that had not been the case.

As always, the first thing I do when new cats arrive is to carefully examine them for fleas, signs of an upper respiratory infection and gender. There were two boys and two girls. Knowing their sex, I could now put on my creative hat and come up with names for them.

Naming the kittens is always something I enjoy doing. In fact, when Mitch and I take road trips, we often brainstorm for clever cat names. I keep a pad and pen handy and write as fast as I can when either of us comes up with a theme or a group of names.

Many litters of kittens have a group name based on where they were found, which makes it simple for the veterinarian to file information about an entire litter. Within the group's folder are details of each kitten. For example, the "sofa kitties" were dug out of a man's couch and the "fireplace group" was retrieved from a lady's woodpile. A particular litter's place of rescue encouraged names like Lazy Boy, Sealy, Duvet, Ottoman and Futon for the sofa group. The kittens from the woodpile were named Mahogany, Aspen, Willow and Maple.

Sometimes we pick a theme that inspires names. The flower-themed kittens were called Tulip, Poppy, Daisy, Sunflower and Petunia. I remember a litter that was all black. That group's name was "Formal Night," so Black-Tie, Bell-of-the-Ball, Tux, Prince Charming and Bow-Tie were fitting names. Orange tabby kittens were easy; Sunny, Cheetos, Ritz and Marigold were perfectly suited for them. Black and white kitties' names were Oreo, Hydrox, Polka Dot, Domino, and Holstein. Other litters were named after Las Vegas hotels, candy bars, constellations and Greek islands. In addition, we played on words with names such as "Purr-cey," "Purr-ty" and "Paw-lynn."

Naming the cats is truly one of the most fun parts of my job.

❧

Each of the Solvang kittens got a name before settling in for their stay at RESQCATS, although, contrary to what I just said, their names were not at all inspired by the winery. Sometimes you just name them what comes to mind!

Jaspurr, the biggest kitten in the litter, was a dark marble tabby male. The two females both had tortoiseshell coloring, but Confetti, the smallest, had short hair while her sister, Picadilly, was long-haired. Lastly, there was Mimosa, an orange and white tabby boy. The four kittens were quite a multicolored group.

❧

Once I was satisfied with their newly given names, I put the kittens in an enclosure lined with new fleece blankets I had sewn. The top sides of the blankets boasted a playful kitten design while the reverse sides had a paw print pattern in coordinating colors.

I placed a heating pad in one of their baskets. Within seconds, all four kittens had piled into their newly-made bed to bask in its comfort and warmth. They were provided with bouncy balls, fake-fur mice and many other toys with which to amuse themselves. And of course, I left plenty of food and water. In other words, the kittens now had all the amenities that they had been deprived of while living under the bushes behind the winery. Before leaving, I picked up the kittens, one by one, to hold each one close to my face, kiss it on the head and whisper, "You're safe now." Then I tucked them in for the night.

By Friday morning, warning signs of trouble were already evident. The kittens had not touched their food during the night. Although not eating is common when young kittens come in off the street, I was concerned. Most often, they are not familiar with kitten food because they have only nursed from their mother. Sometimes they need to be introduced to food by finger-feeding them canned food several times a day. Once the kittens become accustomed to the taste, they make their own way to the food bowl. So, finger-feeding four kittens on a set schedule became my plan.

By Friday afternoon, however, I could see that something more than just not eating was wrong with the tiniest girl, Picadilly. She vomited every time I fed her and had lost over two ounces within twenty-four hours. Her brothers, Jaspurr and Mimosa seemed to be doing okay, but her sister, Confetti, also appeared to be declining.

I made a phone call and scheduled a vet appointment for that afternoon. The kittens' physical exams revealed nothing alarming. The doctor was reassuring and said, "It may just take some time to get them accustomed to eating." He instructed me to continue finger-feeding them every few hours. Hopefully, the taste of the canned food would eventually entice them to eat on their own. He also recommended administering subcutaneous fluids three times daily. Fortunately, I had a lot of experience giving sub-q fluids under the skin.

Kittens' digestive systems are extremely delicate. Since the kittens had only nursed, the sudden diet change could cause some diarrhea and dehydration. Administering the fluids would help.

The doctor emphasized the critical importance of keeping a close eye on Picadilly because of her vomiting. I was up to the task; no problem. I put her on my intensive care watch list. I fed her every three hours, checked her hydration levels and watched her diligently.

Although Jaspurr started eating on his own by Saturday morning and appeared fine, he declined rapidly between Saturday night and Sunday morning. He lost three ounces overnight! While that may not seem like a lot, it is a significant amount for a kitten that weighs less than a pound. It would be akin to a one-hundred pound person losing nineteen pounds in twenty-four hours! Jaspurr appeared to be a thriving, spunky, healthy kitten one day, but by the next morning, he looked like the awful photos you see on ASPCA posters of sick and dying kittens. He became part of my intensive care focus along with Picadilly. I fed him every few hours, gave him sub-q fluids and made sure he stayed warm. When he was not with me, he was on the heating pad in a basket with his siblings.

My previous experiences of dealing with sick kittens were

usually successful. Most of them bounced back after a few days of supportive care. I was heartbroken when I discovered that Jaspurr had died sometime Sunday night. The cause of his death was a mystery, even to the vet.

By Monday, Picadilly and Confetti were fading quickly, so I rushed them to the vet. After their examinations, the vet drew blood and collected a fecal sample for comprehensive tests. Then he suggested giving them blood plasma transfusions to help boost their compromised immune systems. His objective was to give their bodies' immune support while we waited for results of the diagnostic tests. Once we had that information, the appropriate treatment plan could be determined.

The next day, we received conclusive tests results; the kittens had feline distemper. Unfortunately, there was nothing we could do except to continue supportive care and hope that their immune systems would kick in and lead to their recovery.

Fortunately, Mimosa showed no symptoms of this often deadly feline virus.

At this point, Picadilly seemed much worse than her sister, Confetti. She was visibly frail and growing weaker by the hour. In fact, the vet thought he had lost her during her transfusion, but somehow, she had managed to rally. As I left the clinic, he said, "Jeffyne, I think if she makes it through the night, she'll be okay." I heard him distinctly and understood that he was preparing me for the worst, but his tone was also optimistic. I believed that there was a chance she would recover.

By early evening, however, I began to realize that Picadilly would not survive. She became more frail with each passing minute. Sadly, there was nothing more I could do to save her. But I would not let her die alone. I wanted to surround her with the warmth and comfort of my body. It was very important to me that she feel love from my heart until she drew her last breath.

❧

Mitch is a compassionate man and always rises to the occasion when something like this happens at RESQCATS. He is an amazingly thoughtful person who just seems to know what to do during heartbreaking situations. He made a bed for me on the couch knowing that it would be a long night ahead. Once I was comfortably settled, he gently placed Picadilly on my chest, kissed me and told me he loved me. Then he left us alone together.

Lying there, I kissed Picadilly's tiny head and held her close. I was still awake a few hours later when she slipped into a peaceful coma. I tenderly wrapped my hand around her tiny body and gently placed my finger on her heart. I felt it beat for the last time when she died quietly around midnight.

I was overwhelmingly sad and wept silently. But I also remember feeling a sense of relief for Picadilly as she left to become an angel on the Rainbow Bridge. I was grateful that I was with her, so she did not have to die alone.

Little time passed before my attention focused on Confetti. She was failing and did not appear to be too far behind her sister. She was in and out of the hospital many times during the next few days and received another plasma transfusion. I continued her sub-q fluids and antibiotics. Confetti fought hard to sustain life and I did everything humanly possible to save her.

Happily, Confetti made it! The supportive medical care she received was certainly an important factor for her survival, but I also believe that the good wishes, love and support from many people who followed her story greatly contributed to her recovery.

Confetti's brother, Mimosa, seemed to take on the part-time job of caregiver. He gazed at me with curious, melancholy eyes whenever I removed her from their bed. But when I returned Confetti, he resumed his job. He would curl around his sister, providing her warmth and comfort. He soothed her with his hypnotic purr. Confetti and Mimosa became inseparable. I am convinced that his love and the bond they shared was a significant part of her healing.

Confetti and Mimosa were adopted by a couple that keeps in touch with me to this very day. They send photos of the pair sharing the same bed, sitting in a windowsill next to each other, or lying paw-to-paw on the back of the couch watching television. They are always together.

I truly believe that miracles are hidden in this story; not just for the survival of Confetti and Mimosa but also in the loss of Jaspurr and Picadilly.

Although Picadilly did not survive, she still left me precious gifts. She gave me the chance to once again love and nurture. She allowed me the opportunity to provide the hands-on care that I had so desperately missed. She helped to reignite the passion that I had for rescuing cats and kittens.

Picadilly turned on my heart-light and let it shine again!

"Wow! You must have a really cool sanctuary if a stray cat wandering by thinks it looks like a good place to break in, get a free meal and hang out!"

The tale of Houdini is about a stray caught red-handed breaking and entering the RESQCATS sanctuary. His tale is one of respect, patience, trust and everlasting love.

TWENTY-SEVEN

Cat Caught Breaking and Entering

As I walked into the cattery one afternoon, I caught a glimpse of a black and white "flash" dashing down the corridor. I knew immediately that it was a cat, not the occasional skunk that finds its way into the building. As soon as the cat spotted me, he turned and fled towards the outdoor tunnels that connect the inside of the sanctuary to outdoor enclosures.

I thought, "Who is that? That's not one of my cats! How did he get in here?"

Over the next several days, I frequently saw the intruder appear at the rear of the cattery where he had been helping himself to food and water. He was never far from the tunnels that served as his escape route.

I could not fathom how the stranger had gotten into the cattery! The overhead tunnels were securely connected to outdoor enclosures. They were constructed not only to keep my cats inside a safe, yet outdoor, environment, but also to keep other unwelcome critters out.

Sometimes I saw our black and white trespasser in the open space between the adoption enclosure ceiling and the roof overhang, an area I call the penthouse. But that was also sealed; there was no way in or out! Other days, he was nowhere to be found. He was a prowler; a cat caught breaking and entering to avail himself of the free food bounty, then vanishing to who knows where! His sudden appearances followed by his rapid disappearances got to be quite a joke at RESQCATS. Since he seemed to evaporate just as quickly as he materialized, volunteers frequently asked, "Well, Jeffyne, is the prowler in today...or is he out?"

The cat's "magic" disappearing acts reminded me of Harry

Houdini, a Hungarian illusionist born in 1874. Houdini became a legendary magician who was most famous for his sensational escape acts. He gained fame after repeatedly escaping from police handcuffs and jails and was even given certificates from various wardens for escaping from their prisons. He later expanded his repertoire by escaping from straitjackets and coffins. Given our mysterious feline intruder's escape artist talents, I appropriately named him Houdini.

I searched everywhere, but I could not find Houdini's point of entry or exit. To make matters worse, some of the resident cats also discovered the new escape route. They let themselves out to roam in open and dangerous territory whenever they pleased. That is totally against all the cattery rules!

❧

RESQCATS indoor-only policy was something I decided to implement for all adopters after the first few years of becoming a non-profit sanctuary. It was excruciatingly upsetting for me when I was often the first person someone called when their adopted cat had been hit by a car, went missing or was taken by a coyote.

I am baffled as to why anyone would call with such tragic news. Did they somehow feel obligated to let me know? Was I to offer consolation? Did they want to adopt another one? Did they think that I would ever trust them to adopt another cat knowing that history could repeat itself? It never made sense to me why I should be told of their cat's demise.

Those conversations caused me great sorrow and doubt. I took each loss personally. I carried the burden that somehow the tragedy was my fault and I could have prevented it. I questioned my adoption procedure. Should I have handled the process differently? These were caring people who just did not realize that cats die from accidents, pesticides, coyotes, cat fights and more. The list of potential dangers is endless. Up until then, I had encouraged adopters to keep their cats safely indoors, but I did not require a commitment to do so.

But one day, after yet another sad outdoor death, I reached a breaking point. I made the decision to mandate that adopters sign a promise to keep their cats inside. Because of a cat named Papillon, cats and kittens adopted from RESQCATS were to never set a paw outside.

Papillon was a sweet two-year-old black cat that was finally adopted after a lengthy stay at RESQCATS. It is not easy to find someone who will even consider giving an adult cat a home. Then, add the fact that Papillon was black; many people are superstitious of black cats. And to further compound the challenge, it was the middle of kitten season and most potential adopters only want kittens. Papillon was very lucky to have been adopted.

However, less than two months after Papillion went to her new home, I was driving on a busy street when I spotted a black cat lying on the side of the road. It did not move, so I assumed the cat was dead. I remember thinking how sad it was. I thought about continuing past as it is not my habit to pick up deceased animals. But I felt an impulse to stop and see if, by some miracle, the cat was alive and needed help.

As I approached, I recognized Papillion. She was lifeless. Suddenly, it was as if everything was in slow motion. As I moved toward her, my legs became heavy and it felt as if my feet were sinking in wet cement. I was overcome with sadness and began to sob. Was this real, or was it a terrible nightmare? I could only hope that Papillon's death had been instantaneous.

Leaving her on the side of the road was not an option. I retrieved one of the blankets I carry in my vehicle for emergencies. I carefully placed her limp body onto the blanket and wrapped her snugly. I gently lifted her and put her in the back of my car.

I knew that the new owner's apartment building backed up to the busy street. I made my way towards her residence. Then I sat in the parking lot and thought about my options for several minutes. Maybe it would be better if she did not know what had happened. Would I want to know? Yes, I would. With that thought in mind, I knocked on her door. Although it was already past noon, it was apparent I had woken the lady. I wept as I told her what had happened.

Surprisingly, she had no idea if Papillon was in her apartment or outside. The woman claimed that whenever she let Papillon out, the cat never left her outdoor patio. Well, she sure did this time! The news of Papillon's death did not seem to particularly faze the lady. I left feeling extremely angry and decided not to leave Papillon with her.

By the time I returned home, I was hysterical. When I was finally able to articulate what had happened, Mitch took me in his arms while I cried uncontrollably. After I regained my composure, he escorted me to Twilight Park, an area in the backyard where together we buried Papillon.

Twilight Park is a special garden where painted arches rest on six-foot posts. Mitch carved the arches and I painted them in shades of red, orange, yellow, green, blue and purple to create a perfect image of a rainbow. A bird bath with a statue of St. Francis of Assisi, the patron saint of animals, occupies the central area. Stone markers honor the graves of cats and kittens that died while under RESQCATS care. One corner is the final resting place of three special dogs that belonged to close friends. At the back of the park is a bench where the statue of an angel sits and watches over those that have passed.

I gathered a pretty bunch of lilies, roses and lavender, and laid them on Papillon's final resting place.

After Papillon was buried, I headed towards the cat sanctuary. Once inside, I made a verbal promise that from then on, every cat or kitten that came through RESQCATS doors would find homes with people who understood outdoor feline dangers. I vowed that all future adopters would commit to securing their cats' safety by keeping them indoors. It would be a requirement that all adopters guarantee their pledge by signing a contract and since that sad day, there have been no RESQCATS adoptions without that signed pledge.

❧

Greyco, one of the resident cats and the "diplomat" among the felines, happily disobeyed the indoor-only rule after he discovered Houdini's escape route. Greyco was a precocious cat that spent his entire life challenging an open passageway. He was always quick to slip through any opening that led from the cattery to what he perceived as utopia...the great outdoors! It did not matter how slight the gap; he slithered past, scampered out and leaped over the fence before I could react. But he never ran away. I always knew I could find him sitting on the back deck right in the middle of our pack of collies. He considered our dogs to be his dogs!

I always warned new volunteers about Greyco's sneaky getaways, but, more often than not, he would still slip past them on their very first day. I have to admit, I knew that he would take advantage of an inexperienced person.

Realizing that Greyco's escape was inevitable, the well-seasoned volunteers and I stood back, watched and waited for him to pull a fast one on an unsuspecting trainee. The petrified newcomer immediately begged for forgiveness. As bystanders who predicted Greyco's shenanigans, we could not help but chuckle. But not wanting the novice volunteer to feel bad for too long, I was to quick say, "You're now initiated as a true RESQCATS volunteer because Greyco sneaked past you!" I was always pleased when the newcomer recovered and joined in the laughter.

ξ

Soon after Houdini began to come and go at will, I spotted Greyco several times in the yard playing with his collie friends. But there were no volunteers present; no one was in the cattery opening and closing doors. He had no calculated opportunity to escape. So how did he get out?

On another occasion, as I walked outside to get our mail, I found Seacliff comfortably stretched out in the middle of the driveway. He seemed to be in his own personal cat heaven as he rolled back and forth on the warm bricks exposing his orange tabby belly to the bright sun. How long had he been out there sunbathing? And, more importantly, how did he get out of the cattery?

I can still see myself standing in the driveway with my hands on my hips, utterly perplexed. Just what was going on? Did the resident cats not understand that the tunnels and enclosures had been built so they could have the outside experiences without the life-threatening dangers? Apparently that was not the case. To them, Houdini's escape route was their opportunity for liberation!

ξ

It was easy to tell when Houdini was in the cattery. He was not neutered, so the pungent odor that filled the cattery was a sure sign of his presence. The scent of unneutered tomcats is unmistakable! Clearly, two things needed to be done. He was going to get neutered and I had to find his getaway path.

Since Houdini had never allowed anyone to get near him, I felt it was best if he were trapped, neutered and released back into the cattery. He got a clean bill of health at the veterinary clinic and the vet estimated that Houdini was about two years old. Although he was a young cat, he had multiple battle wounds and scars from his harsh life on the streets. He was a large-framed cat, but even from his brief, distant appearances, I could see that he was underweight. His early life as a stray had clearly not been kind to him.

Houdini continued to come and go as he pleased. He ate the food and drank the water from bowls located on the very back shelf, a place where he felt there was a safe enough distance between him and me. On some occasions, I caught his eye. The first few times, we both stopped as if suddenly frozen and stared at each other for a split second. Then suddenly, he would take off like a bolt of lightening. I understood his need for space and did not approach his territory. After several months, he sensed that he did not have to be afraid of me. He stopped darting away and appeared okay when we made eye contact. I was flattered!

Houdini did not act like a feral cat. He showed no signs of aggression. He never hissed or growled at me. He just seemed terribly frightened. I tried not to move toward him, but if I walked too swiftly even in an opposing direction, he felt threatened and raced to safety. I believe he was a stray that had been on his own for a long time without human contact. I honored his boundaries and continued to put food and water in the familiar spot where escape was just a scurry away.

One day, after finding Greyco in the yard with his dogs again, I devised a plan. I returned Greyco to the cattery and then followed him in hopes of determining the exact location of the mysterious escape route. It took less than thirty seconds for Greyco to head towards one of the outdoor enclosures. And there it was! The point of escape! A break in the wire mesh had exposed a hole large enough for a cat to exit...and enter, as well! It was uncharted territory as far as Greyco was concerned and he was not about to miss out on it. He once again raced to freedom!

It appeared that Houdini had pulled the wire mesh that surrounded the outdoor enclosures away from the wooden base boards. It could not have been an easy task because the wire was securely fastened to the wood frame. He apparently had pulled out the staples with his paws and pushed the wire with his head so that he could get in for an easy meal. I did not mind that Houdini wanted something to eat; in fact, I was happy to provide food and water for an obviously hungry cat. The problem, of course, was that it had become an exit for my other cats!

When I told a friend about Houdini, he said, "Wow! You must have a really cool sanctuary if a stray cat wandering by thinks it looks like a good place to break in, get a free meal and hang out!"

On the day that Greyco led me to the break-in point, Houdini was perched in one of the overhead tunnels. Mitch fetched the tool box and went to work repairing and reinforcing the baseboards around each outdoor enclosure. As Houdini watched intently from the tunnel above, I looked at him and said, "Houdini, I don't care if you come or you go, but this is not a revolving door." Of course, I really did care! Once the break was repaired, he was safe inside RESQCATS.

Houdini seemed okay with the new arrangement. In fact, he made himself quite at home. There was plenty of food and water and the penthouse was a retreat where he could watch without fear of me getting too close for his comfort. And most importantly, the other resident cats readily accepted him. Following only Greyco, Houdini became second-in-command in diplomatic duties.

Eight months elapsed before Houdini finally felt at ease exploring the front room of the cattery. That area has several wicker baskets with pillows and heating pads. Six-foot condos offered a respite for any cat that wanted to be alone or preferred to keep an eye on their domain from a high perch. Scratching posts are in every corner. Bubbling water fountains offer a constant, peaceful sound. And toys are abundant.

Imagine my surprise, when one morning, I discovered Houdini curled up in a basket in the main room. He looked ever so content, and well, handsome! The battle scars on his face had faded and were now practically invisible. His thin body had filled out into a muscular, well-proportioned cat. Houdini, by all appearances, was a healthy and happy cat.

Nevertheless, Houdini continued to dictate the distance between us. He did not permit me to get too close, and at this point, I had still never touched him. But I was okay with that.

It was a full two years after becoming a permanent resident before Houdini allowed me to pet him! From that moment on, his trust in me grew. While he remained cautious, he came to enjoy our petting sessions. Eventually, he permitted the volunteers to approach and caress him, too. Those gentle touches progressed into head butts. Over the years, Houdini became more comfortable with RESQCATS visitors, too. He often watched them from the safety of the upper shelf, but on rare occasions, he let some carefully chosen visitors receive the honor of his affectionate head butts.

Years later, after Greyco died, Houdini assumed the title of chief diplomat among the residents. All the cats loved Houdini and took turns sleeping with him. They groomed him as if he were a king and he often returned the favor.

Somehow, I managed to get Houdini into the doctor for his check-ups, but there was always a price to pay. He was not the kind of cat that quickly forgot a vet ordeal. I was not easily forgiven and he punished me for days, or even weeks, by running from me. Every aspect of health care, even something as minor as cleaning an occasional goopy eye, was a major undertaking. I learned early on to respect his wishes. He had made it very clear that medical attention was emotionally distressing. Houdini just wanted to live in the beautiful place that he had chosen, in surroundings where he felt safe, and with people he had come to trust.

❧

Houdini lived at RESQCATS for several years. Still, I was surprised when I woke up one morning and noticed that he had suddenly grown old. I did not want to face it, so I chose not to believe that he had changed into an elderly cat...or that he had become thinner, moved slower, and slept more. He lost his ability to jump to the highest condos and spent most of his time spooning with his feline friends. But there was one thing that did not change; Houdini never lost his gentleness and sweet persona.

I truly did not see him aging. In hindsight, he was obviously an older cat than I originally thought. Or, possibly, time just passed by too quickly.

One day, Houdini abruptly took a turn for the worse. He became weak and suddenly collapsed. Typically, my first inclination would have been to get him to the veterinarian for blood work, x-rays and any other tests that might explain his sudden crisis. But I knew in my heart that Houdini would have not wanted that. Even if I had forced him through blood draws and testing and could have told him it was for his own good, he would have chosen not to be treated. It just was not his way. More importantly, he would have left this world feeling betrayed of the trust and love that we had so painstakingly cultivated.

When Houdini's health failed, he was gone in a day. I am very grateful that he did not suffer a prolonged illness.

Losing Houdini may have been sudden, but his memory lingers on; it has never faded for me. There is not a day that goes by that I do not think of him. He had a profound, yet quiet, presence in the cattery. Now that silence seems almost deafening.

I loved Houdini and I will forever remember our time together. I will always miss him. But he is still with me in a different way. Soon after he died, I had rainbow-colored paw prints tattooed on my forearm. The paw prints remind me of Houdini every day and when people ask about the tattoo, I simply smile and tell them, "That's my Houdini."

I love all creatures with one exception. Fleas! I hate fleas! They are nasty pests that can cause itching, scratching, skin allergies, and worse.

Many people do not realize that something as small as a flea can be extremely dangerous, especially in large numbers; and on a tiny kitten, they can be life-threatening.

When Stellar and Starz arrived, they were infested with these parasites. Had Stellar not had the good fortune of coming to RESQCATS, he probably would have died within a day.

TWENTY-EIGHT

A Gift of Life for Stellar and Starz

Stellar and Starz were rescued by a volunteer from a hoarding situation. RESQCATS had confiscated several kittens from the home and paid for spay and neuter surgeries for the owner's remaining cats. These siblings were the last two to be removed.

As I set up a space for Stellar and Starz, I noticed that they had fleas. It is not an uncommon occurrence, but fleas and all the problems they can cause are not allowed in the cattery. I get rid of them by combing, bathing or using a topical flea treatment before the cats and kittens enter a clean enclosure.

Both Stellar and Starz had long, thick fur that made it difficult to see the tiny pests. With just a single pass of my special flea-removing comb, more than two dozen of the varmints were snared. The kittens' infestation was much too great for just the comb treatment, but a chemical flea treatment was also not an option as kittens should be at least eight weeks old before topical treatments can be applied. These brothers were about four weeks old, each weighing less than ten ounces...much too young to be treated with the toxic chemicals found in anti-flea applications.

A bath with Dawn dish soap should solve the problem. For over thirty years, Dawn has been an important component in the tool kit of rescuers. It has helped in the rescue and release of more than 75,000 wild animals affected by oil pollution. The thick blue liquid contains a grease cutter that also destroys the exoskeleton on fleas.

I gasped at what I saw as I began to bathe the kittens. While I did not count them, I was sure that there were no less than a hundred fleas crawling on each tiny kitten's body.

I was horrified at the sight of the bloody water that ran down the drain. They were so infested that I washed them twice!

Starz acted like a normal kitten; he was energetic and playful. But Stellar appeared lethargic. I had learned that checking the color of a kitten's gums was a valid indication of anemia. Normally, gums should be pink, but both kittens' gums were pale white. This was a convincing sign that their red blood cell counts were down. The fleas were literally sucking the life from the brothers!

I checked on the boys every few hours for the remainder of the day and into the night.

The following morning, Starz was still energetic and eating like a normal kitten. But Stellar was noticeably more fragile than the previous day. I rechecked his gums. I did not think it was possible, but they had less color than the day before. He was pathetically weak and could barely lift his little head.

It was Sunday morning and the regular vet offices were closed. While I do have the cell number of one of the local veterinarians, I realized that this was urgent and required more than a phone call. It often seems like weekends invite emergencies. Thankfully, Santa Barbara has an outstanding twenty-four hour hospital for cases that cannot wait until Monday morning. I wrapped Stellar in a papoose-style blanket, tucked him in my lap, and sped to the hospital. Due to my frequent weekend visits, it was not surprising that the staff at our local emergency facility immediately recognized me!

The veterinarian did a thorough examination of Stellar. I had filled him in on the details...where Stellar came from, when I got him and what had already been done. I realized that Stellar was in trouble. I was deeply worried and wanted answers immediately. "Just tell me what to do and I'll do it," I pleaded. Of course, that is not the way medicine works. The vet remained calm and concentrated on the exam. I guessed he was not a man of many words, or maybe I did not give him a chance to reply. He requested that I leave Stellar with him for additional tests. As I was leaving, the expression on his face was clear; the situation was serious. I drove home with a heavy heart knowing that there might not be a happy ending.

A couple hours later, Stellar's veterinarian phoned with the test results. They were not good. He said that Stellar was suffering from severe flea anemia. A normal red blood cell count for a kitten his age is twenty or higher. Stellar's count was only seven!

The doctor's recommendation was to give him an immediate blood transfusion. The cost of the blood alone was $900 and the estimate for the hospital and after-care would add another $500 to the bill. I pledged from the day I founded RESQCATS that I would never euthanize any cat based on the cost of treatment. To me, every life is a precious gift and it is my job to provide whatever medical care they need. This transfusion could save Stellar's life. The doctor told me that the odds were in Stellar's favor for a full recovery. I immediately gave my approval.

As we had hoped, the transfusion was a success. Stellar returned to RESQCATS the next day and rejoined his brother. My instructions were to bring him back the following day to recheck his blood count.

To keep him company, I took Starz along for Stellar's follow-up appointment. During the consultation, I mentioned to the vet that Starz' gums were pale. Although he was active and eating well, the veterinarian suggested doing a red blood cell count, just to be on the safe side. The doctor and I were surprised when Starz' count was only nine! That was almost as low as Stellar's number had been. Now Starz also needed a blood transfusion! I could not believe it! He had been lively, playful and eating, all good signs of a healthy kitten. But there had been no mistakes on the tests; Starz was in danger. My heart sank.

Without hesitation, I gave the okay for another transfusion.

But headache was added to heartache when the hospital informed me that there was no blood available for Starz! The vet explained that a container of blood is only good for twenty-four hours after it is opened. The bag that had been used for Stellar had expired.

"Okay, I get it," I said. "So open a new bag." But that was easier said than done. The doctor explained that the hospital donor cat was recovering from surgery and would not be able to give blood for several weeks. I was stunned.

What could I do? Paying another $900 for blood and additional hospital charges was not the issue… the issue was that there was no available blood.

As a wave of panic overcame me, the vet asked, "Do you have a big, young, healthy cat that could be a donor?" I mentally ran through the names and ages of my eighteen cats. Certainly, one of them would qualify! Pebbles and Paisley were fat and hearty and they were only three years old. Maybe one of these sisters would be an eligible candidate.

I raced home and bolted into the house yelling, "Who wants to save a life today?!" I spotted Paisley first. She was in her usual spot on the back of the couch napping in the sun. I swooped her up, kissed her and said, "Let's go, Paisley… we're going save a life today!"

Starz' transfusion was not as urgent as Stellar's had been. Despite his test results, the fact that he was energetic and eating well allowed us time to blood-type Paisley. Making sure that the two were blood-compatible reduced the likelihood of potential risks. The lab results could take up to twenty-four hours, but we had the luxury of time without life-threatening consequences. We got the good news; Starz and Paisley were a perfect match!

The following day, they went to the clinic as a team!

When we arrived at the hospital, the veterinarian's advice was to rerun Starz' blood count prior to the transfusion. The procedure required anesthesia, which is always a risk for such a small animal. Earlier, we had no choice with Stellar's critical condition, but we did have time with Starz. To my delight, his count had already started to improve on its own.

"So, does he still need the transfusion?" I anxiously asked. "I think we can wait a couple of more days to see what happens," the vet replied.

Two days later, Starz' red blood cell count was up to thirteen. The elevated level meant that his body was manufacturing red cells and he would not need Paisley's blood. It was truly a miracle!

ι

Stellar was adopted by his emergency room veterinarian. She shares her home with another feline and a dog that loves cats. Starz found a wonderful home with the son of a RESQCATS volunteer.

Because of her blood type, Paisley was recognized as a universal donor. Since then, she has saved the lives of two other cats in need with her "gift of life." Paisley is now hailed and greeted as a hero at the emergency hospital!

Paisley often serves as the backrest for my office chair. Actually, she gets most of the chair while I teeter on the edge! But you will never hear me complain or say one bad word about my extraordinary Paisley. She can sit anywhere she wants! She is my hero, as well!

I would like to be a veterinarian in my next life assuming, of course, that there is a next life. But in my current life, I gladly embrace being an animal rescuer.

One of the most exciting events in rescue is witnessing a mother cat giving birth. It is a miracle to see each tiny baby enter the world.

This is the story of a special mother cat that captured me by the heartstrings from the moment I first saw her.

TWENTY-NINE

Misa – A Pregnant Stray

🐾

It can be challenging not to become attached to every cat and kitten that comes to RESQCATS. If I allowed each one to capture my heart, I would always be in a state of turmoil when they leave to go to their adoptive homes.

In many cases, kittens are a few weeks old when they come to the organization. If they are healthy, they simply need to grow and go through the standard medical protocol. They take less of my time; mostly, my interaction involves trips to the vet for exams, vaccinations and tests for feline leukemia. There is little occasion to become emotionally attached and feel that, "I just can't give this one up!" Once the kittens reach the two pound weight requirement, they are scheduled for spay or neuter surgery. Then they are eligible for adoption.

My priorities are dictated by sick kittens that require my full attention.

I handle rescue work and adoptions from a pragmatic perspective. I see myself as a stepping stone on the kittens' paths. Just as the RESQCATS mission statement says; it is my purpose to rescue, care for and adopt stray and abandoned cats and kittens. I must carefully monitor my emotions or every cat and kitten would stay. When they are adopted, I believe they become the center of someone's life and the adopters are the recipients of all their joy, laughter and unconditional love.

🐾

In the early years of RESQCATS, I was responsible for bottle-feeding motherless kittens. Since the task needed to be repeated every three hours, I was usually half asleep when

I prepared kitten milk replacement during the nighttime feeds. At that time, I housed orphaned litters in the office bathroom. That was more convenient than having to walk through the garage and along the outside walkway to the cattery in the middle of the night. Not only was it closer, but it was more comfortable sitting in the bathroom than on the cattery's cement floor. After all the kittens had been fed, it was a short trip through the house and back to bed.

While I loved bottle-feeding kittens, the schedule was demanding. Besides taking a toll on my much needed sleep, there were additional responsibilities, too. Each kitten had to be monitored daily to make sure it was gaining weight. For the kittens that were less than four weeks old, I had to stimulate them to go to the bathroom. With this fixed timetable of responsibilities and the extra demands on my time and energy, I did not have the luxury of time to get attached to them.

I remember one especially trying year when the season's first three litters needed to be bottle-fed. About the time the first litter was weaned and the kittens were able to eat on their own own, the second newborn group arrived. That meant that the next five to six weeks of my schedule were once again committed to bottle-feeding, weighing, bathroom stimulating and weaning.

Then the third litter arrived and there were seven in that group! Fortunately, they were older, so there would be fewer weeks required to schedule around their mealtimes.

The seven kittens quickly learned that I was their exclusive source of food. Each time I entered their room, all seven rushed towards me, mewing all the while for their food.

After all those non-stop weeks of bottle-feeding kittens, I was exhausted. One day, I was sitting on the bathroom floor feeding the kittens when Mitch overheard me sobbing. He opened the door to see what was wrong. There I sat with tears streaming down my face, futilely trying to feed one kitten while the other six scratched and clawed their way up my body, all demanding the bottle. I looked at Mitch and cried, "I just can't do this anymore!"

Of course, I did get through that temporary crisis and found a way to continue!

By May, I had already bottle-fed three litters and I was worn out. There were still many more months of kitten season to come. Where was I going to find the energy? It seemed I might need to rely on caffeine and pure adrenaline to get me through the remaining eight to nine months!

§

I refer to people who foster but cannot give animals up for adoption as "flunking fostering." My husband is a perfect example.

There have been a number of instances when a kitten was not placed on the adoption list because of him. Several times, I discovered him in the bathroom, not using the facilities, but instead playing with the kittens. When the time came for them to move to the cattery, it was not unusual for him to want to keep one.

But it doesn't stop there! On other occasions, Mitch fell in love with the mother cats, so he wanted to keep a kitten and the mom! I needed to implement a plan for these situations. If I allowed him access to the kittens, it was certain that we would have to have a discussion about why we should not keep some of the adoptable cats or kittens. The easiest solution was to lock the bathroom door, hide the key and avoid the confrontation altogether!

On more than one occasion, I caught Mitch in the cattery visiting with mothers and their kittens. Each time, I tried to give him the benefit of the doubt. Perhaps his curiosity had gotten the best of him and he wondered what I did all day.

After all, he really only sees me for a quick bowl of cereal in the morning and dinner at night. My schedule during kitten season is from dawn to dusk. We finish our evening meal by 6:30 and then move to the living room to watch the news. It is not out of the ordinary for me to be asleep on the couch by 8 o'clock. Mitch has to wake me, so I can "sleepwalk" upstairs to bed.

When I become aware of his presence in the cattery, regardless of his purpose, he is immediately escorted out. My fear is that he will want all the mothers and all the babies!

Perhaps I should clarify my actions, so I do not appear insensitive. I am actually quite emotional when some of the cats find homes. It is particularly difficult to see those leave that I have nurtured back to health. I cannot hide my tears from the adopters. Many are sympathetic and extend an invitation for me to visit, but I recall taking only one person up on the offer. I believe that there comes a time to figuratively cut the cord and move on to helping others.

That being said, once in a while and without warning, I have an immediate connection with a particular cat or kitten. I cannot explain it; the bond is just there.

ł

That was certainly the case when Misa arrived at RESQCATS. She was a pregnant stray that was rescued on the streets in Santa Maria, California. I knew there was something unique about her the moment I saw her.

I preach to the choir, so to speak, about the prejudice of human eyes when people say they want a cat to look a certain way. It is like they place an order for exactly what they want. They tell me the color of fur and eyes they desire and the length of the coat. I recall a lady who requested a tuxedo cat and detailed precisely where she wanted the black and white markings!

I admit that I thought that Misa was beautiful. Her fur was soft beige with lynx point markings. The silver-gray accents around her face and paws were exquisite and she had stunning blue eyes. When she looked at me, I was reminded of the quote by William Shakespeare: "The eyes are the window to your soul." But my attraction to her was not just her beauty. Although she looked like she could give birth at any time, she was still graceful and poised. She had a sweet and gentle disposition. Everything about her was love. And love was going to be easy for me to fall into.

I took Misa to the vet for an exam and a leukemia test. I hoped that an ultra-sound would help determine how far along she was in her pregnancy. Depending on how the babies were situated in her belly, the doctor might also be able to tell how many kittens she was carrying.

I expected everything to be just fine at her first vet appointment. And it was. That is, until she went into labor during the ultra-sound! The vet rushed her back to me and said, "Jeffyne, you have to get her home right now! Misa is about to deliver!"

Suddenly, I understood how expectant fathers must feel. I was excited and apprehensive at the same time. Mostly, I felt a keen sense of duty to get her safely back to RESQCATS!

I vividly recall the speedy drive back. I remained cautious as I sped through the tail end of yellow lights and failed to completely halt at a stop sign. I begged Misa, "Please don't start delivering in the car!" I feared jolting her into giving birth in my backseat, so I slowed down at every turn and bump. I was as anxious as a taxi driver trying to get a pregnant lady to the hospital. I gripped the steering wheel until my knuckles grew pale. My breaths were short and I felt light-headed. While I concentrated on driving, I kept an eye on Misa in the rearview mirror. She did not seem to share my panic as she sat calmly inside her carrier.

Two things came to my mind. First, "I'm not going to win any awards for safe driving today." And second, "Misa is about to give birth." I desperately pleaded, "Misa, please wait ten more minutes."

Once we were safely back at RESQCATS, I put Misa into her enclosure. I quickly gathered my latex gloves and sterile scissors just in case she needed assistance with the babies' umbilical cords. Many young mothers do not have the instinct to cut the cords, which can cause the kittens to become entangled. I wanted to be fully prepared to help. Besides, I needed to practice those procedures for my next life as a veterinarian!

I barely had time to get seated in front of the crate with all my equipment when the first kitten popped out. To my surprise, unlike Misa, it had dark fur. I thought, "That baby sure doesn't look like Misa!" It was as if a fair-skinned, blue-eyed blond woman had given birth to a dark-haired, olive-skinned baby!

As I watched Misa clean her kitten, I noticed that the placenta was underneath her. Fearing potential trouble, I put on the latex gloves and gently moved it into Misa's view. Fortunately, she was able to sever the cord.

Then, as most mammals do, Misa consumed the rich-in-nutrient afterbirth. While it is difficult to watch, that is a normal occurrence in nature.

Thirty minutes later, she gave birth to a second kitten. Another dark tabby entered the world and I exclaimed, "Misa! That one doesn't look like you either!"

Some time passed before there were additional signs of labor. I was not going to leave Misa, so I took the time to sit, reflect and take in the event of the moment.

You see, there was more going on in my life than just watching a mother cat give birth. I was also worried about Journey, one of my elderly collies. She had been very ill and had recently spent a week in the emergency hospital. She was home again now but not doing well. I was not sure she would live through the night.

As I sat in Misa's enclosure, I rode a roller coaster of emotions. I was simultaneously sad and happy. I feared losing Journey and, at the same time, I was witnessing new life being born. The cycle of life…birth and death was happening right before me.

Misa's gift went well beyond watching her give birth. During that time, I found peace and acceptance of what I believed was the imminent loss of my beloved Journey. I was grateful to Misa for providing me that opportunity.

Miraculously, Journey survived the low point of her illness and was with us for more than another year before losing her battle to kidney disease. I embrace her memory while recalling the paradox of that extraordinary day when life and death seemed to go hand in hand.

Misa delivered two more dark long-haired tabbies. She had three boys and a girl. Not one resembled her! I teased her, "Misa, you must have met a tall, dark, handsome stranger in the alley! Too bad it was just a one-night stand!"

Over the following weeks, I watched Misa care for her kittens. She was a wonderful nurturer and her babies were certainly luckier than she had been. Dahlia, Travis, Linus and Dallas grew up in a comfortable, safe environment. They had not faced the dangers of living in the wild, predation by larger animals, hunger or disease. I would like to think that Misa was grateful for what I had provided. As I looked into her soulful eyes, I believed I saw her appreciation.

I tried not to let Misa steal my heart, but she did. I spent many hours with her…petting, brushing and observing her taking care of the babies. Several times, the words, "I'd love to have a kitty like you," slipped past my lips. However, I knew all along that she would not stay.

ê

Many people who visit RESQCATS have commented on the residents. They expressed how lucky the cats are to live in such a wonderful place, but I actually feel quite the opposite. They live at the facility because they were unadoptable for health, attitude or age reasons; no one wanted them. Most would have had terrible lives or been put down if they had not found their way to RESQCATS. However, for me, euthanasia is not an option; I am committed to their lifetime care.

My quandary is always about time and my inability to give the residents my full attention. There are only so many hours in a day and most of it is spent rescuing and providing for stray and abandoned cats. That leaves little discretionary time for the residents.

ê

I wanted more for Misa. She deserved a home with someone who had time to lavish her with love. With all my responsibilities, I was clearly not that person. It seemed selfish to consider keeping her as one of my own. Her gift to me had been timely and unforgettable, but now I needed to give her something back...a home where she could be the focus of someone else's life.

Misa was adopted by a beautiful young lady who also saw her exceptional qualities. I felt confident that she would have a long life of pampering and affection. When I saw Misa a few weeks later for a follow-up vaccination, it was obvious that they were a match made in heaven.

Tragically, all that changed less than a month later when a roommate left a door open. Misa wandered outside and was attacked by the dog that lived next door. Misa's guardian called me, sobbing uncontrollably to let me know. She was obviously devastated and blamed herself for the incident.

It took a moment for me to register what I was hearing. In disbelief, I asked, "Is Misa dead?" Through her tears, the young lady said, "The assault caused such massive internal injuries that even surgery couldn't save her."

The woman and I cried on the phone together. I thanked her for letting me know and tried to reassure her that it was not her fault. It was a catastrophic error, and we all make mistakes. It was a tragedy that just happened without malice or intent.

I know that to be true in my mind; however, in my heart, I cannot seem to find the lesson in such misfortune. My sadness is just as intense now as it was then. I hope that time will eventually bring me peace.

Would I change the deep affection that I felt for Misa just to avoid the pain of loss....not in a million years! Or would I attempt to not love other animals that came into my life simply to escape the hurt of losing them? Never!

Whenever I think of Misa, I am reminded of the famous quote by Alfred, Lord Tennyson: "'Tis better to have loved and lost than never to have loved at all."

Adopting an animal is a lifetime commitment. My expectation is that adopters honor that promise.

In the history of RESQCATS, there has been only one exception to that condition; Liz and her kitties, Lila and Huckleberry.

THIRTY

Lila's Journey Home

Liz, that "little old lady from Pasadena," who had adopted Lila and Huckleberry, and I became friends. Over the years, she called often to give me updates about her cats. I even broke some of my own rules about disconnecting from the cats once they have been adopted. I visited Lila and Huckleberry several times.

At some time later in our relationship, I told Liz that if there were ever a time she could not care for Lila and Huckleberry, they could return to RESQCATS. Understand, I would not have changed my decision allowing her to adopt them for a single minute! But I realized that the likelihood of Liz outliving the kittens was doubtful.

About two years after she drove off with Lila and Huckleberry in her bright yellow sports car, her health declined suddenly. Staying true to my promise to Liz, Lila and Huckleberry returned to RESQCATS.

Lila had adjusted remarkably well in her home with Liz. She spent hours enjoying lap time away from her gregarious, and often annoying, brother, Huckleberry. Although she had come a long way with Liz, Lila regressed quickly after her return to RESQCATS.

Liz's opinion was that Lila would be fine without her rambunctious brother. I had hoped that both could be adopted together again. But I was certainly open to her view, especially since now I needed to find a home for two two-year-old cats during the height of kitten season.

Luckily, Huckleberry was adopted by a wonderful couple almost immediately. But, sadly, Lila remained terrified at RESQCATS for a second time.

Lila was traumatized after leaving Liz's home. She reverted

back to her frightened and distrustful kitten behavior. For weeks, the volunteers worked to socialize her. Over time, she did show improvement but not enough to consider putting her through the ordeal of relocating to a new home. The readjustment in a new place could be too much for her. And what if she did not adjust? What if the adopter wanted to return her? How would that affect Lila? I made the decision to keep her as a RESQCATS resident.

Although she was cautious and preferred to keep to herself, Lila mingled with the other residents. She was watchful as she slept with one eye open. I talked softly as I moved slowly towards her, allowing her to decide when she wanted me within reach. She eventually enjoyed being brushed and petted; however, she always remained guarded.

Several months after Lila became a resident, a volunteer brought her boyfriend to RESQCATS. He had a soft spot for blue-eyed cats and fell in love with Lila the moment he saw the striking Siamese-Himalayan with sapphire-colored eyes. Since Lila was so cautious, it was odd that she responded so quickly to him. She permitted him to approach her without hesitation. Then she gladly accepted the caress of his hand as he stroked her.

At this particular time, I was in Oregon on my yearly sabbatical. I was unaware of the new friendship between the boyfriend and Lila until I received a call from the volunteer. "Jeffyne, my boyfriend is in love with Lila. She relaxes and lets him pet her every time he visits. She is purring with contentment. We'd love to adopt her." I was surprised to say the least!

We had a lengthy conversation about Lila. I made certain that the volunteer and her partner understood Lila's previous circumstances. I explained that it could take a long time for her to adjust to a new home. They would need to give her time. Most importantly, I explained that they were making a lifetime commitment to her. I felt they understood completely. I was overjoyed for Lila. She would have her very own home again where she could live "happily ever after!" Lila went home with the couple in 2009.

Sadly, a year later, the couple broke up. Lila remained with the young man. After all, he was the one who had been love-struck by her.

Unfortunately, in 2012, I was contacted by the local humane society that Lila had been relinquished by the man. His excuses for turning her in were absolutely false! According to him, "When my girlfriend and I broke up, she dumped the cat on me. I never wanted her."

I suspect there was another reason because it had been two years since the couple had separated. I could not imagine any excuse that would satisfy me. I was deeply saddened and very angry. The last thing this excruciatingly shy cat needed was to be relinquished to a shelter. Her history was one of insecurity and fear. The shelter personnel informed him that if Lila was deemed to be unadoptable, she would be euthanized. The man's response was "Well, that's just life!"

No! That is death! To this day, I cannot understand people who have so little compassion for animals.

The Santa Barbara Humane Society is a wonderful organization that I have had the pleasure of working with since I founded RESQCATS in 1997. The employees work diligently to accommodate all my requested surgeries, especially during kitten season. They have spayed and neutered literally hundreds and hundreds of cats and kittens for RESQCATS.

I have the utmost respect for the humane society staff and what they do for the animals they take in. If I were the one standing behind their counter, listening every day to the lame excuses people give when they relinquish their pets, it would be almost impossible for me to remain polite and gracious.

I do appreciate that some people have circumstances that leave them with few options, but in my experience, poor excuses for giving up their pets far outnumber valid reasons.

Fortunately, many of the owner-relinquished animals that the humane society accepts are friendly and easily adopted. However, a timid cat like Lila would present a huge challenge. It could be weeks or months before she responded to the shelter personnel, if at all.

The staff was considerate during our conversations about Lila. Each time I checked in, the reply was always reassuring. "Let's just give her some time, Jeffyne." I am well aware that they have devoted months and even years to some animals waiting for the right person to adopt them.

Three weeks passed and Lila made little progress at the humane society. While I understood that was not a lot of time, something in my heart told me that Lila needed to come back to RESQCATS.

When I returned from the shelter with Lila, she quickly found a basket on the upper shelf. She hid by burying her entire body under a blanket creating an inconspicuous kitty mound. I laid my hand gently across the hump. I began to caress her through the blanket. Then, I whispered, "Lila, you are home."

She started to purr. She is home. And she is still purring!

Fate is defined as "the force or principle believed to predetermine events." If you believe in fate, you accept as true that things in one's life happen at certain times for a reason.

Some people believe in fate, but I have never given much thought to the idea of predestined events or attempted to figure out what they mean.

One must keep an open heart and mind in order to recognize what might be fate. It opens a door beyond everyday reality and offers a different perspective of life that makes us stop, think and appreciate.

This is the story of Sheba and how she prepared me for the marvel of one of life's surprises!

THIRTY-ONE

3:10

It was mid-summer in 2012 when I received a call from a lady who worked at a local Santa Barbara business. She said that a sweet mother cat had given birth to kittens under the bushes next to the employee parking lot. Her litter was a few weeks old and the kittens were just beginning to peer out from under the shrubbery. The woman and her co-workers were worried about the family and they urgently needed my help.

When I arrived at the business, I was surprised by the employees' compassion. They had become quite attached to the mother cat and her little family.

Their concern for the mother cat and her babies, however, was very different from management's outlook. The human resources executive was as unsympathetic a person as I had ever met. To her, the cats were a nuisance. I never understood her dislike of the animals, but judging by her sour demeanor, it appeared that she had more than just a problem with the cats. More likely, her real issue had nothing to do with them and had everything to do with maintaining authority and control. She was aware that the employees were feeding the mother cat and that they obviously cared for her. But she never consulted them to find a satisfactory solution for their concerns. Instead, she had placed "Do not feed the cats" signs around the employee break area and parking lot.

I seriously doubted that she fared any better with her employees on work-related issues. But I decided to give her the benefit of the doubt; after all, she was the human resources executive. And you supposedly have people skills to have been hired for that position.

Being a compassionate animal rescuer, there was obviously nothing about her lack of empathy that I could relate to...no more than her employees might. The workers loved the mother cat and named her Sheba. During lunch and afternoon breaks, they secretively fed Sheba while at their outside recess tables. After first making sure the coast was clear of their heartless boss, some even chose to stay after work hours to feed Sheba canned food.

Sheba's babies were old enough to start weaning from mother's milk and to begin eating solid food. They were also venturing out into the parking lot. It was at this point that the employees contacted me as they were worried about the kittens being run over either in the parking lot or on the adjacent busy street. It was never stated, but perhaps they also feared that the dreaded human resources director would dispose of them.

Sheba must have been worried too. She let the employees know of her need for help in a most unusual way. One morning, before anyone had arrived, she moved her kittens to the doormat just outside the employee entrance. Now it was impossible for her little family to go unnoticed as she nursed them in plain sight...the workers had to step over them to gain entrance to the building! She repeated this routine for several days.

In hindsight, Sheba was especially clever placing her kittens at the employees' entrance rather than at the door where the human resources person entered. The fact that employees and management had separate entrances was very telling about the director.

Sheba developed another incredibly amazing scheme. The employee break bell rang promptly at 3:10 every afternoon. Guess who always showed up? Sheba! She came running at the sound of the bell knowing that the employees would feed her tasty morsels of food. Very smart cat! 3:10...on the dot! She never missed a break.

The lady who had contacted me said that it would be easy to find Sheba and her babies if I arrived around 3:10. I took her advice and got there just before the break bell. The employees had been briefed on who I was and greeted me with great big smiles and handshakes. One lady wrapped her arms around me, hugged me and thanked me several times. It was plain to see just how much the workers had bonded to Sheba and her kittens.

I easily collected three adorable little kittens from under the bushes along with Sheba. Several of the staff cried as I placed the kittens into a carrier, so I stayed a bit longer to reassure them that RESQCATS was a safe and caring sanctuary. I promised that this special family would be loved and well cared for.

It was after I got Sheba and three kittens loaded in my car and was ready to leave that a fourth kitten was found! Thank goodness one of the employees knew there was another one! She assured me that I now had them all.

Coincidently, as I headed towards my car, I came face-to-face with the human resources director. I was polite and took the opportunity to introduce myself and tell her why I was there. To her credit, she did acknowledge my outreached hand. But I could not pull my hand away fast enough when she said, "I'm glad you're getting rid of those nuisances." That comment alone was bad enough, but it got worse when she continued, "I'll gladly pay to have someone get those cats out of here."

❧

There were many times in the past when I spoke up for animals without mincing my words. Those altercations usually proved to be less than productive and the animals were no better off. Sometimes, even if I expressed my opinion in a more constructive way, it was still a waste of time and energy.

I am reminded of the time I was seated next to someone at a business event for Mitch's company. The man hunted deer and elk for sport. He boasted about his skills as an expert shot. He admitted that he never ate the meat of the animals he killed; his hunting was simply his hobby and male bonding time. I tried my hardest to convince him that there is no sport in killing defenseless animals so that their heads can be hung on a wall or that their skins can be displayed under a coffee table.

It turned out to be an excruciatingly long evening for me. As I sat there eating my vegetarian dinner, I thought, "There are six-hundred people in this room. How on earth did I end up sitting next to such a heartless person?"

So, as difficult as it was for me, I remained courteous and professional with the human resources director and I gave her one of my RESQCATS business cards. While I recognized that I probably would not change her callous view, I hoped that she would honor her words and donate to our organization. Afterwards, I mailed her a personal note and a current RESQCATS newsletter. In the message, I thanked the director for allowing me to rescue Sheba and her kittens and complimented the company's caring employees. I informed her that she had prevented a huge problem by allowing RESQCATS to help. Without intervention, Sheba probably would have given birth to another litter by the end of the year. What's more, I wrote, "Sheba's four kittens could have had litters of their own by the following spring."

I also took the opportunity to tell her that RESQCATS is a non-profit organization. I detailed RESQCATS protocol, explaining that Sheba and each kitten would receive vet exams, Felv/FIV tests, worming meds, vaccinations, spay or neuter surgery, a micro-chip and any additional medical care they needed.

"I'll gladly pay to have someone get those cats out of here," is what she had told me. I hoped she would stay true to her words by making a donation. Not surprisingly, I never heard from her. I really did not expect that I would.

❧

Sheba and her kittens were a delightful little family with two girls and two boys. I named the girls Mystery and Gypsy and the boys were called Inky and BlackJack.

With the exception of their blueberry-colored eyes, they were miniature duplicates of their mother. Each was as black as coal without a single white hair. I estimated them to be about five weeks old, not yet mature enough for their eyes to have changed color.

The employees had handled and cuddled them at every opportunity, so they were extremely friendly. They were also beginning to wean from mother's milk and eat on their own.

Although I believe that all kittens are adorable, this litter was truly exceptional. One day, the quadruplets appeared together at the end of the large crate and peered out into their vast unexplored territory. To such tiny kittens, the two-inch step to the floor must have seemed like a plunge into the Grand Canyon! They loved to investigate. Every toy was a new adventure. Everything that moved needed to be inspected. One day, they discovered Sheba's tail. They loved chasing, chewing and attacking it. Once Sheba realized how enamored the kittens were with her tail, she teased them and instigated play, swooshing it back and forth. The tail game went on for hours. I cannot remember a litter that I enjoyed quite as much during that season.

❧

I remained in contact with the staff member who had initially asked for my assistance. She had been tremendously helpful in rounding up Sheba and her babies on the day I rescued them. I felt obliged to keep in touch with the employees and give them progress updates. They had entrusted Sheba and her kittens to me, and after all they had done, I owed that to them.

My contact informed me that the employees planned to host a bake sale to raise money for Sheba and her family. Naturally, I was grateful for any support with the costs, but their effort to help is what truly touched my heart. The employees' dedication was the real treasure. That is something money cannot buy.

A few days after the bake sale, I received a call from the employee summoning me to their business site. She had the money the employees had raised at their bake sale and wanted to give it to me. When I arrived at the agreed-upon time, she met me in the parking lot and handed over a wad of cash.

I was grateful for the sincere effort of the employees and my eyes filled with tears. I hugged and thanked her numerous times.

After I returned to RESQCATS, I took the bundle from my pocket and counted the bills. It added up to three hundred and ten dollars. "Wow! Three hundred and ten dollars," I thought, "that's a lot of cookies and cupcakes!"

Then it dawned on me!

Sheba had appeared when the employee break bell rang at 3:10 each day. And now, I was holding $310 in my hand from the bake sale!

Was it planned? Was it a fluke? Or was it just a coincidence?

Think what you may.

But I know what I believe! It was fate!

The RESQCATS perspective on adoption is to find good, permanent homes for all our cats and kittens. That means I will not adopt kittens to just anyone who comes along. My primary objective is, and always has been, to do what is best for the cats! My job is to find that perfect home for every cat and kitten that passes through our doors. I consider adoption a lifetime commitment. I work conscientiously to find the right homes... no matter how long it takes.

The circumstances surrounding Butch and Sundance were ultimately about refusing to adopt them to a home where they would not be accepted by everyone. I needed to wait for just the right family.

THIRTY-TWO

A Bonded Pair for Life

ረ

It was the summer of 2013. After sixteen years of operating RESQCATS, I should have been accustomed to the reasons people give when they say, "I can no longer keep my cat." I have heard it all, usually many times over, and find most rationales inexcusable. It has always been my belief that adopting an animal is a lifetime commitment.

I received a call from a woman about two one-year-old brothers that she wanted to relinquish to RESQCATS. At that time, every enclosure in our facility was full, so I advised the owner to take the brothers to another rescue. The woman apparently did not heed my suggestion since a couple of weeks later, she was back on the phone with a proposal. "If RESQCATS is willing to pay to have the brothers neutered, I will consider taking them with me when I move to Texas. At least I will think about it." Although the organization would have been happy to pay for their surgeries, I wondered why she thought it was RESQCATS' responsibility to neuter her cats. More importantly, I was not convinced that she would follow through on her stated intention to transport them to Texas. It seemed a strong possibility that she would leave them behind. Since I now had space at RESQCATS, I offered to take them. She happily agreed to relinquish the cats.

ረ

It often amazes me how someone else's lack of commitment can suddenly become my responsibility. I wish I could convince everyone that pets should be treated like family members rather than as disposable property, but I know I am unlikely to ever succeed with that goal. There will always be some people who think that rescues exist solely to step in when it is no longer convenient for them to have an animal. For me, it always comes down to what is best for the cats.

ɭ

When I asked the woman how she could be willing to give up her cats, she replied, "Oh I got them for my kids last year. They were baby kittens, but now they're grown and they aren't as cute." There was a long pause as if she was waiting for me to respond, but I was silent. So she continued, "I had always planned on getting rid of them when they were no longer kittens." Really! That is exactly what she said.

Statements like hers certainly make me angry, but mostly, they make me sad for the cats. The lady's callous and irresponsible conduct also set a poor example for her children. To her, the cats were expendable because they were no longer cute. Since children learn from their parents' behavior, her kids are likely to treat animals in the same way when they grow up. They will think that dumping animals is acceptable behavior.

ɭ

The cats arrived within a few days. I named the boys Butch and Sundance...after Butch Cassidy and the Sundance Kid.

When I met the brothers, it was love at first sight! In all my years of rescue, I had rarely witnessed such an inseparable pair. They spooned when they slept, groomed each other and ate from the same bowl...they were constantly together. It was obvious that they truly loved one another. In my view, animals are capable of love and this pair was living proof. I will never forget watching them sleep, curled around each other as if their bodies were attached by an invisible string.

I knew I had done the right thing by bringing Butch and Sundance to RESQCATS. I felt good about my decision. However, reality set in within a couple of days. Here I was, in the middle of kitten season, with one-year-old bonded brothers that needed a home together. That would not be an easy task when the cattery was filled with younger kittens.

It just seems to be human nature that the youngest kittens in a litter are the first to get adopted. Eight-week-old kittens are chosen before the ten week olds. A litter's one-year-old mother, just barely beyond kittenhood herself, could take months to find a home.

ε

As a rescue person, I have never fully understood most adopters' thought processes. My perspective is that people should adopt the older ones first! Sadly, mine is a minority point of view.

Many people have a pre-conceived notion of what they want in a cat or kitten when adopting. I hear it all the time, "It has to be a kitten," "I only want a tuxedo cat," or "I am interested in any kitten, but it can't be a black one."

Potential adopters' lists of requests are endless. They have requirements about size and looks, "I want the youngest one so that I can mold its personality." The personality of a kitten is already set based on several predetermined factors. "I only want one with blue eyes." I can do that, but it may be weeks or next year! "I want a kitten that's not going to be too big when it grows up." How can I know how large a kitten will become in adulthood?

The requests for certain traits, personality, colors and size are infinite…and exhausting!

I recall a lady who visited RESQCATS with a list that was excruciatingly long and virtually impossible to match. "I want a brother and sister. It doesn't matter what one of them looks like. But the other one must be a brown tabby with a bushy tail and an orange nose. Oh, and it should have long hair, too. I also have kids, so it has to be friendly and get along with my dog." That is what she actually said! I repeated her request back to make sure I had gotten it all. Then I politely asked, "You do understand this is rescue?"

Then there are people who honestly believe that I have something to do with the formation of each kitten's behavior. "I want a cuddly kitten that will sit on my lap." Anyone who has had cats knows that the only time kittens slow down is when they are asleep and that is usually during the day when you are somewhere else. Evenings on the couch watching television with your new kitten curled up on your lap is probably not going to happen on command!

Frequently, people who have insisted on adopting an outgoing, playful, in-your-face kitten will call a few days later looking for advice. Their question usually goes like this: "What can I do to tire out my kitten so I can get some sleep?" I listen patiently, offer suggestions and then just chuckle to myself because they got exactly what they requested.

I really do understand that people want certain characteristics in a kitten. But rescued animals are not like ordering a new car! I have no way of manufacturing them to fit someone's particular desires. They arrive the way they are!

ɚ

I got lucky, or so I thought, when a lady was interested in giving Butch and Sundance the home they needed. She and her family had adopted kittens from RESQCATS thirteen years before. They had lost both of them to old age, so she was ready to adopt again. She said that her kids were grown and she had no interest in going through the whole "kitten thing" again. The boys seemed to be a perfect match.

When she came to sign the adoption papers, the woman did have one request. She said she would be out of town for a week and asked if I could keep Butch and Sundance until after she returned. Under normal circumstances, I would have become suspicious and wondered if she were having some doubts about adopting. Perhaps she was biding her time to think more about it or to talk it over with her family. In any case, I have learned over the years that if an adoption does not go through as planned, it is always in the best interests of the cats. Because this woman was a previous adopter who had kept her cats for thirteen years, I believed she would be a woman of her word. I agreed to keep the brothers for the extra time she had requested. In fact, I was more than happy to love on the boys a few more days.

On the day that Butch and Sundance were to go to their new home, the woman called to set a pick-up time. "We'll be there around four," she said. I was not sure who "we" were and assumed she meant her husband. I was pleasantly surprised when the woman brought her daughter. I introduced myself and then realized that I had met the girl thirteen years before when she was only six years old. When I offered to shake the daughter's hand, she reluctantly did so. I assumed that it was just shyness on her part.

The visit went much different than I had anticipated. From the moment they arrived, it appeared that the daughter was intent on sabotaging the adoption. Her self-absorbed attitude was less about the cats and more about having control over her mother. Throughout the visit, she was offensive and argumentative with her mother. What infuriated me most though were her unsolicited and degrading comments about Butch and Sundance.

At one point during the visit, the mother picked up Butch and cuddled him. It seemed like she was trying to convince her daughter that the boys were great cats. "Look how lovable he is!" she said. The daughter pointed at Butch and retorted, "That one has wicked looking eyes." Of course, Butch's eyes were those of a darling young cat!

Sundance came down from his basket, curled around the mother's legs and began to affectionately lick her toes. When the mother commented on how sweet that was, her daughter recoiled and snapped at her, "That's disgusting! He's going to ruin your pedicure!"

Not appreciating the daughter's unkind remarks, I excused myself pretending that I needed to take care of other business. I hoped that my absence would give the mother and daughter a few minutes to resolve their differences. But I also needed time to think about how to handle this repulsive situation.

During one of her outbursts, the daughter had claimed to be allergic to grown cats. But still, she inquired about adopting two of the eight-week-old kittens in the enclosure next door. To avoid further conflict, I chose not to remind her that kittens grow into adult cats!

The daughter was home from boarding school for two months before she would be leaving for college. Aside from her self-centered attitude, I especially did not like her disparaging comments about Butch and Cassidy. From my viewpoint, it would have been more beneficial if the girl had attended charm school rather than boarding school!

In short, the energy surrounding this adoption was just wrong. Butch and Sundance deserved a home where all family members welcomed and loved them. They had already been rejected and discarded by their first family. I was certainly not going to send them into an obviously negative environment, so I stood my ground and defended the boys. I wanted them to have a home where everyone cherished them.

I finally reached a point where I had to speak my mind. Although it might have been unbecoming, I did not mince my words. I told both mother and daughter exactly what I thought about the young woman's attitude. "The comments you have made are uncalled for and your remarks about Butch and Sundance are disrespectful," I said. "You're a spoiled, self-serving little girl and your condescending attitude will catch up with you someday." At the end of my tirade, mother and daughter hurriedly left in a huff...without Butch and Sundance! I do not regret anything I said; in fact, I am rather proud about speaking my mind...and especially about the outcome!

I promised myself that if it took the rest of kitten season to find the boys the right home, that is what I would do. At times like these, when I need perspective, there is a quote that I hold dear: "Obstacles create opportunity." I was now more determined than ever to find the perfect home for Butch and Sundance.

It was only several days later when I opened an email from a man named Steven. He wrote that he would like to adopt two kittens or cats for his family. I replied with detailed information about two darling twelve-week-old black and white sisters. It was not absolutely necessary that Lil' Dot and Polka Dot be adopted together, but I hoped they could remain a pair. I attached their photos and hit "send."

I have no clue as to what made me reopen his email to read it again, but I did. And there it was...right in front of me. Steven's email clearly stated two kittens *or two cats*. Cats! Yes, it said cats! I carefully composed a second reply with the full details of Butch and Sundance's heartbreaking circumstances. I attached photos of them posing together. Then I followed up with a phone message.

Steven returned my call the following morning. I told him that Lil' Dot and Polka Dot were available for adoption through RESQCATS at a local pet supply store while Butch and Sundance were with me. I invited him and his family to meet both pairs. He said that while he and his wife would be delighted to bring their kids at a later stage, they first wanted to visit the kittens without their children. He knew their children would fall in love with whomever they met. Steven and Joan wanted to make sure the kittens were a match for the family before the kids were involved.

The couple's love for Butch and Sundance was immediate.

They noticed the bond between the brothers right away. I explained to them that this was what I refer to in rescue as, "a pair who really needs a home." There was no mistaking that this was a couple who wanted to make a difference. And they knew that adopting Butch and Sundance would certainly make that difference!

They agreed to visit Lil' Dot and Polka Dot at the pet supply store before making a decision about whether to introduce their children to one or both pairs.

As they were leaving, Steven expressed his affection for Butch and Sundance and his feelings were echoed by Joan. "I know the kids are going to love whichever kitties they meet first," he said. He then asked for my advice, "How should I handle this because I would really like our family to adopt Butch and Sundance?"

I did my best to appear objective even though I really hoped that Butch and Sundance would have a home with his family. "You need to be honest with the kids," I told him. "Explain to them that little kittens always find homes, but it's much harder for the older cats. You have the opportunity to educate them about adopting rescued animals. Then, as parents, you are not only teaching your children, but you're helping the cats."

Then I reassured them, "Just so you know, I'd be comfortable with your family adopting any of our cats or kittens. You're exactly the kind of open-hearted individuals that every rescue person dreams of in an adopter!"

They left for the pet supply store to meet Lil' Dot and Polka Dot.

Two hours later, Steven called back. It had seemed to me more like two days! When I recognized his number, I prepared myself for disappointment. I assumed that the kids had chosen to adopt Lil' Dot and Polka Dot.

Steven said, "I presented both options to my children."

As I listened to his words, my heart skipped a beat. The few seconds between his sentences felt like an eternity.

He was excited to tell me, "The kids have decided that they'd like to give Butch and Sundance a home!" I was elated. I swallowed hard and searched for my voice. When I could finally speak again, I blurted, "I'm so happy for all of you! When would you like to bring the kids to meet Butch and Sundance?"

In less than fifteen minutes, I met Joan and Steven's son and their twin daughters. They were considerate, well-mannered and compassionate. Of course, they were also very excited! This really was a perfect family! Butch and Sundance went home with them that afternoon.

It does not take a genius to understand the important message that Steven and Joan taught their children. As parents, they had set a positive example. When their children grow up, they will pass along that lesson to future generations, and the animals will benefit. This family's message is one of kindness, love and empathy. It is the true meaning of what rescuing animals is all about.

The abandonment of animals is an unforgivable act of cruelty that I cannot comprehend. How can anyone move and leave an animal behind? Does the perpetrator have some preconceived idea that a domestic cat, one that is accustomed to being fed on a daily basis, knows how to hunt? Is there any consideration of where it might find shelter from the cold and rain? Do people just not care that the cat is sure to suffer?

I have no inkling how someone who abandons a pet thinks. And I decided a long time ago that there is nothing about this inexcusable behavior that I want to understand. A reason or acceptable explanation just does not exist!

THIRTY-THREE

Jacquelyn's Message

In May 2014, I was contacted by a young woman about a cat that had been abandoned by the previous renters. She had taken it upon herself to feed it every day and, over time, the lady had also befriended the cat. In fact, the cat looked forward to her daily visits and feeding.

However, the woman was moving. Unlike the former renters, she could not imagine leaving the homeless cat to fend for herself and unfortunately, her new apartment did not allow animals. To make matters worse, her current landlord threatened to have the cat removed and euthanized if something was not done right away.

RESQCATS agreed to take the cat. Since the cat was small in stature, the lady guessed that she was about six months old. She described her as sweet and said she even curled around her legs at feeding time begging for attention.

I thought that I could certainly find a home for a sweet six-month-old kitten!

When the young woman delivered the small cat to RESQCATS, it was apparent that things were very different from what I was expecting. I knew immediately that this was no kitten! "This cat is not six-months-old," I said. "She is more like six years!" I am sure that the compassionate lady had not intentionally misrepresented the feline; she was just inexperienced with cats.

In reality, the little cat appeared to be a frail senior that had seen better days. Her ears were bald and covered with scabs. My previous experience with hairless spots on an animal made me suspicious that it was caused by ringworm, a highly contagious fungus. As a precaution, I set her up in an isolated area where she would have no contact with other cats. There were several other health issues as well. She had a huge bump above her left eye. Her black fur was dull and the outlines of her small undernourished skeleton were clearly visible beneath her skin. She was unstable in her back legs. She limped and seemed unable to jump. I wondered if she may have suffered from a broken leg or hip although she did not appear to be in any pain.

So here she was at RESQCATS! The "kitten" that had been described to me as six months old was considerably older and had some obvious health concerns. I was certainly in for more than I had originally anticipated.

But what was I to do? How could I say no to the young woman who obviously wanted to do the right thing? I would do what I always do...deal with the circumstances and provide the unfortunate, abandoned cat my very best.

I named her Jacquelyn.

I made an appointment to see the veterinarian that afternoon. Based on the poor condition of her teeth, the doctor estimated that Jacquelyn was not six years old, but more like twelve!

She desperately needed to have her teeth cleaned; a front canine tooth was grossly inflamed and would require extraction. It appeared that several other teeth might also have to be removed.

Fortunately, x-rays revealed no broken bones in her legs or hips, and no signs of previous injuries. The unsteadiness in her hind end was probably neurological.

Before we could risk putting her under anesthesia for a dental, the vet recommended a full blood panel and urinalysis. She also suggested that a fluid sample from the large cyst above her left eye be extracted and sent to the laboratory for testing.

ɛ

There is a lingering period that I call the "gray area." During this stretch of time, between tests and results, I wait in limbo until we get answers. I hate the gray area! I am not a patient person, especially when I think a medical condition is going to require a follow-up procedure. I often say, "Just tell me what's going on and let's get started on a treatment program, and let's do it now!" But sometimes I have no choice but to wait, often for days, until results are received.

Fortunately, Jacquelyn's blood work and urinalysis were perfect. She had no kidney issues. That in itself was amazing for a senior cat. Her feline leukemia and FIV tests were negative, so I assumed we could move forward with a dental. "That's great news!" I said to the vet. "When can we schedule her surgery?

The vet's reply stopped me in my tracks. The cyst above her eye was diagnosed as a mass cell tumor. While these growths are usually benign in cats, we needed to determine if it was isolated or if it had developed as a secondary site from somewhere else. More tumors could exist in her abdomen. The only way to know conclusively was to do an abdominal ultrasound, which required a specialist. I quickly realized that following up on the tumor was much more critical than her dental procedure.

Jacquelyn's next appointment was with a veterinarian of internal medicine. Yes, there are vets that specialize in areas of medicine for animals just like those in human medicine. There are cardiologists, ophthalmologists, dermatologists, as well as doctors who focus on orthopedics, oncology and radiology, to mention just a few. In my years of rescue, I have become familiar with many of them and I feel fortunate that we can provide such expert care for our animals.

The ultrasound indicated that the tumor was isolated to

the solitary site above her eye and there was no sign of other tumors inside her abdomen. That was a wonderful report, so I was anxious to move forward with the next step... surgery. However, due to the proximity of the tumor to Jacquelyn's eye, the regular veterinarian was uncomfortable performing the needed operation. Again she suggested a specialist. This time we were sent to a board-certified surgeon.

After Jacquelyn and I met with the surgeon, we developed a plan of action. Much pre-surgery preparation would be necessary. Our goal was to shrink the tumor as much as possible with medication and chemotherapy. Since the cyst was so large and right next to the eye, reducing the size was crucial in order to get it all.

I left the surgeon's office with numerous medications and pills for Jacquelyn's treatment along with instructions to administer them several times a day in a particular order.

What I have neglected to mention until now is that Jacquelyn had attitude...and a whole lot of it! Sometimes she could be very sweet and appear to enjoy being petted. Other times, she was completely unapproachable. To complicate matters, her moods were unpredictable. Many of our petting sessions quickly turned into batting, hissing and an occasional warning bite. She never actually did any serious damage with her teeth, but I certainly had punctures and scratches as proof of our encounters. Jacquelyn reminded me of Dr. Jekyll and Mr. Hyde. One minute she was happy and purring as I massaged her ears, but the next moment she would strike out without warning.

ℓ

I have always prided myself in my ability to pill a cat. I never had to use a pilling gun; I find them to be particularly awkward. Timing is everything and there are just too many things to try and do all at once. I have to balance the pill in the end of the gun, open the cat's mouth, insert the dispenser halfway down the throat and then push. This all has to be done in less than a second! How is a person supposed to be able to do all that with just two hands?

Fortunately, I have small hands with thin fingers, so popping that little pill down a cat's throat is just one of my talents!

The protocol for worming cats and kittens requires inserting a pill all the way down a cat's throat. The suggested regimen is every two weeks. So between deworming tablets and antibiotic capsules, I get a lot of practice. I sometimes follow up with a syringe of water to be certain that the pill does not get lodged in the esophagus. I have performed this task, literally, thousands of times. Admittedly, I do not always get it down the cat's throat the first time, but I do not give up until I am victorious!

Usually, the only occasion when I am not triumphant in pilling a cat is when someone is watching or I am trying to show off! It never fails. A volunteer or adopter will be standing next to me to observe my technique and I just cannot get the pill in the cat's mouth. The cat's teeth become so tightly clenched, especially after two or three attempts, that it would take a crow bar to pry them apart. Other times, the pill will not go down the throat and the cat spits it out. I try again. And again! By this time, the pill has dissolved in saliva and the poor cat is drooling all over itself.

Now I have become the cat's number one enemy! Escaping from me is its primary objective. The cat wiggles and squirms from my grip and runs as far away as possible. I have no choice but to get a new pill and start all over.

At this point, I sheepishly tell the onlooker that I will take care of it later, after the cat has recovered.

One can certainly understand why I choose to pill alone... and then boast of my talents later!

Jacquelyn was another story. While I do love a challenge, pilling her proved to be dangerous for me and miserable for her. I needed a different plan of action. Fortunately for both of us, Jacquelyn loved to have her ears rubbed. The vet had her medications compounded into creams. I was able to massage the drugs into the flaps of her ears where they were absorbed into her body. The written prescription warned me to wear latex gloves when I applied the medication so that they did not get absorbed into my body as well.

Two weeks later, Jacquelyn was back at the clinic for her follow-up exam. All indications were that the chemotherapy drugs had worked! The tumor was smaller, which would definitely make it easier to remove. I was elated and had high hopes that the entire cyst could be eradicated. We scheduled the operation.

Surgery day seemed to pass excruciatingly slowly as I waited to hear news from the veterinarian. Again I found myself in that ambiguous middle ground of apprehension and uncertainty, the gray area.

As always, it was busy at RESQCATS, but this particular day of anticipation seemed to tick away at a snail's pace. The incredibly slow passage of time only added to my anxiety. I thought of all the questions I had not asked the surgeon. "How long will the operation take? What are the anesthesia risks for a senior cat? What if you discover more than you anticipated?" How could I have not asked such important things? Now I had so many questions and too much time to worry about the answers.

Finally, the doctor called. Jacquelyn was in recovery and doing remarkably well. Most importantly, the operation was successful. "We got it all!" the vet told me. I was so happy that I could have danced on a cloud! Jacquelyn needed to stay in the hospital overnight, but if all continued well, she could return to RESQCATS the following morning.

I was exceptionally excited to bring Jacquelyn home. But I was completely unprepared to see her naked face. The fur had been shaved across her forehead and from around her eyes and nose. She looked pitiful. The doctor saw the shock on my face and assured me, "It'll grow back, I promise you. It'll grow back."

It took a moment to recover from the surprise. But my focus quickly changed from surprise to happiness as I remembered that the vet had gotten clean margins. I told Jacquelyn, "It doesn't matter how you look; I'm just grateful that you're going to be okay."

Several weeks passed and Jacquelyn continued to recover. I kept her in a private enclosure isolated from the resident cats. She had been through a great deal and I thought she deserved a quiet place away from the bustling activity in the main quarters. Her room had a window with a view, so she could watch our nine collies in the yard.

Jacquelyn's facial fur gradually grew back. Her eyes again became clear and bright. Her black fur regained its sleek luster due to her healthy appetite. Her added body weight reassured me that she was feeling better.

Her attitude, however, remained sketchy and all of our interactions were still on her capricious terms.

By mid-July, Jacquelyn was strong enough to undergo anesthesia a second time, so the postponed dental surgery was now scheduled. Surprisingly, the only extraction was an infected canine tooth. Her remaining teeth were cleaned and polished to a pearly white sheen. To my surprise, based on the remarkable condition of her teeth, the vet reduced Jacquelyn's age from twelve to ten! Now how often does that happen? You take an animal to the vet in the morning and it returns that afternoon two years younger! It was certainly a first for me!

Once the painful tooth was removed, Jacquelyn blossomed. She must have suffered from the abscess discomfort more than I had realized.

She began to enjoy time with the volunteers, but she was happiest when it was just the two of us. We nurtured a special relationship of respect and understanding. Admittedly, the understanding was mostly on my part because she dictated when she wanted to receive my affection and when she did not. There were numerous occasions when my hasty retreat separated safety from injury!

❚

I now realize that I was in complete denial when I thought I could find a home for Jacquelyn. My steadfast determination led me to believe that there was someone who would adopt her. I posted her on all the Internet sites for adoptable animals. A volunteer even created a video that included photos of Jacquelyn with a musical background. She chose the song "I Feel Good" by James Brown. We had never done anything like that before and I thought it was a clever approach. I was convinced that someone would see the video and call to adopt her.

Sadly, no one responded. I reminded myself, "Who would want a ten-year-old black cat with a feisty attitude in the middle of kitten season?" Undaunted, I continued to update the posts refusing to surrender to the inevitable.

Weeks later, a person called about Jacquelyn but visited with her only briefly. In fact, he was here and gone in less than ten minutes. As he left, I noticed he was sporting scratches on his arm and blood on his jacket. I realized that there was not going to be an adoption that day!

I suppose that Jacquelyn's mind was made up on the first

day that she arrived at RESQCATS. She had chosen me as her forever guardian. I needed to accept her decision and consent to her spending the rest of her life as a resident. By now, she had been with me for five months and I had genuinely come to love her.

ɞ

Recognizing that Jacquelyn was a cat that required her own space, I had a new enclosure constructed for her in the main part of the cattery. It was well-equipped to fit her particular needs. Because of her unstable hind legs, a wide handicap ramp was built making it easier to access the lower shelves. We installed a screened window, so she had a panoramic view of the avocado grove. Just outside her enclosure, she could watch the comings and goings of a busy group of hummingbirds sipping nectar from nearby feeders. Beyond her vision, she could hear the gentle tinkles of a dozen wind chimes when a breeze blew through the trees. I opened the window every morning for fresh air and closed it at night to keep her toasty during cool evenings. At that time, none of the other enclosures had windows, so Jacquelyn was the first RESQCATS resident to have a room with a view!

To my delight, within a couple of days, she adjusted to seeing the other cats and her new surroundings.

Jacquelyn and I continued to spend time together and her trust in me steadily grew. Some of the batting, hissing and swatting was replaced with friendly head butts and affectionate signs of wanting more attention. She lowered her head into the palm of my hand inviting me to rub her. She eventually placed her paw on my lap requesting more time when I tried to leave her enclosure. I sat on the edge of her crate while she perched on her shelf and gently tucked her head under my neck. I hoped she would eventually find her way into my lap.

When I could hear her purr loudly echoing through the

cattery, I knew it was a signal that she was in a friendly mood.

Every day was a ritual for us. As I entered the cattery in the morning, the first thing I said was, "Good morning, Jacquelyn." Evenings were ceremonial as well, ending with a special, "Good-night and sweet dreams, my Jacquelyn."

If there is any question as you read this, let me be very clear. Jacquelyn had captured a very special place in my heart. Every day began and ended with her.

ι

One day in late December, my world with Jacquelyn changed abruptly. I had noticed that one of her eyes had been watering for several days. I attributed it to allergies or perhaps a treatable eye infection. But this particular morning was different. Something seemed to have developed overnight. There was intense swelling under her eye and along the side of her nose.

I took Jacquelyn to the vet immediately. Sadly, x-rays and blood work diagnosed her with an aggressive form of bone cancer. Ironically, her new ailment was totally unrelated to the benign cyst from earlier. This was something different and the doctor said there was absolutely nothing that could be done to treat her.

Within a week, I found Jacquelyn immersing the affected side of her face in her water bowl. She began to spend more and more time hiding in her crate. She became very uneasy and much moodier than usual. It was clear to me that she wanted to be left alone.

I fully realized that she was slipping away. I had two choices. I could let her go before she started to suffer. Or I could wait and watch her slide downhill and experience pain. Postponing euthanasia would have only allowed me a few more days with her. But, to me, that would have been selfish. Providing a dignified and peaceful end of life has always been important to me. I chose to let Jacquelyn go to the Rainbow Bridge sooner rather than later.

My mourning was profoundly deep. How could Jacquelyn have broken my heart in just our short months together? At first, I wept quietly, and alone. The flood of uncontrollable tears came days later and they did not stop. I was grateful that Mitch was there to hold and comfort me. He understandingly listened when I was finally able to pour my heart out.

My custom of opening Jacquelyn's window in the morning and closing it at night continued. I got into the habit of placing a delicate incense bowl on the shelf next to her bed. I often lit incense in the cattery and took that moment to bless the cats. The incense I chose for Jacquelyn was called "Love." It mirrored the intense feelings that we had for each other.

The soft breeze that blew outside the window should have carried the incense smoke away, but it did not. Instead, the smoke playfully swirled around my head and encircled my neck...just as Jacquelyn had curled around me as a sign of her affection. To me, the smoke symbolized that her spirit had not left. I believed that she would stay with me until she knew I was ready to let her go.

❧

Three hours at the beauty shop is pure bliss for me. Having my hair done is one of my few treats during kitten season. My cell phone is turned to the silent position. I close my eyes and feel like I literally melt into the chair. At this time, my gray tabby roots are transformed into my distinctive calico look of blonde, dark brown and wild red streaks.

My hair is washed twice followed by a deep conditioner and a therapeutic head massage. I love the ensuing warmth of the hair-dryer. Its low peaceful rumble blocks out the sounds of the busy world. The whole process is sheer indulgence. It made me feel more relaxed than I had in weeks.

In the midst of chattering ladies, UPS deliveries, a guy selling flowers and the whir of hand-held dryers, the radio was playing my favorite song "Somewhere Over the Rainbow."

The music and lyrics always bring tears to my eyes as I imagine The Rainbow Bridge. It is a magnificent vision of a blissful place where I join all my animals that have passed. As the song played, I knew it was a sign from Jacquelyn. It was time for her to leave…and for me to let go.

At that moment, the sun shone in the mirrors that surrounded me and filled the walls beneath the counter with dozens of reflecting rainbows. I realized then that it was time to free her spirit leaving only her memories in my heart.

I continued to light incense in Jacquelyn's enclosure, but now it was different. The smoke no longer lingered inside. It slowly drifted through the open window, dancing and twirling towards the sky. As I watched, I imagined my pain following the haze as it disappeared into the heavens.

It may be a long time before I can speak of Jacquelyn without feeling such sorrow. Even today, as I retell her story, I can feel those same emotions surge inside me. Tears still come to my eyes, but they are quiet and gentle tears. And a loving smile is not too far behind.

Instinctual behaviors are clearly defined in nature. Mothers of animals in the wild know when something is "just not right" with their offspring. They often abandon sick babies and move on to care for the ones that are well. This is recognized as survival of the fittest.

Although I understand the concept, I find it heartbreaking to witness. Watching programs on the Nature Channel or National Geographic where mothers leave their young to suffer and die greatly sadden me.

The same abandonment behavior is not uncommon when domestic mother cats instinctively know that something is wrong. But allowing kittens to die when human intervention could possibly save their lives is not acceptable.

"Know that the same spark that is within you is within all our animal friends, the desire to live is the same within all of us..."
— *Rae Aren*

THIRTY-FOUR

Winkin and Blinkin

It was May 2014 when two tiny kittens were discovered under a bush. They were curled up next to each other...dying. A feral mom had given birth to three babies, but she had abandoned the pair. The mother cat's instinct told her that something was wrong with the kittens, so she left them behind and continued to care for her remaining healthy offspring. This was certainly a case of survival of the fittest.

It was due to good fortune and kindhearted human intervention that the newborns were given a chance to live.

From the moment the nearly lifeless orange tabby boy and his Siamese-looking sister were rescued, my RESQCATS foster, Deanna, and I realized that the kittens faced a long struggle before they would be healthy. They were only a few days old and needed to be bottle-fed. That was certainly not a problem since bottle-feeding is a normal part of fostering. But as it turned out, that was going to be the easiest part of the job.

Both kittens had terrible eye infections. They were by far the worst we had ever seen. One of the little boy's eyes protruded beyond the eye socket making it impossible for him to close his lid, or even blink. His other eye was crusty and glued shut. Both of the girl's eyes were completely sealed.

I suspected a herpes virus, which is common in kittens. But this clearly needed more than the usual treatment of lysine supplements and eye ointment.

Deanna took the siblings to the veterinarian right away. The vet was just as alarmed by their condition and immediately referred the kittens to an ophthalmologist. The doctor even made a personal call to inform the ophthalmic staff that it was urgent that the kittens be seen right away; we were able to get an appointment that afternoon.

The ophthalmologist was gentle as she carefully examined each tiny kitten. Although it is difficult to prescribe pain relievers for such small animals, she calculated an appropriate dose. She also prescribed nine different eye medications that needed to be administered at scheduled intervals around the clock. The specialist's optimism about saving both the boy's eyes made me optimistic, too. Her confidence gave us reason for hope.

Since both kittens had eye issues, Deanna fittingly named them; she chose Winkin for the pretty little girl and Blinkin for the sweet boy.

As a foster, Deanna has taken care of hundreds of kittens. She has years of experience bottle-feeding and dispensing medication to newborns. She faithfully followed the vet's explicit instructions and returned to the ophthalmologist numerous times for follow-up exams.

Based on her observations during each visit, the doctor continued to adjust the medications. Unfortunately, the vet appointments indicated that Blinkin was not getting better. One eye remained swollen and neither eye showed improvement. The doctor felt that to alleviate Blinkin's pain, both of his eyes should be surgically removed.

Our hearts sank. I realized that this was the most compassionate route for Blinkin, but I had a lot of questions. How long would he be under? How could a four-week-old kitten handle the required anesthesia? What are the chances that he would not survive the surgery?

I knew that the length of the recommended surgery could be dangerous to such a small kitten and the doctor agreed. We were putting Blinkin's life in jeopardy, but it was a risk we had to take.

Fortunately, the surgery was successful. "I can't believe it," Deanna cheerfully reported to me, "Blinkin purred all the way home! He must have been in more pain than we realized, but now he's a happy boy!" Blinkin was well on his way to recovery.

A few days later, I visited Blinkin at Deanna's home. When

I first saw him without his eyes, I was shocked. I felt sorry for all he had endured. But Deanna assured me that he felt fine and I could see that he was energetic and playful. She kept him in a large kennel where he quickly learned to maneuver to his food and litter box. He jumped and played like any seeing kitten. By the time the visit ended, I realized that being blind did not appear to cause him any problems.

Winkin's eyes did not seem to be as severe, so the veterinarian wanted to continue her treatment. Although one eye showed all indications of needing to be removed, the other one looked somewhat encouraging. She appeared to see light and shadow, which was a good sign. Perhaps more time would give her a chance for improvement.

Her regimen of medications continued for many weeks but, by the end of July, all hope was lost. Both eyes, even the one in which she had some sight, had deteriorated. Once again, the doctor recommended surgery to remove both of Winkin's eyes.

I was brokenhearted. "Had I waited too long and caused her undue discomfort?" I asked the vet. "Will her recovery be prolonged because we have waited until now?" The doctor was reassuring. She reminded me that Winkin was eleven weeks old and the risks of anesthesia and surgery were greatly reduced.

Deanna and I spoke several times on the day of the operation. She was waiting at the hospital to hear the results of the surgery and hoping that all had gone well. We knew that Winkin's chances were good for a positive outcome, but worrying just seems to come with the territory of rescuing animals.

I was on the phone with Deanna when the surgeon came to tell us that the procedure had gone well. We were relieved and happy at the same time.

Winkin now faced another problem. Prior to the surgery, she had used her one eye that saw light and shadow to get around. Now that light and shadow had become total darkness. Her adjustment to this complete blindness was one of hesitancy and caution. She relied solely on Blinkin to show her the way. Fortunately, he did just that!

Meanwhile, Blinkin had adapted to not having his sight. He was confident...running, jumping, and climbing. Winkin depended on Blinkin's lead to guide her. As time passed, and with Blinkin's coaching, Winkin also became more self-confident. The two kittens became closely bonded; in fact, they were an inseparable pair.

Now my focus shifted. Both kittens had recovered from their surgeries and Deanna felt that they were ready to come to RESQCATS. I wondered how they would adjust to a new environment. Did I need to make special preparations for them? The reality of finding an adopter for a bonded pair of blind kittens weighed heavily on me. Would anyone consider adopting sightless siblings when there were so many "perfect" kittens available? What if someone was willing to take one but not both? How would I explain that Winkin and Blinkin must be adopted together? I had no experience with blind cats, so what adjustment protocol could I recommend? The reality of seeking an adopter did not truly sink in until after they arrived.

I was incredibly nervous on the day Deanna brought the pair to RESQCATS. I feared for their safety inside the four by eight foot enclosure. The driftwood ramps that enable kittens to go from the floor to an upper shelf could be potentially hazardous to kittens with no sight! Deanna assured me that they were able to maneuver ramps, stairs and even leap off condos like any kitten with perfect vision. "Just show them once and they'll be fine," she said. She demonstrated by lifting Blinkin from the ground onto a low condo. Before I knew it, he had jumped down and was back on it again! I did not believe it until I saw it!

I was still uneasy with Winkin and Blinkin climbing to the elevated shelf. I worried that they could fall a distance to the cement floor below that could cause serious injury!

As a precaution, Deanna and I stretched a large blanket that mimicked a hammock across the width of the enclosure. It would catch them if they fell. Blinkin led Winkin straight up the incline to the upper shelf. They not only found the hammock, but they loved to curl up in it to nap! Within a day, they easily moved everywhere. Like any other normal kittens, they wrestled and played chase with each other.

❧

I had spent weeks concerned about their medical condition. When that had been resolved, I worried about their ability to adjust to a new environment. Now I had to face the challenge of finding a home for Winkin and Blinkin. How would people react when they looked at them? What would they say when they saw the hollow places where eyes had once been? Would it help to explain that it was good fortune that they had been discovered and not died?

Over the following days, I watched the siblings in amazement and I began to see things from a new perspective. Blinkin and Winkin did see...just in a different way. The kittens saw their world through touch, smell and what seemed to be an inexplicable sixth sense.

Their lesson became clear to me. I now understood that "beauty is in the eye of the beholder." Our eyes are the most prejudiced organ in our body. As humans, we judge people by how they look; we are attracted to each other, at least initially, by appearance.

Much of what we consider beautiful in others is through our vision. For example, consider the entertainment business. Attractive people are cast in the hottest soap operas and movies. We are inundated by commercial ads in magazines and on television for products that promise us youthful appearances. The perfectly-proportioned bodies of models set the standards of how we can all look through diet and exercise and, sometimes, through even more extreme measures. Too often, outer beauty becomes our focus.

In reality, there is beauty in everyone we meet that goes

beyond the external appearance. It comes from within and is much more significant than just being handsome or pretty. That is even more obvious to me now because of Winkin and Blinkin.

I realized that educating people about sightless kittens could be a futile task. Cat sanctuaries exist around the country for unwanted blind cats. Did their existence mean that I was right and that Winkin and Blinkin would not be adopted? Or would someone see the beauty in their spirit, playfulness, boundless energy and the lessons they could teach... just as I had?

Although some people challenged my position, I stayed optimistic. Many had followed Winkin and Blinkin on Facebook and posted negative opinions. To stay true to my positive outlook, I deleted all negative comments. The most common unconstructive remark was, "Blind kittens! Why don't you just put them down?" I thought, "If they could see Winkin and Blinkin, then they would understand why that was never a consideration."

Others did not appreciate that Winkin and Blinkin were a bonded pair. A vet tech who had seen them during each doctor visit wanted Blinkin, but not Winkin. How could she not realize that they needed to be adopted together?

Regardless of the opinionated comments from far-removed onlookers about what I should have done, not done or let happen to Winkin and Blinkin, I continued to believe that most people have good intentions. There are many sympathetic hearts in the world. I just needed one of those kind people to step forward and adopt the kittens.

I suspect that Kim had been following Winkin and Blinkin on Facebook for months. When it came time to find them a home, I placed them on the adoption list. She called the same day.

Kim had adopted a kitten, Levon, the year before. When she identified herself, I knew immediately who she was. She said, "Jeffyne, I'm calling because I recently lost two senior cats and

I feel that I have the heart and the home to give to Winkin and Blinkin."

I was speechless. Had I heard her correctly? Or was I just dreaming? My heart started to pound and my head began spinning. When the lump in my throat cleared, I responded. I explained their circumstances in full detail anticipating that Kim would need time to reconsider. But after some discussion, I knew that Kim was serious about adopting Winkin and Blinkin.

We planned a time for her to meet them. I was careful to leave an "out" for her; I made certain that she understood that I was not assuming that she would adopt them. I realized the importance of spending time and observing them before making such a commitment.

But to my great pleasure, Kim had already made up her mind well before her visit. She arrived with a brand new carrier and two collars engraved with their names. The siblings went home with Kim that day.

Their new best friend is Levon. He plays with his new buddies and sleeps next to them. He has taken on the role of personal guardian and made it his duty to be their guide.

I will always be grateful to Kim for giving two special-needs kittens their forever home. While others might have turned away, Kim was able to look past Winkin and Blinkin's imperfections to recognize their inner beauty. She saw them as I did...loving and playful normal kittens. And just as importantly, she saw them as beautiful.

I will forever be indebted to Winkin and Blinkin. They reminded me of a valuable life lesson. Despite being different physically, spiritually or emotionally, we are all worthy of love and compassion because truly...beauty is in the eye of the beholder!

Sometimes, rescuing animals can feel like a lonely pursuit. Most often, I save cats and kittens that have been abandoned by negligent owners. Other times, I rescue strays that were ignored by people who just did not care.

I frequently feel overwhelmed and wonder if anyone else shares the same compassion for animals that I do.

THIRTY-FIVE

Bella Baker... A Renewal of the Human Spirit

Rescuing and caring for cats and kittens often results in some very long days. The daily tasks and responsibilities are frequently overwhelming. By the time kitten season is half over, even people have begun to tire me. At this point in the year, I have heard many stories of neglect and abandonment, and I often become disillusioned by the lack of compassion in the human race.

Please do not misunderstand me. I love what I do. It is my passion. But it is not unusual for rescuers like me to lose sight of the good we do to make animals' lives better. Instead, we continually worry about the animals in perilous situations that we cannot help. I have no doubt that many people who rescue animals experience this same profound disappointment and sense of isolation. These feelings become the rescuers' universal bond.

Sometimes, during these difficult periods, a person will come into my life to remind me that there are others in the world willing to go the extra mile for animals.

It was mid-June and kitten season was in full swing. This particular year, our normally hectic schedule was even more demanding. An increased number of kittens were coming to RESQCATS due to changes in the local trap, neuter and return organization. The discontinuation of the group's foster and adoption program meant that RESQCATS needed to accommodate more feral kittens. This situation created greater challenges than we had ever faced.

RESQCATS had already cared for eleven stray kittens and three mother cats with severe upper respiratory issues. They had lived with people who did not want to be bothered by the cats. When they arrived, the mothers and babies were extremely sick and undernourished. They all required many weeks of treatment and supportive care before they could go to their forever homes.

We had also rescued many kittens that were being sold on Craigslist. And we had taken in mother cats with babies from owners who did not have the resources to cover the cost of spaying the mother. RESQCATS often pays to have an owner's cats fixed as a means to curb the pet overpopulation problem.

In addition, we had spent many weeks working with a family that had a mother cat and four unaltered one-year-old kittens. The mother had already given birth to a second litter of six. To make matters worse, one of the daughters from her first litter was about to deliver. I feared that the other two females might also be pregnant.

I wondered if anyone else felt accountable for their animals. Sick cats and kittens were ignored by their owners and were dying without intervention. Some people saw kittens as a commodity and sold them to make money. Others did not seem to understand the importance of spaying and neutering. While the well-being of domestic animals rests with people, it did not appear to me that many were taking their responsibility seriously.

By this time, I was frustrated and clearly did not have humans at the top of my favored list!

My regular routine includes checking my email several times a day to keep up with adoption requests and the general business that goes along with operating a non-profit organization.

It was during this busy time that I opened an email from John Baker, a man who needed assistance. Although we share a mutual acquaintance, that was not the only reason I quickly responded to his message. I could almost hear the urgency in his voice through his written words. John was desperate to help a pregnant cat that he had befriended in the Korcatown section of Los Angeles. He was determined to get her off the streets and into a safe place. I returned his email with a phone call. During our conversation, it became clear that he deeply cared about animals. Given our mutual love and concern for animals, it was not surprising that our souls connected immediately. I gladly agreed to take the cat.

John offered to drive the cat to Santa Barbara. In the meantime, he would arrange for a safe temporary place for her. We concluded that it was a good plan and I expected to hear from him the following day. I became concerned when there was no call and no email. Several days later, he explained the cause for the delay.

As he shared the story, I could still hear the alarm in his voice. "I took the cat to my friend's apartment, where I thought she'd be safe," John said. "But somehow, she escaped. Jeffyne, I was out all night looking for her! It was a strange neighborhood and I thought I'd never see her again!" Knowing John as I do now, I can imagine how inconsolable he must have felt. I am sure he had a long, sleepless night.

But John continued, "To my surprise, the cat showed up the next day!" Now just think about that. This was an unfamiliar area for the cat. She had only been in the friend's apartment briefly before escaping. She had spent the night in unknown territory but, amazingly, found her way back to the apartment.

John and the cat arrived at RESQCATS the next day.

He was tall, well-built and very outgoing, but there was something else about him that struck me. From the moment I met him, I could tell that he was someone special. His compassion for animals surpassed anyone I had met in a long time.

I had prepared a large isolated room for the expectant cat.

It was away from the main part of the cattery and would be a quiet, more comfortable place for her to deliver her kittens. Together, John and I got her settled. The cat immediately made herself at home and appeared content in her new environment.

Now we needed to decide on a name. She was a gorgeous brown tabby with large, jade-colored eyes. Since she had been found in Koreatown, we considered a Korean name that meant beautiful. John did some research on the Internet and we quickly ruled out that possibility since neither of us could pronounce the Korean word for beautiful!

Then John suggested that we call her Bella, which means beautiful in Italian. I told him, "I once had a long-time resident named Bella, but we could incorporate your last name and call her Bella Baker!" So the mother-to-be was named Bella Baker.

John spent most of the afternoon with Bella Baker. He was in no hurry to go home in the LA traffic. I was glad he stayed; it gave us a chance to talk. We got to know each other by telling stories of past rescues. Over the years, John had helped many stray dogs find homes. Bella Baker was his first experience with a stray cat. I felt enormously energized by our conversation. It was nice to connect with someone who had similar feelings.

It was difficult for John when the time came for him to go home. I knew he was happy with Bella Baker's arrangements, but it was still hard for him to leave her. After all, he had poured his heart and soul into her rescue. While I invited him to visit Bella Baker anytime, fighting the LA traffic for two-and-a-hours would not make frequent visits easy.

The next day, which also happened to be Father's Day, Bella Baker gave birth to seven kittens. She had been brought to RESQCATS just in the nick of time! On that particular day of celebrating fathers, it was extraordinary to see kittens being born. I often wonder who the fathers are. Sometimes, it seems like RESQCATS is nothing more than a temporary home for unwed mothers!

John and I texted messages back and forth between the births of each kitten. We celebrated every new arrival on our phones with smiley faces and big red hearts! During the following weeks, we spoke often as I kept him up-to-date with lots of photos of Bella Baker and her babies.

Several weeks later, John made a second trip to Santa Barbara to visit Bella Baker and her kittens. As we sat admiring the new family, we exchanged more sentiments about what had taken place. We spent several hours sharing our respective life stories. The more we talked, the more I felt like we had been friends for years.

As the kittens grew, they followed the usual RESQCATS medical protocol. When they were old enough to find permanent homes, two were adopted together. Then another found a home...and another...and then one more. Finally, only Bella Baker and her daughter, Karma, were left.

Typically, kittens are adopted first. In fact, many people do not seem to even notice the mother cats. But Bella Baker was still a kitten herself! She was a year old when she had gotten pregnant and had missed out on kittenhood. Although she was busy raising a family, she still loved to play and wrestle with her babies. I thought to myself, "Wouldn't it be nice, just once in a while, if a mother and one of her babies found a home together?"

Although some people were interested in adopting Karma, I rejected the idea of sending her with anyone that wanted only a kitten. My desire was that someone would come along and take both of them. In my view, if I stood by my conviction long enough, mother and daughter would go home together.

Sometimes, wishes do come true. LaRea was looking to adopt a kitten when she met Bella Baker and Karma. In her mind, it was impossible to separate the mother-daughter duo. Without my suggesting that they remain together, she approached me about wanting to adopt both of them. Honestly, I don't know who was more excited...LaRea or me.

Bella Baker and Karma went home with LaRea.

As I look back, I can see how Bella Baker brought happiness to many people. That sweet stray cat from Koreatown had delivered beautiful kittens. When she and her kittens were adopted, I believe that they changed peoples' lives through their gifts of joy and unconditional love.

But Bella Baker's greatest gift was to me. She brought some very special people into my life.

I am especially grateful to LaRea for her kindness. She opened her heart to a mother cat and her daughter.

As for John, I feel that we are kindred spirits. To this day, we remain good friends.

And Bella Baker will forever have a place in my heart. She renewed my faith in people and reminded me that there is goodness in the human spirit. Whenever I think of her, I realize that I am not alone. There truly are others who share a deep compassion for animals...just like me.